# Neuropathy Demystified: A Comprehensive Guide from Diagnosis to Targeted Treatment for Optimal Wellness

Authored by

**Sumaira Kanwal**
*Department of Bioscience*
*COMSATS University Islamabad*
*Sahiwal Campus*
*Sahiwal, Pakistan*

&

**Shazia Perveen**
*Department of Zoology*
*The Women University Multan*
*Mattital Campus, Multan, Pakistan*

**Neuropathy Demystified: A Comprehensive Guide from Diagnosis to Targeted Treatment for Optimal Wellness**

Authrors: Sumaira Kanwal and Shazia Perveen

ISBN (Online): 979-8-89881-183-9

ISBN (Print): 979-8-89881-184-6

ISBN (Paperback): 979-8-89881-185-3



Published by Bentham Science Publishers Pte. Ltd. Singapore, in collaboration with Eureka Conferences, USA. 

First published in 2025.

**Bentham Science Publishers Pte. Ltd.**
No. 9 Raffles Place
Office No. 26-01
Singapore 048619
Singapore
Email: subscriptions@benthamscience.net

BENTHAM SCIENCE

# CONTENTS

# PREFACE

Neuropathy is a complex disorder that affects millions of lives worldwide. It can manifest in a multitude of ways, from tingling and numbness to excruciating pain, profoundly altering the lives of those it touches. Yet, despite its prevalence and its profound impact, neuropathy remains a condition often misunderstood and overlooked.

This book was born out of a deep commitment to shed light on the complexities of neuropathy, offering a comprehensive guide to understanding, managing, and ultimately finding relief from its grasp. Within these pages, we embark on a journey—one that delves into the intricacies of the nervous system, explores the multifaceted causes of neuropathy, and unveils a myriad of strategies for living a fulfilling life despite its challenges.

Our intention is clear: to empower the readers with knowledge. Neuropathy doesn't discriminate; it affects people of all ages, backgrounds, and socioeconomic statuses. Whether you're newly diagnosed, a long-time sufferer, a caregiver, or simply curious, this book aims to provide the information you need to make informed decisions and regain control of your life.

Throughout this book, you'll find:

Understanding Neuropathy: We'll delve deep into the science behind neuropathy, explaining the intricacies of the nervous system and how neuropathy disrupts its delicate balance.

Types and Causes: Neuropathy is not a single disorder but a family of conditions. We'll explore the various types of neuropathy and the diverse factors that can trigger or contribute to their development.

Symptoms and Diagnosis: Recognizing neuropathy is the first step toward managing it. We'll help you identify the telltale signs and explain the diagnostic process.

Treatment Options: From conventional medical treatments to complementary therapies and lifestyle modifications, we'll outline a comprehensive range of strategies to alleviate symptoms and promote healing.

Living with Neuropathy: Life doesn't stop with a neuropathy diagnosis. We'll offer guidance on how to adapt, find support, and maintain a high quality of life.

Hope and Inspiration: Real-life stories of individuals who have conquered neuropathy will serve as a beacon of hope, illustrating that healing is possible.

Remember, this book is not a replacement for professional medical advice. It is a roadmap, a companion on your journey to understanding and managing neuropathy. We encourage you to work closely with your healthcare team and explore the strategies outlined here in collaboration with them.

Neuropathy may be a formidable adversary, but it is not invincible. Armed with knowledge, support, and determination, you can navigate the path to healing. This book is here to guide you.

May it serve as a source of knowledge, inspiration, and empowerment as you embark on your journey towards wellness.

With compassion and hope,

**Sumaira Kanwal**
Department of Bioscience
COMSATS University Islamabad
Sahiwal Campus
Sahiwal, Pakistan

&

**Shazia Perveen**
Department of Zoology
The Women University Multan
Mattital Campus, Multan, Pakistan

# CHAPTER 1

# Understanding Neurological Disorders: A Comprehensive Overview

**Abstract:** Neurological disorders encompass a range of conditions that affect the nervous system, comprising the brain, spinal cord, and peripheral nerves. These disorders can manifest in various ways, including cognitive impairments, motor dysfunction, sensory anomalies, and autonomic disturbances, which significantly impact an individual's quality of life. Common neurological disorders include Alzheimer's disease, Parkinson's disease, epilepsy, multiple sclerosis, and migraines. Understanding the underlying mechanisms of these conditions is crucial for developing effective treatments and improving patient outcomes. Neurological disorders arise from many causes, each impacting the nervous system in distinct ways. Genetic factors play a significant role, with inherited conditions and mutations leading to disorders such as Huntington's disease and certain epilepsies. Infections, including bacterial meningitis and viral encephalitis, can result in severe neurological damage. Traumatic injuries to the brain and spinal cord, such as those from accidents, are common causes of neurological impairments. Degenerative diseases, including Alzheimer's and Parkinson's diseases, involve the progressive loss of nerve cells. The treatment landscape for neurological disorders is multifaceted and continually evolving, reflecting the complexity of these conditions. Pharmacological interventions play a crucial role, with medications targeting specific neurotransmitter systems to alleviate symptoms and slow disease progression. For example, dopamine agonists and levodopa are mainstays in managing symptoms of Parkinson's disease, while antiepileptic drugs aim to control seizures in epilepsy patients. Additionally, advancements in neuroimaging techniques and surgical interventions offer innovative treatment approaches. Deep brain stimulation, for instance, provides targeted electrical stimulation to alleviate symptoms in movement disorders, such as Parkinson's disease.

**Keywords:** Degenerative diseases, Huntington's disease, Neurological disorders, Parkinson, Sensory anomalies.

## INTRODUCTION

Neurological disorders are broad terms encompassing an extensive variety of conditions that distress the neurological system, including the brain, spinal cord, and peripheral nerves. Such disorders can originate from a variety of causes, including heredity, viruses, distress, autoimmune reactions, metabolic disorders,

**Sumaira Kanwal & Shazia Perveen**

or unknown factors. Neurological disorders can manifest in diverse ways, including cognitive impairment, movement disorders, sensory disturbances, or autonomic dysfunction. Examples of neurological disorders include Alzheimer's disease, Parkinson's disease, multiple sclerosis, epilepsy, and stroke.

## Neuropathies

Neuropathy specifically refers to a variety of diseases that lead to damage or improper functioning of one or more peripheral nerves. Peripheral nerves transfer signals between the vital nervous structure (spinal cord and brain) and the remaining body, including limbs, organs, and muscles. Neuropathies can arise from various factors such as diabetes (diabetic neuropathy), infections (*e.g.*, HIV-associated neuropathy), autoimmune diseases (*e.g.*, Guillain-Barré syndrome), physical trauma, exposure to toxins, or hereditary conditions. Symptoms of neuropathy may include pain, numbness, insensitivity, and dullness, with the affected areas becoming numb.

It is characterized by the damaging or improper functioning of these peripheral nerves, resulting in symptoms such as pain, numbness, tingling, weakness, and loss of sensation in the affected areas. Neuropathy may arise from various factors as well as diabetes, infections, autoimmune diseases, toxins, trauma, or hereditary conditions.

- **Multiple Sclerosis (MS):** It is a neurological disorder caused by damage to the myelin sheath, the protective covering of nerve fibers in the brain and spinal cord. Peripheral neuropathy can occur in some individuals with MS, either due to direct nerve damage or as a side effect of medications used to manage the condition.
- **Guillain-Barré Syndrome (GBS):** GBS is an autoimmune condition that affects the peripheral nervous system, resulting in muscle weakness, tingling sensations, and loss of movement. An infection often precedes it, and the immune system mistakenly attacks the peripheral nerves, causing neuropathy.
- **Charcot-Marie-Tooth Disease (CMT):** CMT is an inherited disorder that affects the peripheral nerves, resulting in muscle weakness, muscle wasting, foot deformities, and sensory impairment. It is among several inherited neuropathies. These examples illustrate how neuropathy can be a component of various neurological disorders, either as a primary feature or as a secondary complication. Understanding and managing neuropathy within the context of neurological disorders is crucial for the appropriate diagnosis, treatment, and management of these conditions.

Nervous system disorders that affect the brain, spinal cord, and nerves distributed throughout the body. These disorders can manifest in various ways and have diverse causes, symptoms, and treatments. Some common neurological disorders include:

## ALZHEIMER'S DISEASE AND OTHER DEMENTIAS

Alzheimer's disease and other memory loss are neurodegenerative conditions specified by progressive mental deterioration and disability in daily functioning. Here's an overview of Alzheimer's disease and common types of memory loss:

### Vascular Dementia

It is the second most common type of memory loss, accounting for about 20% of cases.

This result is due to the improper flow of blood to the brain, which is caused by strokes or small vessel disease. It leads to damage in brain areas responsible for cognitive function.

The severity of symptoms depends on the location and condition of vascular damage. It also includes problems with attention, executive function, and gait disturbances.

### Lewy Body Dementia

It is caused by the presence of abnormal protein deposits in the brain, known as Lewy bodies.

It shows similar characteristics with both Alzheimer's disease and Parkinson's disease, showing common symptoms including difficulties in learning, false perception in visual, motor symptoms, and REM sleep behavior disorder.

LBD is often challenging to diagnose due to its overlapping features with other dementias.

**Parkinsonism** refers to a group of nervous system disorders that lead to movement problems similar to those observed in Parkinson's disease. It is the commonest cause of Parkinsonism; other conditions can present with similar symptoms. Here's an overview:

**Parkinson's Disease (PD)** is a degenerative neurological condition characterized by the gradual decline of neurons responsible for producing dopamine. in the substantianigra region of the brain. This leads to motor symptoms, including trembling, bradykinesia, rigidity, and an inability to maintain position. Non-motor symptoms also include thinking problems, mood disturbances, and improper functioning of the autonomic system.

## Parkinson's Disease and Symptoms

A neurodegenerative condition that causes the movement to slow. Its symptoms vary from person to person and become more severe over time. The primary motor symptoms of Parkinson's disease include:

**Tremor:** Resting tremor is the major symptom of Parkinson's disease, which usually starts in one hand or arm and often involves a rhythmic shaking movement. The tremor may appear as a pill-rolling tremor, where the thumb and fingers move backward and forward as if rolling a pill.

**Bradykinesia:** Slowness of movement is another symptom of Parkinson's disease. Individuals with this disease may have difficulty initiating movements, experience reduced range of motion, and perform tasks more slowly than usual.

**Rigidity:** Stiffness of muscles is common in Parkinson's disease, which can affect different parts of the body. It causes stiffness or shows resistance to passive movement, which make it difficult for individuals to move their limbs smoothly.

**Postural Instability:** As Parkinson's disease progresses, individuals may develop problems with balance and coordination, leading to difficulties with posture and gait. They have more chances to fall, particularly when turning or changing direction. In addition to these motor symptoms, Parkinson's disease can also involve a range of non-motor symptoms, which may include:

**Loss of Smell (Hyposmia):** Many individuals with Parkinson's disease experience a reduced ability to detect or identify odors.

**Sleep Disturbances:** Parkinson's disease causes various sleep problems that include sleep disorders, restless legs syndrome, and rapid eye movement (REM).

**Cognitive Changes:** Individuals with Parkinson's disease may experience cognitive impairment, characterized by difficulties in memory, attention, and executive function. In later stages, dementia may occur in some cases.

**Mood Disorders:** Depression and anxiety are common in Parkinson's disease and occur as a result of changes in brain chemistry, and show the effect of living with a chronic illness.

**Autonomic Dysfunction:** Parkinson's disease can affect the autonomic nervous system, leading to symptoms such as orthostatic hypotension (low blood pressure upon standing), constipation, urinary problems, and sexual dysfunction.

**Speech and Swallowing Difficulties:** Parkinson's disease can affect the functions of muscles involved in speech and swallowing, resulting in a change in voice quality, slurred speech, and difficulties with chewing and swallowing.

The individuals with Parkinson's disease do not show all the symptoms, and the severity of symptoms differs from person to person. Treatment for Parkinson's disease aims to deal with symptoms. To improve quality of life, individuals often employ a blend of medications, physical therapy, occupational therapy, and lifestyle adjustments (Fig. **1**).

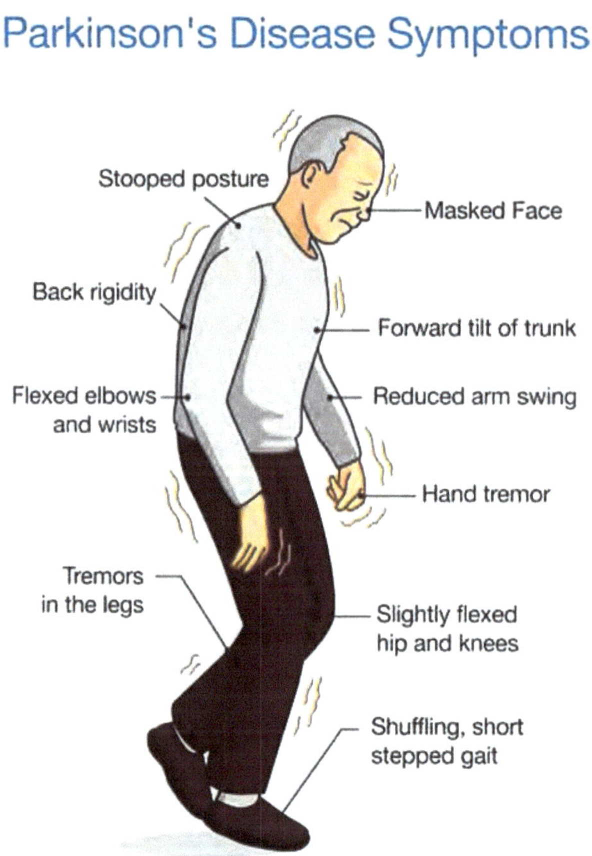


**Fig. (1).** Clinical symptoms of parkinson's disease.

**Parkinson-Plus Syndromes:** These are a group of neurodegenerative disorders that share some features of PD but have additional symptoms and a more rapid progression. Examples include Multiple System Atrophy (MSA), Progressive Supranuclear Palsy (PSP), Corticobasal Degeneration (CBD), and Dementia with Lewy Bodies (DLB). These conditions typically have more widespread damage in the brain and often present with more severe symptoms than PD.

**Drug-Induced Parkinsonism:** Some medications, such as antipsychotic drugs and certain antiemetics, can also cause Parkinsonism as a side effect. Drug-induced Parkinsonism usually resolves once the medication is discontinued.

**Vascular Parkinsonism:** This type of Parkinsonism is caused by small strokes or other vascular lesions in the brain that disrupt the normal function of the basal ganglia and related structures. Symptoms may resemble those of PD but often progress more slowly.

**Toxin-Induced Parkinsonism:** Contact with some toxins, like pesticides, herbicides, or industrial chemicals, can lead to Parkinsonism. These toxins may damage dopaminergic neurons or interfere with dopamine production or function in the brain.

**Metabolic Disorders:** Unusual metabolic disorders, such as Wilson's disease and mitochondrial diseases, can occasionally present with Parkinsonian symptoms due to irregularities in copper metabolism or mitochondrial function, respectively.

The evaluation of Parkinson's disease entails a comprehensive clinical examination, which encompasses reviewing the medical history, conducting physical assessments, and analyzing symptoms. Neuroimaging studies, such as MRI or DaTscan, may be used to help differentiate between various causes of Parkinson's disease. Treatment varies depending on the underlying cause but often includes medications to manage symptoms, physical therapy, and lifestyle modifications. Individuals with Parkinsonism should receive comprehensive care from a multidisciplinary team, including neurologists, movement disorder specialists, and other healthcare professionals.

**Alzheimer's Disease**

It is the most common form of memory loss that accounts for 60-70% of cases.

It is used due to the accumulation of abnormal proteins in the brain, including beta-amyloid plaques and tau tangles, which leads to neuronal damage and loss [1]. Symptoms include loss of memory, language problems, improper functioning in judgment, and changes in behavior and personality. Alzheimer's disease usually progresses gradually over several years, with signs of aggravation as the disease progresses.

**Multiple Sclerosis (MS)**

Multiple Sclerosis (MS) is a persistent autoimmune condition that impacts the Central Nervous System (CNS), comprising the brain, spinal cord, and optic nerves.It is characterized by inflammation and demyelination, which involves damage to the protective myelin sheath surrounding nerve fibers, along with the formation of scar tissue (sclerosis) in the Central Nervous System (CNS). MS can vary widely in its presentation and progression, with symptoms that range from mild to severe and fluctuating over time.

Here are some key points about multiple sclerosis [2].

**Symptoms**

Symptoms of MS can vary depending on the site and degree of damage within the central nervous system. Typical symptoms include:

- Fatigue
- Muscle failing or stiffness
- Loss of sensation or itchy in the limbs
- Difficulty with coordination and balance
- Hazy or double vision
- Problems with speech or swallowing
- Bowel and bladder dysfunction
- Cognitive impairment, including difficulties with memory and concentration
- Mood changes, such as depression or anxiety

**Types of MS**

**Relapsing-Remitting MS (RRMS):** It is the most common form of MS, characterized by periods of relapse (exacerbations) during which new symptoms develop or previously present symptoms become severe, leading to periods of remission during which symptoms improve or stabilize.

**Secondary Progressive MS (SPMS):** In SPMS, the disease transitions from the relapsing-remitting phase to a progressive phase, marked by a severity of symptoms and disability, with or without relapses.

**Primary Progressive MS (PPMS):** It is characterized by a slow progression of symptoms and disabilities from the onset, without distinct relapse-remission cycles.

**Causes and Risk Factors:** The accurate basis of MS is not completely understood, except that it is believed to involve a combination of inherited, environmental, and genetic factors. Risk factors for MS include a family history of the disease, certain viral infections (such as Epstein-Barr virus), smoking, vitamin D deficiency, and geographic location (MS is more common in temperate climates).Diagnosis: MS can be diagnosed with the help of medical history, neurological examination, and different tests that include magnetic resonance imaging (MRI) to detect areas of CNS damage, cerebrospinal fluid analysis after lumbar puncture (spinal tap) for immune markers, and evoked potential tests to measure nerve signal transmission.

**Treatment:** Although there is no cure for MS, various treatments exist to aid in symptom management, diminish disease activity, and decelerate progression. These may encompass disease-modifying therapies (DMTs) aimed at suppressing the immune system and mitigating inflammation, symptomatic treatments to alleviate specific symptoms, rehabilitation therapies to improve mobility and function, and lifestyle interventions such as exercise, healthy diet, and stress management. Early diagnosis and access to suitable treatment are essential in addressing the substantial impact that MS, a complex and unpredictable condition.

**Epilepsy:** Epilepsy is a neurological condition characterized by recurrent, unprovoked seizures. These seizures result from abnormal electrical discharges in the brain, leading to temporary disturbances in normal brain function [3, 4].

**Types of Seizures:** There are different types of seizures, which can be divided into two major categories:

**Generalized Seizures:** Such seizures can cause loss of consciousness and impact both sides of the brain. Tonic-colonic seizures (formerly called grand mal), absence seizures (previously called petit mal), and tonic, colonic, and atonic seizures are among the subtypes (Fig. **2**).

**Focal (Partial) Seizures:** These seizures, which originate in a specific brain region, may or may not involve a loss of consciousness. Focal seizures can be further divided into two types: focal onset impaired awareness seizures (formerly known as complex partial seizures) and focal onset aware seizures (formerly known as simple partial seizures).

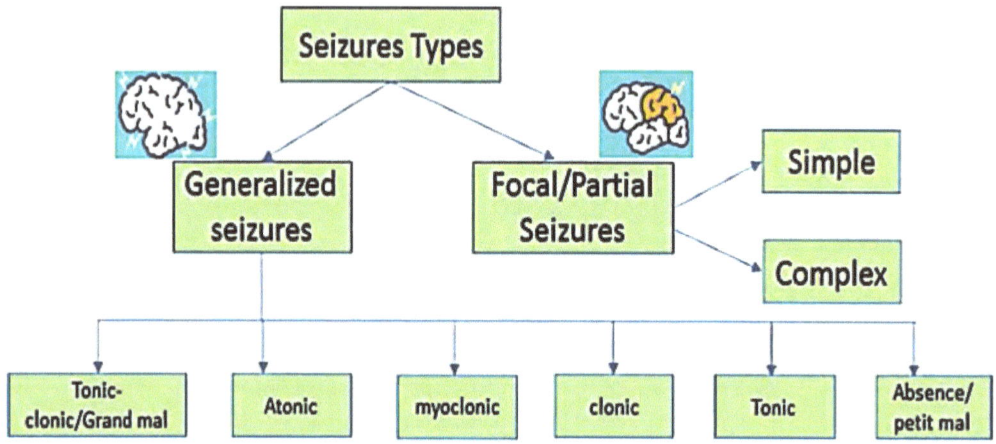


**Fig. (2).** Category and subcategories of seizures.

**Causes:** Epilepsy can have various causes, including genetic factors, brain injury or trauma, brain tumors, stroke, infections (such as meningitis or encephalitis), developmental disorders, and certain metabolic or neurodegenerative conditions.

**Diagnosis:** Epilepsy can be diagnosed with the help of medical history, neurological examination, and diagnostic tests such as electroencephalography (EEG) to measure electrical activity in the brain, MRI or CT scans to detect structural abnormalities, and blood tests to rule out metabolic or infectious causes.

**How Do Seizure Occur?**

Seizures occur due to abnormal electrical activity in the brain. Usually, the brain sends electrical signals in a coordinated manner to control various functions, such as movement, sensation, and cognition. However, when there is a sudden burst of electrical activity that disrupts this typical pattern, it can lead to a seizure. There are various causes of seizures, including:

**Epilepsy:** This is a neurological disorder characterized by recurrent seizures. It is due to genetic factors, brain injury, or structural abnormalities in the brain.

**Brain Injury:** Traumatic brain injury, stroke, brain tumors, infections, and other brain conditions can disrupt regular brain activity and lead to seizures.

**Genetic Factors:** Some individuals have a genetic susceptibility to seizures or epilepsy.

**Metabolic Disorders:** Imbalances in electrolytes (such as sodium and potassium), glucose levels, or other metabolic disturbances can initiate seizures.

**Infections:** Certain infections, such as meningitis, encephalitis, or brain abscesses, can cause brain swelling and may lead to seizures.

**Toxins:** Exposure to certain toxins, such as lead, carbon monoxide, or certain medications or drugs, can trigger seizures.

**Withdrawal:** Abruptly stopping certain medications, alcohol, or drugs can lead to withdrawal seizures.

During a seizure, the specific symptoms can depending on which part of the brain is affected, as well as the severity of the abnormal electrical activity. Seizures can manifest as convulsions, muscle spasms, loss of consciousness, staring spells, or altered sensations. Treatment typically involves medications to control seizures, lifestyle modifications, and sometimes surgery in cases where seizures are resistant to medication.

**Treatment:** Treatment for epilepsy focuses on diminishing both the frequency and severity of seizures, while also minimizing adverse effects and enhancing overall quality of life. Common treatment approaches comprise [5].

**Antiseizure Medications (Antiepileptic Drugs):** These medications are the primary treatment for epilepsy and work by stabilizing the electrical activity in the brain.

**Ketogenic Diet:** This high-fat, low-carbohydrate diet is effective in reducing seizures, particularly in children with certain types of epilepsy.

**Vagus Nerve Stimulation (VNS):** VNS therapy involves inserting a device that sends electrical impulses to the vagus nerve, which can help reduce **seizure** frequency in some individuals.

**Surgery:** If seizures are not controlled with medicine, then surgery to remove or disconnect the part of the brain responsible for seizures (epilepsy surgery) may be considered.

**Lifestyle Management:** Managing epilepsy often involves lifestyle modifications to reduce seizure triggers and improve overall health. This may include getting enough sleep, avoiding alcohol and drugs that may lower seizure threshold, managing stress, and adhering to medication regimens.

Living with epilepsy may present challenges, but with a suitable diagnosis and treatment. Regular follow-up, adherence to treatment plans, and seizure safety precautions are important aspects of epilepsy management. Additionally, raising awareness and reducing stigma surrounding epilepsy can help promote understanding and support for those affected by the condition.

## CONCLUSION

In conclusion, neurological disorders present complex challenges that require a multifaceted approach encompassing research, diagnosis, treatment, and support. By advancing our understanding and addressing the diverse needs of individuals affected by neurological conditions, we can strive towards better outcomes and an improved quality of life for those living with these conditions. Support from family, friends, and support groups plays a vital role in coping with neurological disorders. Providing education, empathy, and practical assistance can help individuals and their caregivers navigate the challenges posed by these conditions.

## REFERENCES

[1] Bouhy D, Timmerman V. [Animal models of Charcot-Marie-Tooth disease and their relevance for understanding the disease in humans]. Rev Neurol (Paris) 2013; 169(12): 971-7.
[http://dx.doi.org/10.1016/j.neurol.2013.07.027] [PMID: 24238786]

[2] Oh J, Vidal-Jordana A, Montalban X. Multiple sclerosis: clinical aspects. Curr Opin Neurol 2018; 31(6): 752-9.
[http://dx.doi.org/10.1097/WCO.0000000000000622] [PMID: 30300239]

[3] Beghi E, Giussani G, Sander JW. The natural history and prognosis of epilepsy. Epileptic disorders: international epilepsy journal with videotape. 2015; 17(3): 243-53.
[http://dx.doi.org/10.1684/epd.2015.0751]

[4] Kim LG, Johnson TL, Marson AG, Chadwick DW. Prediction of risk of seizure recurrence after a single seizure and early epilepsy: further results from the MESS trial. Lancet Neurol 2006; 5(4): 317-22.
[http://dx.doi.org/10.1016/S1474-4422(06)70383-0] [PMID: 16545748]

[5] FitzPatrick L, Bird A. Genetic therapies for neurological disorders. Hum Genet 2022; 141(5): 1085-91.
[http://dx.doi.org/10.1007/s00439-021-02399-5] [PMID: 34807307]

# CHAPTER 2

# The Central Nervous System: Gateway to Understanding Mind and Body

**Abstract:** The Central Nervous System (CNS) encompasses the brain and spinal cord and performs the role as the command center of the body, regulating an innumerable number of physiological and cognitive functions.

Structure: The CNS is organized into discrete regions, each with specialized roles in processing sensory information, coordinating motor responses, and regulating higher cognitive functions. The brain consists of interconnected areas, including the cerebral cortex, cerebellum, and brainstem. The spinal cord serves as a conduit for sensory and motor signals between the brain and the peripheral nervous system.

Function: The CNS integrates sensory inputs from the environment and internal organs to generate appropriate motor responses, maintain homeostasis, and facilitate adaptive behavior. Neurons, the fundamental units of the CNS, communicate through complex networks of synaptic connections, allowing for rapid information processing and transmission.

**Keywords:** Brain, Neurons, Neurotransmitters, Nerve impulse, Spinal cord, Synaptic cleft.

## INTRODUCTION

Human neurological coordination can be separated into the central nervous system and peripheral nervous system. It comprises the common sense and the spinal cord. It significantly influences various bodily functions. In processing and synchronizing information received from the body's sensory organs and sending out commands to muscles, glands, and organs to execute appropriate responses.

## COMPONENTS OF INNERMOST NERVOUS COORDINATION

The Central Nervous System (CNS) contains two main components: the brain and the spinal cord (Fig. **1**).

**Sumaira Kanwal & Shazia Perveen**

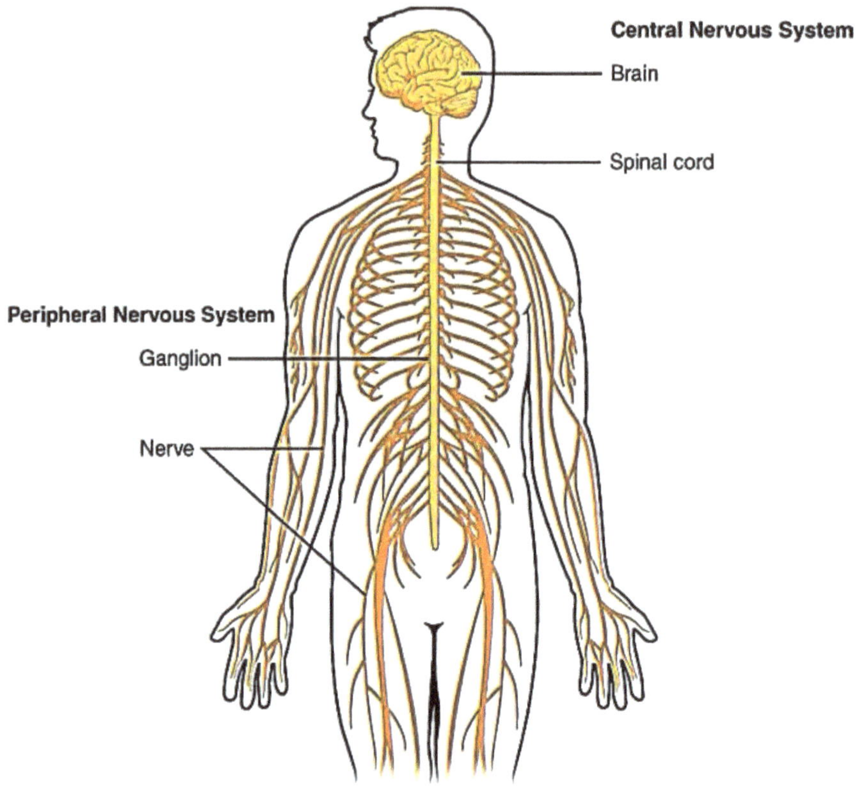


**Fig. (1).** Schematic representation of the peripheral nervous system in orange and the central nervous system in yellow.

**Brain:** It serves as the central command center of both the CNS and the entire nervous system, comprising multiple distinct regions, each dedicated to particular functions (Fig. **2**) [1, 2]:

## Regions of the Brain

- **Cerebrum:** It's the significant fraction of the intelligence, which is separated into several distinct parts, each with its specialized functions. Here are the main parts of the cerebrum:
- **Frontal Lobes and Functions:** These are the largest lobes of the brain's cerebrum and are located at the front of each cerebral hemisphere. These perform various functions such as:
- **Executive Functioning:** The frontal lobes play a central role in executive functions, which include abilities such as planning, decision-making, problem-solving, reasoning, and cognitive flexibility. These functions are crucial for goal-directed behavior and adaptive responses to changing circumstances.

- **Motor Control:** The key motor cortex, positioned in the posterior part of the frontal lobe, is responsible for controlling voluntary movements of skeletal muscles throughout the body. It sends signals to the muscles, initiating and coordinating movement.
- **Speech Production:** Broca's area, typically located in the anterior prefrontal lobe, is involved in the production of verbal communication and language. Damage to this area can result in Broca's aphasia, characterized by difficulty in producing spoken language while comprehension remains intact.
- **Personality Expression and Social Behavior:** The frontal lobes are implicated in regulating personality traits and social behavior. Damage to the frontal lobes can lead to changes in personality, impulsivity, disinhibition, and difficulties in social interactions.
- **Emotional Regulation:** The frontal lobes play a crucial role in regulating emotions and emotional responses. They help modulate emotional reactions to stimuli and play a role in emotional self-regulation.
- **Primary Motor Cortex:** Located in the posterior part of the frontal lobe, it is involved in controlling the voluntary movements of skeletal muscles.
- **Prefrontal Cortex:** It is involved in higher cognitive functions, including decision-making, planning, problem-solving, and social behavior. It also plays a role in personality expression and the regulation of emotions.
- **Broca's Area:** It is located in the left frontal lobe (usually), and it is involved in the production of speech and the processing of language.
- **Parietal Lobes:** The Parietal lobe integrate somatosensory inputs such as pressure, touch and proprioception to create an accurate spatial representation of the body and environment. They also contribute to visuospatial processing, attention and the conversion of sensory signals into motor intentions supporting the coordinated action.
- **Primary Somatosensory Cortex:** Located in the anterior part of the parietal lobe, it receives and processes sensory information from the skin, muscles, and joints, allowing for perception of touch, pressure, temperature, and pain.

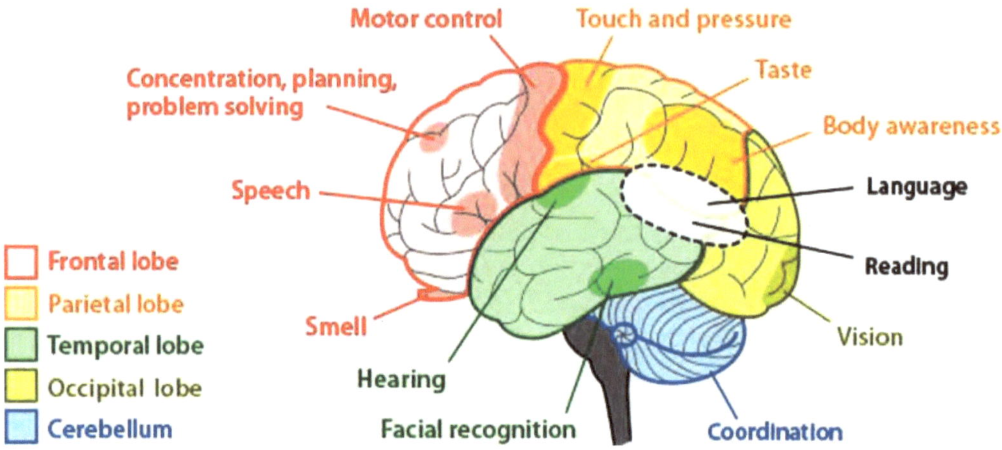


**Fig. (2).** Different regions of the brain.

**Parietal Region:** In charge of processing bodily sensations such as touch, pressure, warmth, and pain. It also affects perception and spatial awareness.

- **Temporal Lobe:** Involved in processing auditory information, memory formation, language comprehension, and emotion regulation. The hippocampus, a structure located within the temporal lobe, plays a crucial role in memory consolidation.
- **Occipital Lobe:** first and foremost, accountable for processing the chart in sequence from the eyes and interpreting illustration stimuli (Fig. **1**).
- **Cerebellum:** Coordinates and regulates voluntary movement, balance, posture, and muscle tone. It assists in refining motor skills and contributes to motor learning and memory.

### Brainstem

- **Medulla Oblongata:** Regulates vital autonomic functions, including heartbeat, breathing, blood pressure, and reflexes such as coughing, sneezing, and swallowing.
- **Pons:** Acts as a bridge between different parts of the brain and is involved in regulating sleep, breathing, and facial expressions.
- **Midbrain:** Functions as a relay center for auditory and visual information and plays a role in controlling eye movement and reflexes.

### Diencephalon

- **Thalamus:** It acts as a relay station for sensory information, transmitting signals to the appropriate areas of the cerebral cortex for further processing.

- **Hypothalamus:** Regulates homeostasis by controlling hunger, thirst, body temperature, and the sleep-wake cycle. It also plays a role in regulating hormone secretion from the pituitary gland.

Each region of the brain works together in a highly coordinated manner to process sensory input, generate appropriate motor responses, regulate physiological functions, and support higher cognitive functions such as memory, learning, and emotion.

- **Spinal Cord:** The spinal cord, elongated and tubular, stretches from the base of the brain down through the vertebral column. Its primary purpose is to transmit nerve signals flanked by the brain and the body's various parts. The spinal cord also coordinates reflexes, which are rapid, involuntary responses to stimuli (Fig. **2**).

## Unit of the Innermost Nervous Organization

The Central Nervous System (CNS) doesn't have a unit in the conventional sense. Instead, it's a complex network of interconnected neurons and support cells that includes the brain and spinal cord. These structures work together to process and integrate information received from sensory organs, coordinate motor responses, regulate physiological functions, and support higher cognitive functions, including thinking, memory, and emotions. So, while we don't refer to the CNS in terms of units, it's a fundamental system that plays a critical role in the functioning of the human body and mind.

It integrates incoming signals from dendrites and determines whether to generate an action potential [3].

**Dendrites:** Dendrites are branching extensions that take delivery of signals beginning other neurons or sensory receptors. They increase the surface area available for receiving incoming signals and transmit these signals toward the cell body.

**Axon:** An electrical impulse is carried by the axon, a long, thin projection, from the cell body to nearby neurons, muscles, or glands. It can be myelinated, which means that a fatty material called myelin surrounds it, speeding up signal transmission.

**Axon Terminals (Synaptic Terminals):** At the end of the axon, there are small structures called axon terminals or synaptic terminals. These terminals form synaptic connections with other neurons or target cells. Upon arrival of an action potential at the axon terminals, it initiates the discharge of neurotransmitters into the synapse. These neurotransmitters subsequently attach to receptors located on the postsynaptic membrane of the receiving neuron or target cell.

**The Functions of Neurons Include**

Neurons serve several essential functions in the nervous system:

- **Signal Transmission:** Neurons convey electrical signals, termed action potentials, through their axons. This mechanism facilitates swift communication among diverse regions of the nervous system, enabling the coordination of sensory perception, motor function, and advanced cognitive processes.
- **Integration of Information:** Neurons gather input from neighboring neurons *via* their dendrites. The cell body then processes this incoming information and decides whether to generate an output signal based on the combined input it receives. This process of integration enables neurons to process and interpret complex patterns of sensory information and to generate appropriate responses.
- **Communication:** Neurons interact with each other and with target cells, such as muscles or glands, through specialized junctions known as synapses. Upon reaching the axon terminals of a presynaptic neuron, an action potential prompts the release of neurotransmitters addicted to the synapse. These neurotransmitters attach to receptors on the postsynaptic cell, causing alterations in its membrane potential, which may potentially initiate an action potential in the postsynaptic neuron.

**Control of Physiological Processes:** Neurons regulate various physiological processes, including movement, sensation, cognition, and emotion. Different types of neurons have specialized functions that contribute to the overall functioning of the nervous system. For example, sensory neurons pick up environmental cues and send them to the central nervous system. In contrast, motor neurons provide impulses to muscles and glands in the CNS that cause movement or secretion.

- **Learning and Memory:** Neurons play a vital role in the processes of learning and memory. Synaptic connections between neurons can undergo strengthening or weakening in response to experiences, a phenomenon known as synaptic plasticity. This adaptive capability of the nervous system enables learning from previous encounters, thereby establishing the foundation for memory formation and learning.

In essence, neurons serve as the fundamental components of the nervous system, tasked with transmitting, processing, and assimilating information to oversee various physiological and cognitive functions.

## Cognitive Functions of Neurons

Neurons are fundamental to cognitive functions, which encompass a wide range of mental processes involved in acquiring, processing, storing, and retrieving information. While neurons themselves don't engage in cognitive processes in the way that higher brain structures do, they are essential for supporting these functions through their role in transmitting and processing information within neural circuits. Here's how neurons contribute to cognitive functions:

**Information Processing:** Neurons receive input from sensory organs or other neurons through their dendrites. They integrate this incoming information and generate output signals, known as action potentials, if the combined input is sufficient to reach the neuron's threshold. This process of information processing enables neurons to analyze and interpret sensory input, generating appropriate responses.

**Memory Formation:** Neurons play a crucial role in memory formation, which involves the encoding, storage, and retrieval of information. Changes in synaptic strength, known as synaptic plasticity, underlie the formation of memories. Neurons within specific brain regions, such as the hippocampus and cortex, form interconnected networks that support the encoding and retrieval of different types of memories, including episodic memories, semantic memories, and procedural memories.

**Attention and Concentration:** Neurons play a crucial role in controlling attention and concentration by modulating the activity of neural circuits involved in these processes. Neurons within the prefrontal cortex and other brain regions help filter irrelevant information, sustain attention on task-relevant stimuli, and shift attention between different tasks or stimuli.

**Language Processing:** Neurons in language-related brain regions, such as Broca's area and Wernicke's area, support language processing by encoding and decoding linguistic information. Neurons within these regions form specialized circuits involved in speech production, comprehension, and other aspects of language processing.

**Executive Functions:** Neurons within the prefrontal cortex and other brain regions support executive functions, which include abilities such as planning, decision-making, problem-solving, and cognitive flexibility. These functions are crucial for goal-directed behavior and adaptive responses to changing circumstances.

**Perception and Cognition:** Neurons within sensory processing regions of the brain, such as the visual cortex, auditory cortex, and somatosensory cortex, support perception by encoding and processing sensory information. Neurons within higher-order cognitive regions of the brain, such as the association cortices, integrate sensory input with stored knowledge and memories to support complex mental processes, including reasoning, imagination, and problem-solving.

Overall, while neurons themselves do not engage in cognitive functions in the same way that higher brain structures do, they are essential for supporting these functions through their role in transmitting and processing information within neural circuits.

**Physiological Functions of Neurons**

The physiological functions of neurons encompass a broad range of activities vital for the performance of the nervous system and the entire body. Here are some key physiological functions of neurons:

**Signal Transmission:** Neurons propagate electrical signals, referred to as action potentials, along their axons. This mechanism facilitates swift communication among diverse regions of the nervous system, thereby coordinating sensory input, motor responses, and advanced cognitive functions.

**Integration of Information:** Neurons receive stimuli from other neurons *via* their dendrites. The cell body synthesizes this inward information and concludes whether to produce a response signal based on the combined input it receives. This process of integration enables neurons to process and interpret complex patterns of sensory information, generating appropriate responses.

**Synaptic Transmission:** Neurons communicate with one another and with target cells, such as muscles or glands, through specialized junctions called synapses. When an action potential arrives at the axon terminals of a presynaptic neuron, it initiates the discharge of neurotransmitters addicted to the synapse. These neurotransmitters then bind to receptors on the postsynaptic cell, causing alterations in the membrane potential of the postsynaptic cell and potentially triggering an action potential in the postsynaptic neuron.

**Regulation of Membrane Potential:**Neurons maintain a resting membrane potential, indicating the electrical charge difference between the interior and exterior of the cell. This baseline potential plays a crucial role in generating and transmitting action potentials. Neurons utilize ion channels and pumps to regulate the movement of ions across their cell membranes, thereby controlling their membrane potential.

**Neurotransmitter Release:** Neurons synthesize and release neurotransmitters, which are chemical messengers that send signals across synapses to other neurons or target cells. Different neurotransmitters have specific effects on postsynaptic cells, ranging from excitatory (depolarizing) to inhibitory (hyperpolarizing).

**Neuronal Plasticity:** Neurons demonstrate plasticity, which refers to their capacity for structural and functional adjustments in reaction to experiences or activities. This adaptability is fundamental to mechanisms such as learning and memory, as well as the nervous system's ability to accommodate environmental changes or recover from injuries.

**Metabolic Functions:** Neurons have high metabolic demands to support their electrical activity and maintain cellular functions. They require a constant supply of oxygen and glucose to produce the energy needed for action potentials and other cellular processes.

At its core, neurons hold a pivotal position in the operations of both the nervous system and the entire body, facilitating sensory perception, motor control, cognition, and various other physiological processes vital for sustaining life.

### Types of Neurons

Neurons are categorized into several types based on their structure, function, and location within the nervous system. Here are the major categories of neurons:

- **Sensory Neurons (Afferent Neurons):** These neurons transmit information from sensory receptors (such as those for touch, pain, temperature, vision, hearing, and taste) to the Central Nervous System (CNS). They are typically unipolar neurons with long dendrites extending to sensory receptors and an axon that carries signals to the CNS.
- **Motor Neurons (Efferent Neurons):** These neurons send signals to or after the CNS to muscles, glands, and other effector organs, controlling movement and other physiological responses (Fig. **3**).
- Motor neurons can be subdivided into somatic motor neurons, which innervate skeletal muscles, and autonomic motor neurons, which innervate smooth muscle, myocardium, and glands (Fig. **3**).
- **Interneurons (Association Neurons)**: Interneurons are found entirely within the CNS and act as connectors between sensory and motor neurons. They

integrate and process signals from multiple sources and relay information within local circuits. Interneurons, the most abundant type of neuron in the nervous system, are essential for tasks such as information processing, coordination, and higher cognitive functions (Fig. **3**).

Additionally, neurons can be classified based on their morphology:

- **Unipolar Neurons:** Unipolar neurons have a single ss extending from the cell body, which bifurcates into two outgrowth branches: one acts as a dendrite, receiving signals from sensory receptors, while the other functions as an axon, transmitting signals to the CNS.
- **Bipolar Neurons:** Bipolar neurons have two processes extending from the cell body: one dendrite that receives signals and one axon that transmits signals. Bipolar neurons are commonly found in specialized sensory organs such as the retina of the eye and the olfactory epithelium of the nose.
- **Multipolar Neurons:** These neurons have multiple dendrites that extend from the cell body and a solitary axon. The predominant type of neuron in the Central Nervous System (CNS), they play pivotal roles in various functions such as motor control, sensory perception, and cognitive processes [4].

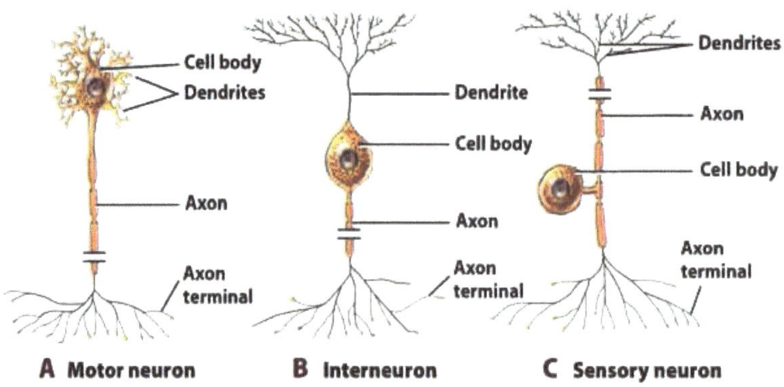


**Fig. (3).** Types of neurons.

These classifications provide a framework for understanding the diversity of neurons in the nervous system and their specialized roles in mediating sensory perception, motor control, cognition, and other physiological processes.

## Structure of a Neuron

The structure of a neuron consists of several specialized components that enable it to transmit and process information. Here's a breakdown of the major parts of a neuron:

**Compartment Body (Soma):** neuron's central component, the cell body, houses the nucleus and a variety of organelles crucial for the neuron's metabolic activities. It consolidates incoming signals from dendrites and initiates outgoing signals.

**Dendrites:** Dendrites are branching extensions that radiate out from the cell body. Dendrites gather signals from neighboring neurons or sensory receptors and convey these signals towards the cell body. Their function is to augment the surface area available for receiving synaptic input.

**Axon:** Electrical impulses are carried *via* the axon, a long, thin projection that extends from the cell body and travels to neighboring neurons, muscles, or glands. A neuron can range from a few millimeters to over a meter in length. Specific axons are myelinated, indicating they're enveloped by a fatty substance called myelin, which increases the speed of the signal.

## Spinal Cord

The spinal cord serves as a crucial component of the Central Nervous System (CNS), facilitating the transmission of signals between the brain and the body. It is an elongated, slender, tubular structure composed of nervous tissue and supportive cells, running from the base of the brain through the vertebral canal within the spinal column (Fig. **4**).

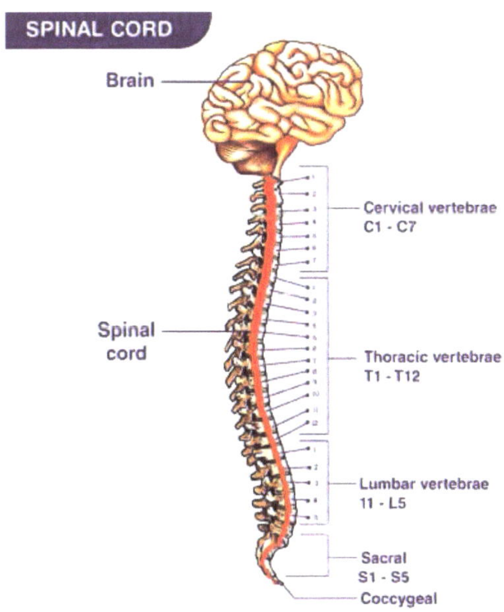


**Fig. (4).** Detailed structure of the spinal cord.

Key functions of the spinal cord include:

**Transmission of Nerve Signals:** Sensory nerves carry signals from the body's periphery to the brain, conveying information about sensations such as touch, temperature, and pain. Motor nerves convey signals from the brain to muscles and glands, controlling movement and various bodily functions.

**Reflexes:** The spinal cord is capable of generating reflex actions independently of the brain. For example, when you touch something hot, sensory neurons in the skin send a signal to the spinal cord, which then quickly sends a signal back to the muscles, causing you to pull your hand away before the brain has even processed the sensation.

**Coordination:** While the brain handles higher-level coordination and executive functions, the spinal cord plays a pivotal role in orchestrating fundamental reflexes and motor patterns, particularly in activities such as walking and running.

Injuries to the spinal cord can have severe consequences, potentially leading to paralysis or loss of sensation below the level of injury. Research into spinal cord injuries and disorders is ongoing, with efforts focused on understanding the mechanisms of injury and developing treatments to promote recovery [5].

**Neurotransmitters:** Neurotransmitters are chemical agents that facilitate the transmission of signals across synapses, the connections between neurons (nerve cells) within the nervous system.

These molecules are released from the terminal of one neuron (the presynaptic neuron). They traverse the synaptic gap and attach to designated receptors on the membrane of the neighboring neuron (known as the postsynaptic neuron), triggering a reaction within it.

Different neurotransmitters exhibit unique functions and exert specific effects on both behavior and physiology. Examples of neurotransmitters include:

**Acetylcholine:** Involved in muscle control, memory, and attention.

**Dopamine:** Plays a role in reward, motivation, motor control, and mood regulation.

**Serotonin:** Regulates mood, appetite, sleep, and some cognitive functions.

**Norepinephrine (noradrenaline):** Involved in the body's “fight or flight” response, alertness, and attention.

**Gamma-Aminobutyric Acid (GABA):** It functions as an inhibitory neurotransmitter, decreasing neuronal excitability and fostering relaxation.

**Glutamate:** Acts as an excitatory neurotransmitter, facilitating communication between neurons and playing a key role in learning and memory. Extra synaptic NMDA receptors are glutamate-gated neurotransmitter receptors that are localized to non-synaptic sites on the surface of neuronal cells.

These neurotransmitters work together in complex ways to regulate various physiological and psychological processes in the body. Disruptions in neurotransmitter levels or function are associated with a wide range of neurological and psychiatric conditions, including depression, schizophrenia, and Parkinson's disease.

### Production and Storage of Neurotransmitters

The production and storage of neurotransmitters are vital processes within neurons that ensure the proper functioning of neuronal communication. Here's a general overview of how it works: Synthesis of neurotransmitters occurs within the neuron *via* diverse biochemical pathways.

The precursor molecules required for neurotransmitter synthesis are often obtained from the diet or through metabolic processes. For example, the amino acid precursor tyrosine is converted into dopamine, norepinephrine, and epinephrine, while tryptophan is converted into serotonin.

**Enzymatic Conversion:** Enzymes within the neuron catalyze the conversion of precursor molecules into neurotransmitters. These enzymes are specific to each neurotransmitter and are often regulated by cellular signaling pathways to control the levels of neurotransmitters.

**Packaging into Vesicles:** Once synthesized, neurotransmitters are transported into synaptic vesicles, which are small, membrane-bound organelles found within the presynaptic terminal. Vesicular transport proteins mediate this process and requires energy in the form of ATP.

**Storage:** Neurotransmitters are stored in synaptic vesicles until they are released in response to neuronal activity. This storage helps to regulate neurotransmitter levels and ensures rapid availability for synaptic transmission.

### Pre-Synaptic Neuron

The presynaptic neuron, alternatively referred to as the presynaptic cell, plays a critical role in neuronal communication throughout the nervous system. It refers to the neuron that sends a signal across a synapse to another neuron, known as the postsynaptic neuron, or to an effector cell, such as a muscle cell or a gland cell.

**Here's a Breakdown of its Role and Functions**

**Transmission of Signals:** The presynaptic neuron receives input signals from other neurons *via* its dendrites and cell body. The signals may induce excitation or inhibition, depending on the neurotransmitters involved and the receptors present on the presynaptic neuron.

**Generation of Action Potentials:** If the input signals received by the presynaptic neuron attain sufficient strength to surpass the threshold potential, they can initiate the production of an action potential. Subsequently, this action potential propagates along the axon of the presynaptic neuron toward the presynaptic terminal [6].

**Release of Neurotransmitters:** On reaching the presynaptic terminal, the action potential initiates the activation of voltage-gated calcium channels. This influx of calcium ions into the presynaptic terminal prompts the merging of synaptic vesicles, which contain neurotransmitters, with the presynaptic membrane. Consequently, neurotransmitters are released into the synaptic cleft (Fig. **5**).

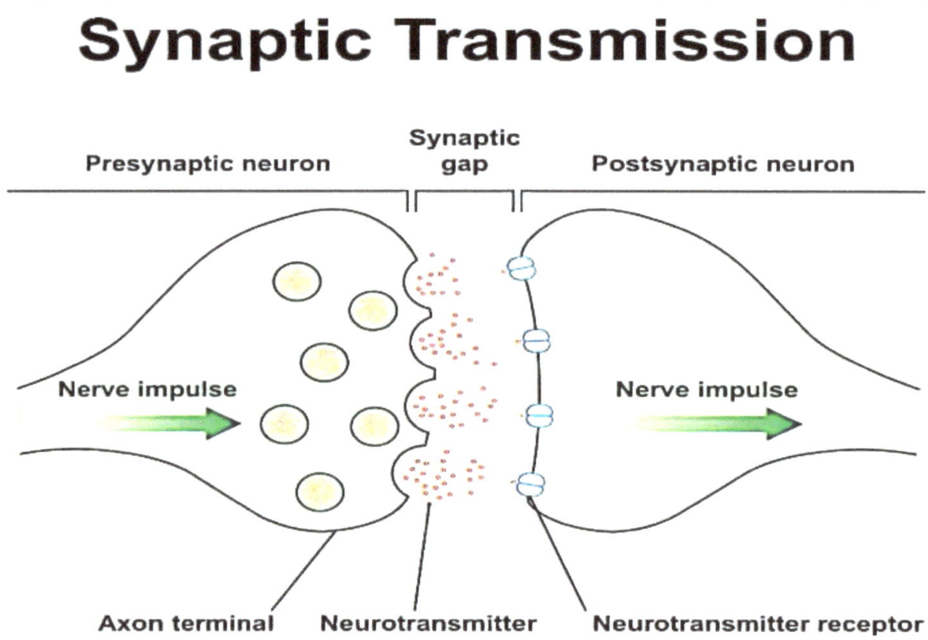


**Fig. (5).** Synaptic cleft.

**Modulation of Synaptic Transmission:** The presynaptic neuron can modulate synaptic transmission through various mechanisms. For example, it can regulate the amount of neurotransmitter released in response to an action potential, a process known as presynaptic facilitation or inhibition.

**Plasticity and Learning:** The involvement of presynaptic neurons is vital in synaptic plasticity, which refers to the capability of synapses to undergo strengthening or weakening over time in reaction to activity. This mechanism is fundamental to the establishment of learning and memory in the brain.

**Integration of Information:** Presynaptic neurons integrate incoming signals from multiple sources and determine whether to transmit an excitatory or inhibitory signal to the postsynaptic neuron based on this information.

In summary, the presynaptic neuron serves as the initiator of synaptic transmission, releasing neurotransmitters that carry signals to the postsynaptic neuron or effector cell, thus facilitating communication within the nervous system.

**Post-synaptic Neuron**

The postsynaptic neuron, alternatively referred to as the postsynaptic cell, is responsible for receiving signals transmitted from the presynaptic neuron across a synapse. It serves as an essential element in neuronal communication within the nervous system. Here is an outline of its role and functions:

**Reception of Neurotransmitters:** Neurotransmitters released by the presynaptic neuron bind to specific receptors located on the membrane of the postsynaptic neuron. These receptors can be ionotropic receptors, which, upon binding of a neurotransmitter, directly unlock ion channels, or metabotropic receptors, which activate intracellular signaling pathways.

**Generation of Postsynaptic Potentials:** When neurotransmitters attach to receptors on the postsynaptic neuron (Fig. **6**), it can result in alterations to the membrane potential of the postsynaptic cell. Excitatory neurotransmitters typically depolarize the postsynaptic membrane, producing excitatory postsynaptic potentials (EPSPs), while inhibitory neurotransmitters typically hyperpolarize the membrane, producing inhibitory postsynaptic potentials (IPSPs).

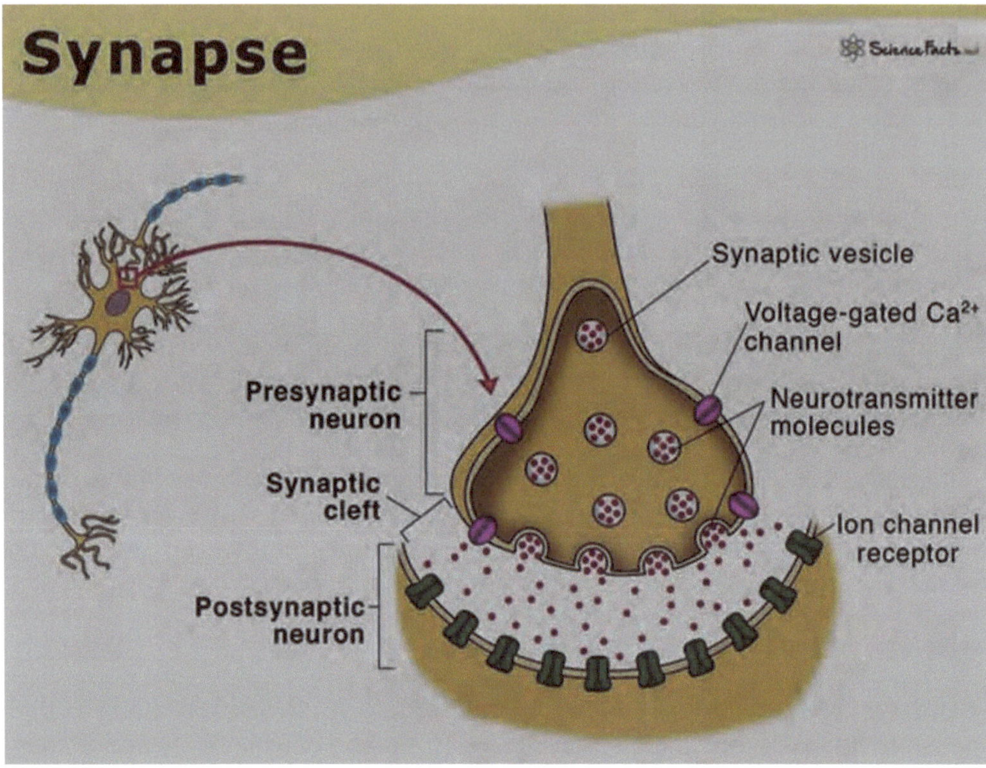


**Fig. (6).** Pre synaptic and postsynaptic neurons and synaptic Cleft.

**Integration of Signals:** The postsynaptic neuron receives signals from multiple presynaptic neurons, both excitatory and inhibitory. The combination of excitatory postsynaptic potentials (EPSPs) and inhibitory postsynaptic potentials (IPSPs) dictates whether the postsynaptic neuron will produce an action potential.

**Propagation of Signals:** If the summation of EPSPs reaches the threshold for action potential generation, an action potential is triggered in the postsynaptic neuron. This action potential then propagates along the axon of the postsynaptic neuron, continuing the signal transmission to downstream neurons or effector cells.

**Synaptic Plasticity:** Postsynaptic neurons are also involved in synaptic plasticity, which denotes the ability of synapses to modify their strength in response to activity over time. Long-Term Potentiation (LTP) and Long-Term Depression (LTD) represent types of synaptic plasticity that encompass alterations in the efficiency of synaptic transmission at the postsynaptic neuron.

**Signal Amplification and Divergence:** Postsynaptic neurons can amplify signals received from multiple presynaptic neurons and also diverge signals to numerous downstream neurons, allowing for complex sequential dispensation and neural network function.

In summary, the postsynaptic neuron receives and integrates signals from presynaptic neurons, determining whether to generate an action potential and propagate the signal further within the nervous system.

**Release:** Upon arrival of an achievement possible at the presynaptic terminal, voltage-gated calcium channels are activated, enabling calcium ions to enter the terminal. This calcium influx prompts the merging of synaptic vesicles with the presynaptic membrane, consequential in the discharge of neurotransmitters into the synaptic cleft. **Reuptake and Recycling:** Following release, neurotransmitters have the ability to bind to receptors located on the postsynaptic neuron and trigger a response. They can also be taken back up into the presynaptic neuron through reuptake transporters, where they can be recycled or degraded by enzymes.

**Degradation:** Some neurotransmitters are broken down by enzymes within the synaptic cleft or within the presynaptic terminal itself. For example, acetylcholine is hydrolyzed by the enzyme acetylcholinesterase into acetate and choline.

Overall, the production and storage of neurotransmitters are tightly regulated processes that ensure the precise control of neuronal communication in the nervous system. Dysregulation of neurotransmitter synthesis, storage, or release can lead to neurological and psychiatric disorders.

**Synaptic Cleft**

The synaptic cleft, also known as the synaptic gap, is a miniature gap or breathing space between the presynaptic incurable of one neuron and the postsynaptic membrane of another neuron. It serves as a pivotal location for inter-neuronal communication within the nervous system. Here is an outline of its features and roles:

**Location:** The synaptic cleft is located at chemical synapses, which are specialized junctions between neurons. It separates the presynaptic neuron, which releases neurotransmitters, from the postsynaptic neuron, which receives the neurotransmitter signals.

**Size:** The synaptic cleft is tiny, typically only about 20-40 nanometers wide. This narrow space ensures that neurotransmitters released from the presynaptic neuron can efficiently reach and bind to receptors on the postsynaptic membrane.

**Composition:** The synaptic cleft contains a variety of molecules, including neurotransmitters released by the presynaptic neuron, receptor proteins embedded in the postsynaptic membrane, and various extracellular matrix proteins that help maintain the structure of the synapse.

**Transmission of Signals:** Upon the arrival of an action potential at the presynaptic terminal, neurotransmitters are released into the synaptic cleft, where they diffuse and attach to designated receptors on the postsynaptic membrane. This attachment triggers a cascade of biochemical processes within the postsynaptic neuron, leading to alterations in its membrane potential and the transmission of the signal.

**Termination of Signaling:** After neurotransmitters have transmitted their signals, they are rapidly removed from the synaptic cleft, thereby terminating synaptic transmission. This removal can occur through processes such as enzymatic degradation, reuptake into the presynaptic neuron or surrounding glial cells, and diffusion away from the synapse.

**Regulation of Synaptic Transmission:** The characteristics of the synaptic cleft, including its dimensions, constituents, and the presence of molecules such as neurotransmitters and neuromodulators, can regulate synaptic transmission. Variations in synaptic cleft properties may adjust the potency and effectiveness of synaptic communication among neurons [7].

In summary, The synaptic cleft constitutes a specialized microenvironment facilitating the transmission of neurotransmitter signals from the presynaptic neuron to the postsynaptic neuron. This process enables communication and information processing within the nervous system.

## CONCLUSION

So, being the center of the body, every function is performed under the command and coordination of the central nervous system. A neuron is the basic unit of the Brain; its structure plays an important role in the transfer of information from one part of the body to another in the form of nerve impulses produced by neurotransmitters.

In the case that the external structure of a neuron is damaged, various complications can be observed, including weak stimuli or sometimes the weakening of muscles.

A healthy nervous system enables a person to perform their functions effectively. Otherwise, several diseases can arise, which can affect the quality of life of the affected person.

## REFERENCES

[1] Robertson LT. Memory and the Brain. J Dent Educ 2002; 66(1): 30-42. [http://dx.doi.org/10.1002/j.0022-0337.2002.66.1.tb03506.x] [PMID: 12358099]

[2] Ding Q, Zhao H. Long-term effects of SARS-CoV-2 infection on human brain and memory. Cell Death Discov 2023; 9(1): 196. [http://dx.doi.org/10.1038/s41420-023-01512-z] [PMID: 37380640]

[3] Tabata H. Crosstalk between blood vessels and glia during the central nervous system development. Life (Basel) 2022; 12(11): 1761. [http://dx.doi.org/10.3390/life12111761] [PMID: 36362915]

[4] Ahmad, A. Multimodal neuron classification based on morphology and electrophysiology (Master's thesis, West Virginia University), 2023. [http://dx.doi.org/10.33915/etd.11808]

[5] Gordineer EA, Stokic DS, Krenn MJ. Distinguishing reflex from non-reflex responses elicited by transcutaneous spinal stimulation targeting the lumbosacral cord in healthy individuals. Exp Brain Res 2024; 242(4): 959-70. [http://dx.doi.org/10.1007/s00221-024-06790-2] [PMID: 38416179]

[6] Godavarthi SK, Hiramoto M, Ignatyev Y, *et al.* Postsynaptic receptors regulate presynaptic transmitter stability through transsynaptic bridges. Proc Natl Acad Sci USA 2024; 121(15): e2318041121. [http://dx.doi.org/10.1073/pnas.2318041121] [PMID: 38568976]

[7] Sherlock ME, Baquero Galvis L, Vicens Q, Kieft JS, Jagannathan S. Principles, mechanisms, and biological implications of translation termination–reinitiation. RNA 2023; 29(7): 865-84. [http://dx.doi.org/10.1261/rna.079375.122] [PMID: 37024263]

# CHAPTER 3

# CNS and Nerve Impulse Process

**Abstract:** Generally, there are three sorts of neurons based on their functions. When stimuli such as touch, sound, or light impact the cells in the sensory organs, sensory neurons react by sending signals to the brain or spinal cord. The brain and spinal cord send impulses to motor neurons, which regulate everything from glandular secretion to muscular contractions. Neurons in the same area of the brain or spinal cord communicate with one another through interneurons. A neural circuit is formed when several neurons are functionally coupled to one another. Specialized cells known as neurons are composed of certain components that are shared by all other eukaryotic cells, including the Golgi apparatus, mitochondria, smooth and rough endoplasmic reticulum, nucleus, and cell body (soma). Synapses, which are specialized connections that often require minuscule quantities of chemical neurotransmitters to bridge the synaptic gap and transfer electrical signal from the presynaptic neuron to the target cell. When a neuron is exposed to a chemical stimulus, a nerve impulse is initiated. As an electrical action potential, the nerve impulse passes through the axon membrane and reaches the axon terminal. Neurotransmitters that convey the nerve impulse to the subsequent cell are released from the axon terminal. The following elements can influence or initiate a nerve impulse: Axon Diameter, temperature, neurotransmitter concentration, myelination, threshold potential, neurotransmitter diseases, drug use, and general health. Depolarization, repolarization, and hyperpolarization are the three primary steps of the action potential. When voltage-gated sodium channels open and positively charged sodium ions flow into a neuron, depolarization occurs. The shutting of sodium ion channels and the opening of potassium ion channels result in repolarization. Nerve cells are also made up of an axon, body (soma), dendrites, and myelin sheath. A nerve cell is protected from harm by its fatty-protein coating, which functions similarly to the plastic sheath that covers an electrical cord's wires. It enables electrical impulses to travel swiftly and effectively across different nerve cells. When there is damage, the electrical signal slows down or stops due to slowed conduction, Decreased Signal Strength, Increased Energy Expenditure, and neurological symptoms, among others. This damage can also cause serious disorders, such as Multiple Sclerosis (MS), GBS, CIDP, ADEM, and NMO. Causes of myelin sheath damage may consist of genetic factors, infection, radiation therapy, physical trauma, vitamin deficiencies, and other factors affecting nerve Conduction Velocity (CV), which is the speed at which an electrochemical impulse propagates down a neural pathway. Conduction velocities are affected by a wide array of factors, including age, sex, and various medical conditions. Axonopathy is a disorder affecting the functioning of axons. Nerve impulse affects it by Slowed Conduction Velocity. Conduction block, Signal Degradation, *etc.* Demyelinating diseases, such as Multiple Sclerosis (MS), cause damage or destruction to the myelin sheath that surrounds the axons.

**Sumaira Kanwal & Shazia Perveen**

**Keywords:** Demyelinating diseases, Multiple sclerosis, Neurological symptoms, Presynaptic neuron, Voltage-gated sodium channels.

## INTRODUCTION

Neuropathy is a condition characterized by nerve damage, often resulting in symptoms such as pain, numbness, tingling, or weakness, typically affecting the hands and feet. There are various types of neuropathy, including peripheral neuropathy, which affects the peripheral nerves outside the brain and spinal cord, and autonomic neuropathy, which affects the nerves that control involuntary bodily functions, such as heart rate, digestion, and bladder control. Causes can range from diabetes and infections to trauma and certain medications. Treatment may involve addressing the underlying cause, using medications to manage symptoms, undergoing physical therapy, and adopting a healthy lifestyle. Neuropathy is a comprehensive term encompassing damage or impairment of one or multiple nerves throughout the body. It can affect nerves in various parts of the body, including the peripheral nerves (those outside the brain and spinal cord) and the autonomic nerves (those that control involuntary bodily functions) [1 - 3].

A neuron, also called a nerve cell. It is the basic structural and functional unit of the nervous system. It is composed of different key parts:

- **Cell Body (Soma):** This central element, characterized by an axon has the core and majority of the organelles. It functions to integrate information from neighboring neurons.
- **Dendrites:** These are the extensions of the cell body that accept signals (chemical or electrical) from other neurons or sensory receptors and transmit them toward the cell body.
- **Axon Terminal (Terminal Bouton):** At the axon end, small structures are present that are called axon terminals or terminal boutons. These structures contain neurotransmitters, which are released into the synapse to send signals to additional neurons or target cells.
- **Synapse:** This is the junction flanked by the axon fatal of a solitary neuron with the dendrites or cell body of another neuron. Neurotransmitters released from the axon terminal diffuse across the synapse to transmit signals to the next neuron.
- **Myelin Sheath:** Some neurons are insulated by a fatty substance called myelin. It surrounds the axon.

It involves increasing the velocity of voltaic impulses along the side of the neuron.

- **Nodes of Ranvier:** Gaps that are present in the myelin sheath along the axon are called nodes of Ranvier. They are involved in the rapid conduction of nerve impulses.

Neurons vary in different shapes and sizes depending on their function within the nervous system, but they all share basic structural components [4, 5].

## Chemical Composition of a Neuron

The chemical composition of a neuron includes various molecules and substances that play crucial roles in its structure and function. Here is a breakdown:

- **Water ($H_2O$):** Water is the most abundant molecule in neurons, constituting about 70- 80% of the total mass. It provides the medium for various biochemical reactions and maintains the structural integrity of the neuron.
- **Proteins:** Neurons contain a wide array of proteins, including enzymes, structural proteins, and receptors. Proteins are essential for the structure, function, and signaling processes within neurons.
- **Lipids:** Lipids, including phospholipids, cholesterol, and glycolipids, are major components of the cell membrane and myelin sheath. They provide structural support, regulate membrane fluidity, and serve as energy storage molecules.
- **Nucleic Acids:** Neurons contain DNA and RNA, which are involved in storing genetic information and regulating DNA expression. RNA plays a critical function in the creation of proteins within neurons.
- **Neurotransmitters:** These are chemical messengers that neurons use to communicate with each other and with other cells. Examples include dopamine, serotonin, glutamate, and gamma-aminobutyric acid (GABA).

## Nerve Impulse

It is also known as an action potential. It is an electrochemical signal that travels along a neuron. It is involved in the transmission of information within the nervous system. When a neuron is stimulated, typically by neurotransmitters released from neighboring neurons, ion channels in the neuron's membrane open, allowing ions to

flow in and out of the cell, (Fig. **1**). This creates a change in the neuron's membrane potential, generating an electrical signal that travels down the length of the neuron. Once the impulse reaches the end of the neuron, it is involved in releasing the neurotransmitters into the synapse, which allows the signal to be transmitted to the next neuron in the circuit. This process is necessary for different physiological functions, including sensory perception, motor control, and cognitive processes [6].

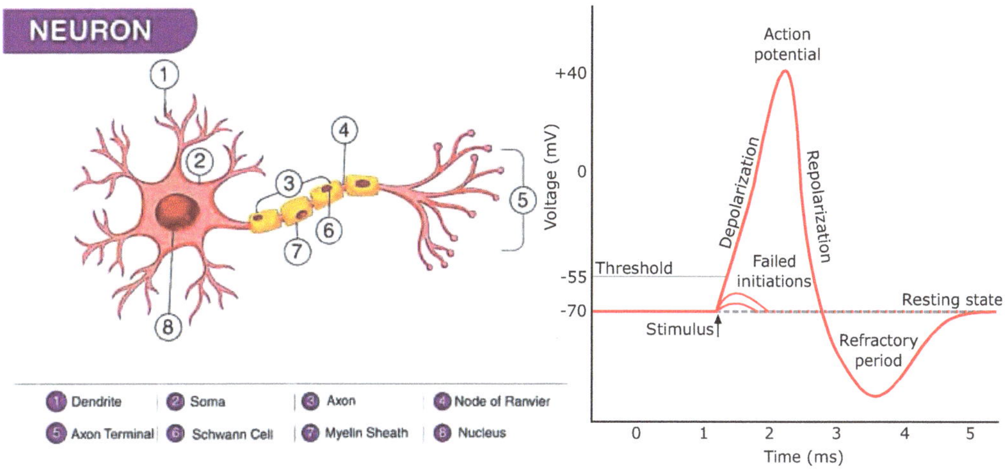


**Fig. (1).** Nerve impulse and action potential phenomenon.

## How Nerve Impulse Travels

The transmission of a nerve impulse, or action potential, occurs through a process called "propagation." Here's how it typically happens:

- **Resting Potential:** A neuron maintains a resting membrane potential due to the unequal distribution of ions across its membrane. The within, along with the neuron, be extra harmful as compared to the exterior, typically around -70 millivolts.
- **Depolarization:** When a stimulus, like a neurotransmitter that binds to receptors on the neuron's membrane, initiates the opening of ion channels. This allows the positive charged ions, such as sodium ($Na^+$), to enter the neuron, resulting in membrane depolarization. Upon reaching a specific threshold (approximately -55 mV), this depolarization initiates the opening of voltage-gated sodium channels.
- **Action Potential:** Voltage-gated sodium channels rapidly open after the threshold is crossed, allowing sodium ions to enter the neurons and further depolarize the membrane. The membrane potential increases quickly as a result, usually reaching +40 mV.
- **Repolarization:** Voltage-gated potassium channels open when the sodium channels shut down after peaking. The neuron releases potassium ions ($K^+$) into the extracellular space, which repolarize the membrane and restore its negative charge.
- **Hyperpolarization:** Sometimes, for a limited period, the membrane potential falls below the resting potential. The prolonged opening of potassium channels

is the cause of this. Potassium channels eventually close, allowing the membrane to revert to its resting potential.

- **Proliferation:** The depolarization at one point on the neuron triggers depolarization in adjacent regions of the membrane. This occurs because of inside movement of positive ions spreads along the membrane, creating a local current that depolarizes adjacent areas, leading to the propagation of the action potential along the length of the neuron.
- **Refractory Period:** After an action potential, the neuron enters a refractory period during which it is less responsive to further stimulation. This period ensures that action potentials travel in one direction and helps regulate the frequency at which neurons can fire.
- This sequence of events repeats as the action potential travels down the length of the neuron, allowing for the transmission of signals over long distances within the nervous system.

### Factors Affecting Nerve Impulse

- **Myelination:** Myelin is a fatty substance that covers the axons of some neurons, forming a myelin sheath. This insulation speeds up the transmission of nerve impulses by allowing the impulse to "jump" from one node of Ranvier to the next, a process called saltatory conduction. Therefore, myelinated neurons conduct nerve impulses faster than unmyelinated neurons.
- **Axon Diameter:** The diameter of an axon also affects the speed of transmission of a nerve impulse. The axons with larger diameters show less resistance to the flow of ions during depolarization, allowing for faster propagation of action potentials.
- **Temperature:** Nerve impulses generally travel faster at higher temperatures due to increased kinetic energy, which speeds up the movement of ions across neuronal membranes.
- **Concentration of Ions:** The concentration gradients of ions across the neuronal membrane affect the speed and efficiency of nerve impulse transmission. For example, higher concentrations of ions, such as potassium and sodium, beyond the body's cells can increase the rate of depolarization.
- **Threshold Potential:** It is the membrane potential that must be reached to trigger an action potential. Factors that affect the ability of a neuron to reach this threshold, such as the intensity of a stimulus, can influence nerve impulse transmission.
- **Neurotransmitters:** The presence and activity of neurotransmitters at the synapses between neurons can modulate the transmission of nerve impulses. Excitatory neurotransmitters increase the chances of an action potential occurring, while inhibitory neurotransmitters decrease it.

- **Pathologies and Drugs:** Certain diseases, injuries, or drugs can interfere with nerve impulse transmission. For example, diseases like multiple sclerosis damage the myelin sheath, slowing down nerve impulses. Drugs that block ion channels or neurotransmitter receptors can also disrupt nerve signaling [7, 8].

**Orthodromic:** Orthodromic nerve impulses are action potentials that propagate in the normal direction along the axon of a neuron, beginning in the compartment stiff in the direction of the neuron terminals. This is the typical direction of nerve impulse transmission in most neurons.

**Antidromic:** Antidromic nerve impulses are action potentials that propagate in the opposite direction along the axon, from the axon terminals back toward the cell body. Antidromic transmission can occur under certain experimental conditions or pathological states, but is not the typical mode of nerve impulse propagation in healthy neurons.

Additionally, nerve impulses can be classified based on their functional properties:

**Action Potential**

An action potential, often referred to as a nerve impulse, is a point of voltaic change that as to movements along the film of an axon. It is the basic unit of communication within the nervous system. Here's a breakdown of the key stages of an action potential:

**Resting State:** The neuron maintains a resting membrane potential, typically around -70 millivolts (mV), due to the unequal distribution of ions across its membrane. At rest, there are more sodium ions ($Na^+$) outer surface of the axons, in addition to more potassium ions ($K^+$) inside [9].

**Depolarization:** When a stimulus reaches a neuron to activate the latent potential in the direction of becoming less negative (depolarized), voltage-gated sodium channels in the membrane open. This allows sodium ions to charge up on the neuron, further depolarizing the membrane. If the depolarization holds out a certain verge (around -55 mV), it triggers the next stage.

**Rapid Sodium Influx:** Once the door is opened, voltage-gated sodium channels unlock fully, leading to a rapid influx of sodium ions into the neuron. This causes a reversal of the membrane potential, making the inside of the neuron temporarily more positive than the outside.

**Repolarization:** As the membrane potential becomes positive, voltage-gated potassium channels open, allowing potassium ions to flow out of the neuron. This repolarizes the membrane, restoring the negative resting potential.

**Hyperpolarization:** Sometimes, the membrane potential for a brief period surpasses the resting potential in negativity. Because potassium channels stay open longer than necessary, hyperpolarization results. Potassium channels eventually close, allowing the membrane to revert to its resting potential.

**Refractory Period:** After the period of action potential, the neuron enters a refractory period during whichit is less responsive to further stimulation. This ensures that action potentials move in a single direction, which helps to regulate the frequency at which neurons can fire.

The action potential spreads along the length of the neuron, from the dendrites to the axon terminals, without a loss of strength. Once it reaches the axon terminals, it initiates the release of neurotransmitters into the synapse, allowing communication with the next neuron in the circuit. This sequence of events is essential for the transmission of signals in the nervous system.

**Excitatory:** Excitatory nerve impulses result in the depolarization of the postsynaptic membrane, which makes it more likely for an action potential to occur in the postsynaptic neuron. Excitatory neurotransmitters, such as glutamate, typically initiate excitatory nerve impulses.

**Inhibitory:** Inhibitory nerve impulses result in hyperpolarization of the postsynaptic membrane, making it less likely for an action potential to occur in the postsynaptic neuron. Inhibitory neurotransmitters, such as gamma-aminobutyric acid (GABA) and glycine, mediate inhibitory nerve impulses.

These classifications help describe the directionality and functional effects of nerve impulses in neuronal communication.

### Structural Composition of a Nerve Cell

A nerve cell is also known as a neuron. It is a specialized cell that plays a crucial role in the functioning of the nervous system. Neurons have a prominent structural composition that allows them to transmit electrical and chemical signals throughout the body. Here's an overview of the structural components of a typical neuron:

**Cell Body (Soma):** It is the foremost fraction of the neuron, having the origin and most of the cell's organelles. It communicates the signals that are coming from dendrites and, based on this input, generates outgoing signals to the axon.

**Dendrites:** These are branch-like extensions from the compartment that take delivery of signals from other neurons or sense organs. Dendrites are enclosed within synapses, specialized structures where communication with other neurons occurs.

**Axon:** It is a long, slight outcrop with the intention of extending the unit body. It controls electrical impulses going to create the cell body en route to supplementary neurons, muscles, otherwise glands. Some neurons have myelin sheaths, a fatty insulation that speeds the transmission of nerve impulses along the axon.

**Axon Terminals** (Axon Endings or Boutons): At the end of the axon, there are terminal branches that form synaptic connections with other cells. These terminals release neurotransmitters, chemicals that transmit signals across the synapse to the dendrites of the next neuron or to different target cells.

**Synapse:** The synapse is the junction between two neurons or between a neuron and its target cell, such as a muscle cell or gland. It consists of the presynaptic terminal (axon terminal), the synaptic cleft (a small gap between the presynaptic and postsynaptic cells), and the postsynaptic membrane (often on a dendrite or cell body).

**Myelin Sheath:** In some neurons, especially in vertebrates, the axon is sheathed by a myelin covering, which is formed by dedicated cells called Schwann cells in the peripheral nervous system and oligodendrocytes in the central nervous system. It helps to speed up the transmission of nerve impulses along the axon (Fig. **2**).

### Role of the Myelin Sheath in Nerve Impulse

The myelin sheath plays a critical role in the propagation of nerve impulses along the axon.

Here's how it contributes to this process:

**Insulation:** It is composed of layers of fatty substances twisted by particular cells known as Schwann cells in the peripheral nervous system, along with oligodendrocytes in the central nervous system. This insulation acts as an electrical insulator, preventing the leakage of electrical currents from the axon and facilitating the rapid conduction of nerve impulses.

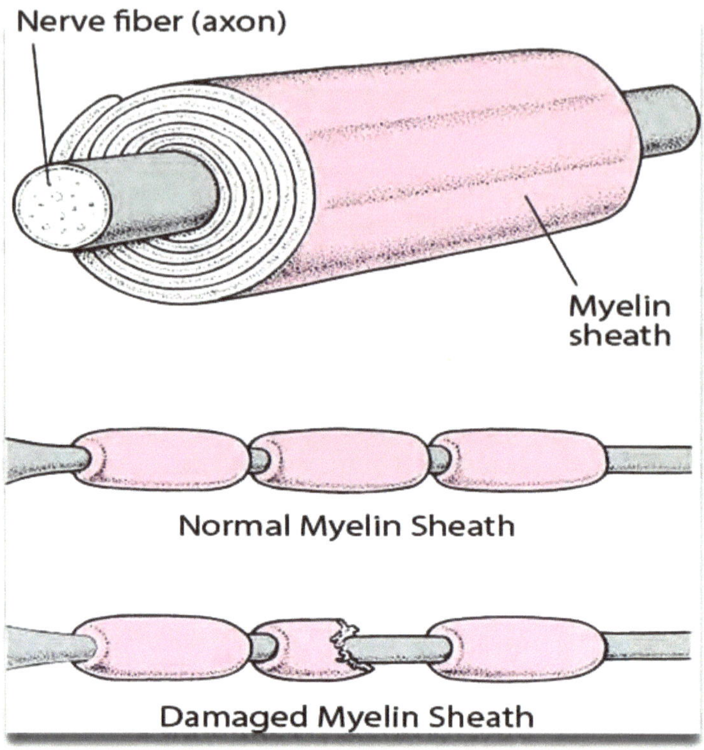


**Fig. (2).** Normal *vs* damaged myelin sheath.

**Saltatory Conduction:** In myelinated axons, the nerve impulses "jump" commencing solitary lump of Ranvier on the way to the subsequently, a development known as saltatory conduction. This jumping of the nerve impulse significantly speeds up the transmission of the signal along the axon compared to unmyelinated axons. Instead of propagating continuously next to the whole extent of the axon, the action potential is regenerated at each node, allowing it to travel faster between nodes.

**Energy Efficiency:** Saltatory conduction conserves energy for the neuron because action potentials are only regenerated at the nodes of Ranvier, where ion channels are concentrated. This reduces the energy required for maintaining the electrical potential across the axonal membrane.

**Preservation of Signal Strength:** The myelin sheath prevents the dissipation of the electrical signal by keeping it confined within the axon. This helps to preserve the strength and integrity of the nerve impulse as it travels along the axon, ensuring efficient communication between neurons.

Overall, the myelin sheath facilitates rapid and efficient transmission of nerve impulses, enabling quick communication within the nervous system. Disorders that affect the myelin sheath, such as multiple sclerosis, can impair nerve conduction and lead to neurological symptoms.

**Nodes of Ranvier:** Gaps that are present in the myelin sheath along the length of the axon are called nodes of the Ranvier. Action potentials, or nerve impulses, jump from one node to the next, which speed up the transmission of the signal along the axon (Fig. **3**).

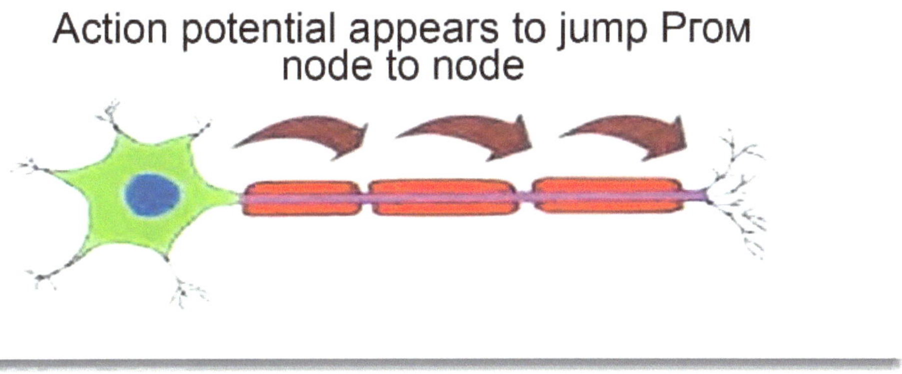


**Fig. (3).** How nerve impulse travels.

**Sensory Receptors:** Some neurons have specialized endings, such as in the skin or sense organs, that detect stimuli from the environment and convert them into electrical signals that the nervous system can transmit.

These structural components work together to enable neurons to transmit and process information throughout the nervous system, which allows for diverse roles such as sensory sensitivity, speed control, and cognitive processes.

## Effect of Damaged Myelin Sheath on Nerve Impulse

Damage to the myelin sheath can have significant effects on nerve impulse transmission and overall nervous system function as shown in Fig. (**4**). Here are some of the key impacts:

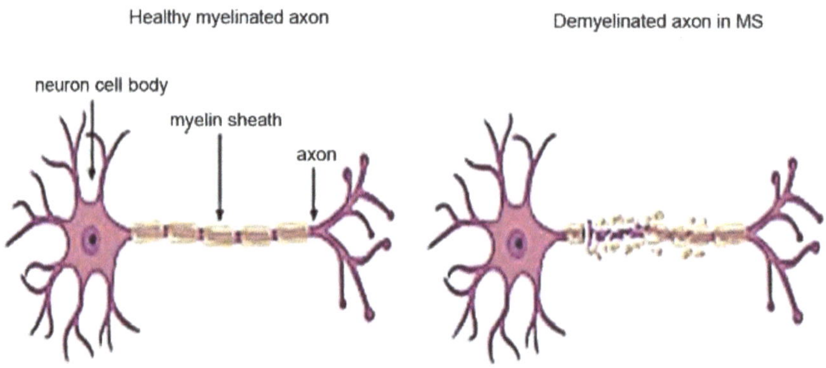


**Fig. (4).** Myelinated *vs* demyelinated axons in multiple sclerosis.

**Slowed Conduction:** When the myelin sheath is damaged, nerve impulses cannot propagate as efficiently along the axon. Without the insulation provided by the myelin sheath, the electrical signal leaks out, and the conduction velocity of the nerve impulse is slowed down. This can lead to delays in signal transmission and impaired communication between neurons.

**Decreased Signal Strength:** Damage to the myelin sheath can result in a decrease in the strength of the nerve impulse. Without proper insulation, the electrical signal may dissipate as it travels along the axon, leading to reduced amplitude of the action potential. This can impair the ability of neurons to transmit signals over long distances effectively.

**Increased Energy Expenditure:** In demyelinated axons, nerve impulses may require more energy to propagate due to increased leakage of ions across the axonal membrane. The neuron may need to expend additional resources to maintain the electrical potential and regenerate action potentials along the length of the axon.

**Impaired Saltatory Conduction:** Damage to the myelin sheath disrupts saltatory conduction. It is the process by which nerve impulses jump from one node of Ranvier to the next in myelinated axons. Without proper insulation, the nerve impulse cannot efficiently leapfrog along the axon, resulting in slower transmission speeds and decreased signal conduction efficiency.

**Neurological Symptoms:** Damage to the myelin sheath can lead to a variety of neurological symptoms that depend on the location and extent of damage. Familiar symptoms of demyelinating diseases, such as multiple sclerosis, may include muscle weakness, sensory disturbances, coordination difficulties, and cognitive impairments.

Overall, damage to the myelin sheath can have profound effects on nerve impulse transmission, resulting in disruptions to neural communication and the manifestation of neurological symptoms. Maintaining the integrity of the myelin sheath is essential for the proper functioning of the nervous system.

## Diseases Associated with a Damaged Myelin Sheath

Damage to the myelin sheath is associated with several diseases, known as demyelinating diseases, which can affect the central nervous system (CNS) or the peripheral nervous system (PNS). Here are some notable examples: (Fig. **1**).

**Multiple Sclerosis (MS):** MS is a chronic autoimmune disease characterized by inflammation and demyelination of the CNS, including the brain and spinal cord. The protected organization strikes the myelin casing, leading to the formation of scar tissue (sclerosis) and disruptions in nerve impulse transmission. MS can cause a lot of symptoms such as fatigue, muscle weakness, vision problems, sensory disturbances, and cognitive impairment.

**Guillain-Barré Syndrome (GBS):** GBS is an acute inflammatory disorder of the PNS, primarily affecting the myelin sheath of peripheral nerves. It is often triggered by infections or other immune system-related factors. GBS typically manifests as rapidly progressive muscle weakness, tingling sensations, and, in severe cases, paralysis. Most individuals with GBS experience spontaneous recovery, although some may have residual neurological deficits.

**Chronic Inflammatory Demyelinating Polyneuropathy (CIDP):** CIDP is a chronic autoimmune condition characterized by inflammation and demyelination of peripheral nerves. It is similar to GBS but has a more gradual onset and longer duration. CIDP leads to progressive weakness, sensory loss, and impaired reflexes, primarily affecting the limbs. Treatment typically involves immunosuppressive therapy to reduce inflammation and slow the progression of the disease.

**Acute Disseminated Encephalomyelitis (ADEM):** ADEM is an inflammatory demyelinating disorder of the CNS that usually occurs following viral or bacterial infections or vaccinations. It is characterized by widespread inflammation and demyelination in the brain and spinal cord, resulting in neurological symptoms such as headaches, fever, confusion, seizures, and motor deficits. ADEM is typically treated with corticosteroids to reduce inflammation.

Neuromyelitis Optica (NMO) or Devic's Disease: NMO is an autoimmune disorder primarily affecting the optic nerves and spinal cord, resulting in inflammation and demyelination. It is characterized by episodes of optic neuritis (inflammation of the optic nerve) and transverse myelitis (inflammation of the spinal cord), resulting in visual impairment, muscle weakness, and sensory disturbances. Treatment may involve immunosuppressive therapy and plasma exchange.

These diseases underscore the significance of the myelin sheath in preserving proper nerve function and the diverse range of symptoms that can result from its damage. Treatment approaches often focus on reducing inflammation, suppressing the immune system, and managing symptoms to improve life standards.

### Causes of Myelin Sheath Damage

The causes of myelin sheath damage can vary depending on the specific condition or circumstance. Here are some common causes:

- **Autoimmune Disorders:** Anywhere the protected coordination wrongly attacks the body's own tissues can lead to damage to the myelin sheath. For example, in Multiple Sclerosis (MS), the immune system targets the myelin sheath in the central nervous system, causing inflammation and demyelination.
- **Infections:** Certain infections can trigger an immune response that damages the myelin sheath. For instance, Guillain-Barré Syndrome (GBS) often occurs following a bacterial or viral infection, such as Campylobacter jejuni or the Epstein-Barr virus.
- **Genetic Factors:** Certain hereditary conditions can lead to defects in the production or maintenance of the myelin sheath.
- **Toxic Exposure:** Exposure to certain toxins or chemicals can damage the myelin sheath. For instance, exposure to heavy metals like lead or mercury, or certain industrial chemicals, can cause demyelination and neurological symptoms.
- **Vitamin Deficiencies:** Deficiencies in certain vitamins, particularly vitamin B12 and vitamin E, can lead to damage to the myelin sheath and result in neurological symptoms.
- **Physical Trauma:** Traumatic injuries, such as spinal cord injuries or severe concussions, can cause damage to the myelin sheath and disrupt nerve function.
- **Radiation Therapy:** Radiation therapy used to treat cancer can sometimes damage nearby healthy tissues, including the myelin sheath, leading to neurological complications.
- **Other Diseases:** Certain diseases or conditions, such as Acute Disseminated Encephalomyelitis (ADEM) or Neuromyelitis Optica (NMO), can cause inflammation and demyelination in the central nervous system.

The specific cause of myelin sheath damage varies depending on the individual and the underlying condition. Treatment approaches often focus on addressing the underlying cause, reducing inflammation, and managing symptoms to improve quality of life.

## Myelin Sheath and Saltatory Conduction

The myelin sheath plays a significant role in facilitating saltatory conduction, a process by which nerve impulses jump from one node of Ranvier to the next along a myelinated axon. Here's how the myelin sheath contributes to saltatory conduction (Fig. **5**).

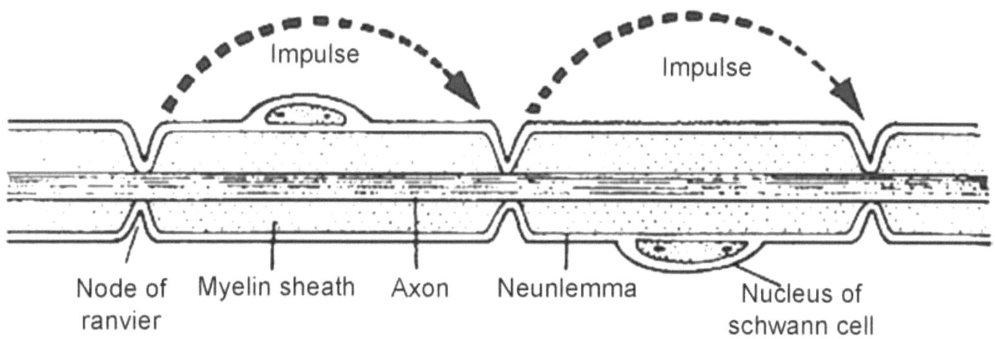


**Fig. (5).** Saltatory conduction in myelinated fibers.

**Insulation:** The myelin sheath provides electrical insulation to the axon. Because myelin is composed of layers of fatty substances, it acts as an insulator, preventing the leakage of ions across the axonal membrane and reducing the capacitance of the axon. This insulation helps to maintain the electrical potential difference between the inside and outside of the axon, facilitating rapid and efficient propagation of nerve impulses.

**Nodes of Ranvier:** The myelin sheath is interrupted at regular intervals by small gaps called nodes of Ranvier. These nodes are critical for saltatory conduction. Unlike the myelinated regions, the axon membrane at the nodes of Ranvier is not covered by myelin. Instead, it contains a high concentration of voltage-gated ion channels, particularly sodium ($Na^+$) and potassium ($K^+$) channels.

**Action Potential Regeneration:** When a nerve impulse reaches a node of Ranvier, voltage-gated $Na^+$ channels on the axonal membrane open, allowing $Na^+$ ions to enter the axon. This triggers depolarization of the axonal membrane, leading to the generation of an action potential. Because the axon is myelinated between the nodes of Ranvier, the electrical signal is insulated and can propagate rapidly to the next node.

**Saltatory Propagation:** At the node of Ranvier, where the action potential is regenerated, the depolarization of the axonal membrane triggers the notch of voltage-gated $Na^+$ channels at the adjacent node, initiating a new action potential. This process repeats itself as the nerve impulse "jumps" from one node to the next along the axon. By skipping the myelinated regions and propagating only at the nodes of Ranvier, the nerve impulse can travel much faster compared to continuous conduction along an unmyelinated axon.

Overall, the myelin sheath enhances the efficiency of nerve impulse transmission by facilitating saltatory conduction. This mechanism conserves energy and facilitates rapid signal propagation along the axon, enabling efficient communication within the nervous system.

### Why Extremities are Affected in a Damaged Myelin Sheath

When the myelin sheath is damaged, particularly in peripheral nerves, it can lead to symptoms that predominantly affect the extremities (arms, legs, hands, and feet). Here are several reasons why this occurs:

- **Length of Axons:** Peripheral nerves that innervate the extremities tend to have longer axons compared to those that innervate other parts of the body. Longer axons are more susceptible to the effects of demyelination because the nerve impulse has to travel a greater distance, increasing the likelihood of signal degradation.
- **Vulnerable Areas:** The peripheral nerves in the extremities are often located closer to the body surface and are more exposed to potential sources of damage, such as trauma or compression. Additionally, these nerves may be more susceptible to immune-mediated attacks, as seen in conditions such as Guillain-Barré Syndrome (GBS) or Chronic Inflammatory Demyelinating Polyneuropathy (CIDP).
- **Blood Supply:** Peripheral nerves require an adequate blood supply to obtain oxygen and nutrients. Damage to the myelin sheath can impair blood flow to the nerves, leading to ischemia (reduced blood supply) and exacerbating nerve damage, particularly in the longer axons of the extremities.
- **Mechanical Stress:** Extremities are subjected to frequent mechanical stress and movement, which can exacerbate damage to already compromised nerves with a damaged myelin sheath. For example, repetitive motions or pressure on the nerves can worsen symptoms in conditions like carpal tunnel syndrome, where the median nerve is compressed at the wrist.
- **Temperature Sensitivity:** Some demyelinating diseases, such as Multiple Sclerosis (MS), may worsen symptoms in response to changes in temperature. Extremities are more susceptible to temperature variations, which can

exacerbate symptoms like numbness, tingling, or weakness associated with demyelination.

- **Functional Implications:** Damage to the myelin sheath in peripheral nerves can result in sensory disturbances (*e.g.*, deadness, scratchy) and motor deficits (*e.g.*, weak point, loss of harmonization) that significantly impact the functional use of the extremities for activities of daily living.

Overall, the susceptibility of extremities to damage from a compromised myelin sheath is multifactorial, involving factors related to the anatomy, physiology, and functional demands of these body parts. As a result, symptoms of peripheral neuropathy or demyelinating diseases often manifest more prominently in the extremities.

## Nerve Conduction Velocity

It is a measure of how fast an electrical impulse travels along a nerve fiber. It is typically measured in meters per second (m/s) or feet per second (ft/s). Several factors, including the diameter of the nerve fiber and the presence or absence of a myelin sheath influence NCV.

Here's how nerve conduction velocity is determined:

- **Myelination:** Myelinated nerve fibers conduct electrical impulses faster than unmyelinated fibers. This is because the myelin covering plays a role as a protector, allowing the electrical signal to travel in the direction of "fly" from one node of Ranvier to the next, a process known as saltatory conduction. As a result, nerve impulses travel more rapidly along myelinated fibers compared to unmyelinated fibers.
- **Nerve Fiber Diameter:** Larger-diameter nerve fibers conduct impulses faster than smaller-diameter fibers. This is because larger fibers have less resistance to the flow of electrical current, allowing for the faster transmission of nerve impulses.
- **Temperature:** Nerve conduction velocity increases with higher temperatures and decreases with lower temperatures. This is due to the temperature's effect on the speed of ion channel gating and the kinetics of action potential propagation.
- **Pathological Conditions:** Certain medical conditions, such as demyelinating diseases like Multiple Sclerosis (MS), can slow down nerve conduction velocity by disrupting the integrity of the myelin sheath or damaging the nerve fibers themselves.

NCV testing, also known as Nerve Conduction Studies (NCS), is a standard diagnostic test used to assess the function of peripheral nerves. During NCV testing, electrodes are kept on the skin overlying the nerve of interest, and through electrical impulses are applied to stimulate the nerve. The time it takes for the electrical impulse to travel between two points along the nerve is measured, allowing for the calculation of the nerve conduction velocity.

NCV testing can provide valuable information about the health of peripheral nerves, identify abnormalities in nerve function, and aid in diagnosing conditions such as peripheral neuropathy, carpal tunnel syndrome, and other nerve-related disorders.

### Axonopathy

In axonopathy, the transmission of nerve impulses along affected axons can be disrupted or impaired. It is a condition characterized by damage or improper functioning that primarily affects the axons of neurons. Axons are the long, slender projections of neurons that transmit electrical signals from the cell body to other neurons, muscles, or glands. When axons are damaged or dysfunctional, it can lead to abnormalities in nerve impulse transmission. Here's how nerve impulses are affected in axonopathy:

- **Conduction Block:** In some cases of axonopathy, the damage to axons can result in conduction blocks, where the transmission of nerve impulses is interrupted or blocked along the affected portion of the axon. This can occur due to disruptions in the axonal membrane or alterations in ion channel function, preventing the propagation of action potentials along the axon.
- **Slowed Conduction Velocity:** Damage to axons can also lead to a reduction in nerve conduction velocity, meaning that nerve impulses travel more slowly along the affected axons. This can occur due to disruptions in the integrity of the axonal membrane, alterations in ion channel function, or abnormalities in axonal transport mechanisms.
- **Signal Degradation:** In some cases, axonopathy can result in the degradation of nerve impulses as they propagate along the affected axons. This can lead to distortions or alterations in the shape, amplitude, or duration of action potentials, resulting in abnormalities in the transmission of sensory or motor signals.
- **Functional Impairments:** The abnormalities in nerve impulse transmission associated with axonopathy. It can result in a variety of functional impairments that depend on the specific nerves affected. Symptom included muscle weakness, sensory disturbances (such as numbness, tingling, or loss of sensation), muscle atrophy, impaired reflexes, and autonomic dysfunction.
- **Secondary Changes:** In addition to abnormalities in nerve impulse transmission, axonopathy may also be associated with secondary changes in other components of neurons, such as the cell body or dendrites. These

secondary changes can further contribute to neurological dysfunction and the clinical manifestations of the condition.

Overall, axonopathy can disrupt the transmission of nerve impulses along affected axons, leading to a variety of neurological symptoms and functional impairments. Treatment of axonopathy typically involves addressing any underlying medical conditions.

Nerve conduction speed difference in demyelination and axonopathy.

In demyelination and axonopathy, there are distinct patterns of nerve conduction speed differences due to the nature of the damage to nerve fibers.

**Demyelination**

In demyelinating conditions, such as Multiple Sclerosis (MS), the myelin sheath surrounding the axons is damaged or destroyed. This damage disrupts the nerve fibers' ability to conduct electrical impulses efficiently.

The primary effect of demyelination on nerve conduction is a reduction in conduction velocity. Without the insulating properties of the myelin sheath, the nerve impulses propagate more slowly along the affected axons.

However, despite the reduction in conduction velocity, the amplitude of the action potential remains relatively preserved in demyelinating conditions. This is because demyelination primarily affects the insulation of the nerve fibers, rather than directly damaging the axons themselves.

Nerve Conduction Studies (NCS) in demyelinating conditions typically show prolonged distal latencies and slowed conduction velocities, often with preserved or slightly reduced Compound Muscle Action Potentials (CMAPs) or Sensory Nerve Action Potentials (SNAPs).

**Axonopathy**

Axonopathy involves damage or dysfunction primarily affecting the axons of neurons, which can occur due to various causes such as genetic disorders, metabolic abnormalities, toxic exposures, infections, or inflammatory conditions.

In axonopathy, the integrity of the axons themselves is compromised, leading to abnormalities in nerve impulse transmission.

The primary effect of axonopathy on nerve conduction is a reduction in the amplitude of the action potential. Damage to the axons results in decreased axonal membrane integrity and a decrease in the number of functioning ion channels, leading to decreased depolarization and reduced amplitude of the action potential.

Additionally, in severe cases of axonopathy, there may be a reduction in conduction velocity as well, although to a lesser extent compared to demyelinating conditions.

Nerve conduction studies in axonopathy typically show reduced Compound Muscle Action Potentials (CMAPs) or Sensory Nerve Action Potentials (SNAPs), along with evidence of slowed conduction velocities if the axonal damage is severe enough to affect conduction properties.

## CONCLUSION

In summary, while both demyelination and axonopathy can result in abnormalities in nerve conduction, the specific patterns differ due to the nature of the damage to nerve fibers. Demyelination primarily affects conduction velocity with preserved action potential amplitude, while axonopathy primarily affects action potential amplitude with potential effects on conduction velocity, particularly in severe cases.

## REFERENCES

[1] Pena SA, Iyengar R, Eshraghi RS, *et al.* Gene therapy for neurological disorders: challenges and recent advancements. J Drug Target 2020; 28(2): 111-28. [http://dx.doi.org/10.1080/1061186X.2019.1630415] [PMID: 31195838]

[2] Hanewinckel R, Ikram MA, Van Doorn PA. Peripheral neuropathies. Handb Clin Neurol 2016; 138: 263-82. [http://dx.doi.org/10.1016/B978-0-12-802973-2.00015-X] [PMID: 27637963]

[3] Drukarch B, Holland HA, Velichkov M, *et al.* Thinking about the nerve impulse: A critical analysis of the electricity-centered conception of nerve excitability. Prog Neurobiol 2018; 169: 172-85. [http://dx.doi.org/10.1016/j.pneurobio.2018.06.009] [PMID: 29981394]

[4] Monje M. Myelin plasticity and nervous system function. Annu Rev Neurosci 2018; 41(1): 61-76. [http://dx.doi.org/10.1146/annurev-neuro-080317-061853] [PMID: 29986163]

[5] Gibson EM, Geraghty AC, Monje M. Bad wrap: Myelin and myelin plasticity in health and disease. Dev Neurobiol 2018; 78(2): 123-35. [http://dx.doi.org/10.1002/dneu.22541] [PMID: 28986960]

[6] Kondiles BR, Horner PJ. Myelin plasticity, neural activity, and traumatic neural injury. Dev Neurobiol 2018; 78(2): 108-22. [http://dx.doi.org/10.1002/dneu.22540] [PMID: 28925069]

[7] Tavee J. Nerve conduction studies: Basic concepts. Handb Clin Neurol 2019; 160: 217-24. [http://dx.doi.org/10.1016/B978-0-444-64032-1.00014-X] [PMID: 31277849]

[8] Khodorov BI, Timin EN. Nerve impulse propagation along nonuniform fibres. Prog Biophys Mol Biol 1975; 30(2-3): 145-84.

[PMID: 792950]

[9] Barnett MW, Larkman PM. The action potential. Pract Neurol 2007; 7(3): 192-7. [PMID: 17515599]

# CHAPTER 4

# Understanding Peripheral Nerve Disorders

**Abstract:** Neuropathy is characterized as a condition that involves nerve damage, frequently associated with symptoms such as numbness, pain, tingling, or weakness, particularly in the hands and feet. There are several types of neuropathy, including peripheral neuropathy, which affects the nerves located in the periphery, external to the brain and spinal cord, and autonomic neuropathy, which affects the nerves involved in controlling involuntary bodily functions, such as digestion, heart rate, and bladder control. These causes range from diabetes and infections to trauma and along with positive medications. Cure and treatment may involve addressing the fundamental cause, medications to alleviate symptoms, physical therapy, and lifestyle modifications. Neuropathy is recognized as a general term that describes the injury to one or more nerves within the body. It can affect nerves in numerous parts of the body, including the peripheral nerves located outside the brain and spinal cord, as well as the autonomic nerves that control involuntary bodily functions. Neuralgia, flaccidity, and numbness in more than one part of your body is known as neuropathy, and there are numerous types of neuropathy, including peripheral neuropathy, diabetic neuropathy, autonomic neuropathy, and cranial neuropathy.

**Keywords:** Autonomic neuropathy, Cranial neuropathy, Diabetic neuropathy, Neuralgia, Neuropathy, Peripheral neuropathy.

## INTRODUCTION

Neuropathy occurs when nerve impairment leads to neuralgia, flaccidity, and peripheral sensory loss in more than one body part. At times, no cause is at work. Neuropathy refers to the damage or dysfunction of one or more nerves, typically resulting in symptoms such as pain, tingling, numbness, or weakness. It can affect any type of nerve in the body, including sensory, motor, and autonomic nerves [1].

There are numerous types of neuropathy, including:

### Peripheral Neuropathy

Peripheral neuropathy affects the nerves located outside the brain and spinal cord, often in the limbs. Diabetes, traumatic injuries, infections, exposure to toxins, or certain treatments and medications frequently cause it.

**Sumaira Kanwal & Shazia Perveen**

Peripheral neuropathy becomes more common with increasing life expectancy, but general population occurrence estimates are lacking, as shown in Fig. (**1**) [1].

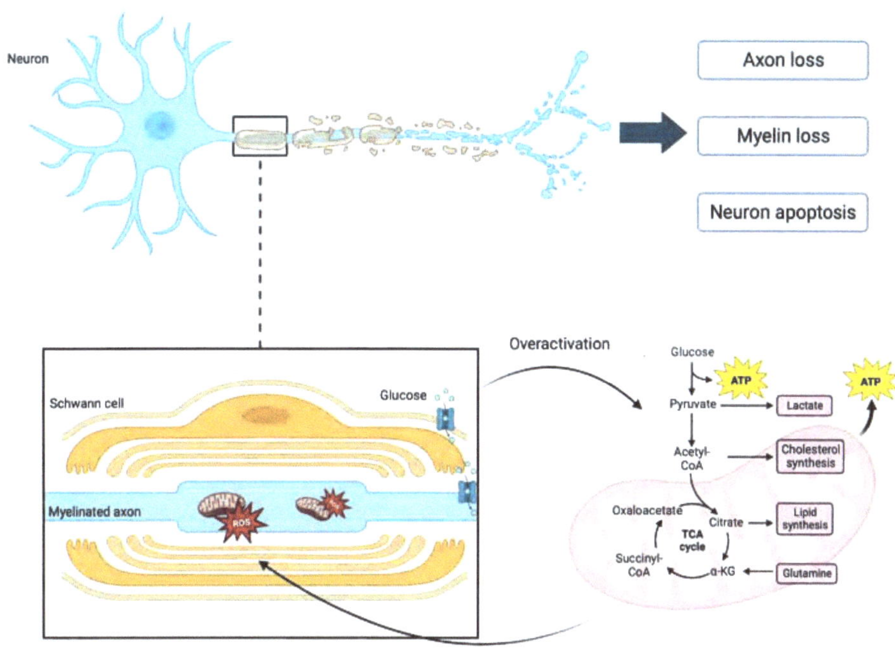


**Fig. (1).** Mechanism of peripheral neuropathy [3].

## Diabetic Neuropathy

This type of neuropathy targets explicitly individuals with diabetes. Prolonged high levels of blood sugar can cause nerve damage all over the body, specifically in the legs and feet. Diabetic neuropathy ranks high among the prevalent, persistent diabetic complications. Concomitant diabetic retinal pathology, diabetes related foot pathology and diabetes-associated atherosclerotic complications as well. Both central and peripheral nerves may be involved in the disease, with peripheral nerves being predominantly affected, known as peripheral diabetic neuropathy, which affects approximately one-third of people experiencing peripheral nerve dysfunction [2].

## Epidemiological Investigation

The significant chronic illness and global epidemic, Diabetes, has emerged as the primary cause of mortality and morbidity worldwide, imposing an increasing disease burden across the globe. Global prevalence of diabetes is rising annually, while the rates of screening, treatment, and control remain suboptimal. Large-scale epidemiological surveys have shown mainland Chinese inhabitants-based results that prove nearly half of the adult population exhibits atypical blood sugar levels [2].

## Mechanism

Diabetic neuropathy, characterized by an irregular pattern of dispersion and symmetric distal polyneuropathy. It results from the demyelination of myelinated fibers, unmyelinated nerve impairment, axonal degeneration, and several other mechanisms, displayed as a pretentious nerve conduction velocity and abnormal sensory function [3].

## Medicament

Currently, in medical practice, a range of pharmaceuticals are used for diabetic treatment, classified based on their function, such as symptomatic relief agents, disease-modifying therapies, and those that address the disease mechanism. Finally, no drug exists that can reverse the course of diabetic neuropathy [3]. Moreover, supportive therapeutic approaches include psychological interventions, acupuncture, Transcutaneous Electrical Nerve Stimulation (TENS) or muscle stimulation, and physiotherapy [4]. The present pharmacological arsenal consists of antiepileptic (gabapentin, pregabalin), tricyclic antidepressants (amitriptyline) and serotonin-noradrenaline reuptake inhibitors (duloxetine) [5].

## Autonomic Neuropathy

In most cases of generalized peripheral neuropathy, autonomic neuropathy involves damage to autonomic nerve fibers. While this involvement is moderate or subclinical, still specific group of peripheral neuropathies exists that selectively or predominantly cause damage to unmyelinated fibers. This type disturbs the nerves that control involuntary functions. It can lead to symptoms such as digestive problems, dizziness or trouble with variable blood pressure [6].

## Cardiac Autonomic Neuropathy

Cardiac autonomic neuropathy can be characterized as a serious complication of diabetes mellitus that is strongly connected with around five times increased risk of cardiovascular death. Cardiac autonomic neuropathy presents in a spectrum of conditions, ranging from hidden tachycardia and stable heart rate to improvement in myocardial infarction, exhibiting silent features [7].

## Diabetic autonomic Neuropathy

In autonomic neuropathy, diabetes mellitus is the shared cause of this abnormality in the developed world. Diabetic autonomic neuropathy causes a collection of symptoms and signs that affect the gastrointestinal, urogenital, cardiovascular, sudomotor, thermoregulatory, and pupillomotor systems [8].

## Cranial Neuropathy

This type of neuropathy involves impairment to the cranial nerves, which arise directly from the brain and control numerous functions, such as facial. Cranial neuropathy involves the destruction of the cranial nerves, which originate from the brain and regulate functions such as hearing, vision, eye movement, taste, facial sensations, and movement. Tumors, trauma, infections and autoimmune diseases are included in the causes and reasons of cranial neuropathy [9].

# CONCLUSION

Neuralgia, flaccidity, and peripheral sensory loss that affects several body parts of a person is described as neuropathy. Several types of neuropathy are recognized, and this chapter includes a few of them, such as autonomic neuropathy, diabetic neuropathy, and peripheral neuropathy.

# REFERENCES

[1] Bouhy D, Timmerman V. [Animal models of Charcot-Marie-Tooth disease and their relevance for understanding the disease in humans]. Rev Neurol (Paris) 2013; 169(12): 971-7. [http://dx.doi.org/10.1016/j.neurol.2013.07.027] [PMID: 24238786]

[2] Oh J, Vidal-Jordana A, Montalban X. Multiple sclerosis: clinical aspects. Curr Opin Neurol 2018; 31(6): 752-9. [http://dx.doi.org/10.1097/WCO.0000000000000622] [PMID: 30300239]

[3] Beghi E, Giussani G, Sander JW. The natural history and prognosis of epilepsy. Epileptic disorders: international epilepsy journal with videotape. 2015; 17(3): 243-53. [http://dx.doi.org/10.1684/epd.2015.0751]

[4] Kim LG, Johnson TL, Marson AG, Chadwick DW. Prediction of risk of seizure recurrence after a single seizure and early epilepsy: further results from the MESS trial. Lancet Neurol 2006; 5(4): 317-22. [http://dx.doi.org/10.1016/S1474-4422(06)70383-0] [PMID: 16545748]

[5] FitzPatrick L, Bird A. Genetic therapies for neurological disorders. Hum Genet 2022; 141(5): 1085-91. [http://dx.doi.org/10.1007/s00439-021-02399-5] [PMID: 34807307]

[6] Robertson LT. Memory and the Brain. J Dent Educ 2002; 66(1): 30-42. [http://dx.doi.org/10.1002/j.0022-0337.2002.66.1.tb03506.x] [PMID: 12358099]

[7] Ding Q, Zhao H. Long-term effects of SARS-CoV-2 infection on human brain and memory. Cell Death Discov 2023; 9(1): 196. [http://dx.doi.org/10.1038/s41420-023-01512-z] [PMID: 37380640]

[8] Pena SA, Iyengar R, Eshraghi RS, *et al.* Gene therapy for neurological disorders: challenges and

recent advancements. J Drug Target 2020; 28(2): 111-28.
[http://dx.doi.org/10.1080/1061186X.2019.1630415] [PMID: 31195838]

[9] Hanewinckel R, Ikram MA, Van Doorn PA. Peripheral neuropathies. Handb Clin Neurol 2016; 138: 263-82.
[http://dx.doi.org/10.1016/B978-0-12-802973-2.00015-X] [PMID: 27637963]

# CHAPTER 5

# A Historical Journey Through Neuropathy

**Abstract:** Neuropathy is a medical condition that primarily affects the peripheral nerves. Symptoms include pain, numbness, tingling, and weakness of muscles, especially in the extremities. The history of neurological disorders is as old as human history itself, with evidence of various conditions and their manifestations dating back to ancient civilizations. Ancient texts from cultures such as Mesopotamia, Egypt, Greece, and China contain descriptions of symptoms that are now recognized as neurological disorders. Conditions like epilepsy, stroke, and paralysis were observed and often attributed to supernatural causes. Ancient Mesopotamian medical texts, such as the "Diagnostic Handbook" and the "Therapeutic Treatises," offer valuable insights into the medical practices of the time. These texts contain descriptions of symptoms such as pain and weakness, which could potentially be related to neuropathic conditions. In ancient Greece, physicians such as Hippocrates and Galen made significant contributions to medical knowledge, including the understanding of neurological disorders. Treatments recommended by these physicians included dietary interventions, exercise, and medicinal herbs, based on the principles of balancing bodily humors and restoring bodily harmony. Traditional Chinese Medicine (TCM) dates back thousands of years and includes a rich repository of knowledge about various medical conditions and their treatments. While there is no direct evidence of neuropathy in ancient Chinese texts, TCM does recognize the concept of "bi" syndrome, which encompasses symptoms such as pain, stiffness, and numbness in the limbs.

**Keywords:** Ancient civilizations, History of neuropathy, Mesopotamia, Therapeutic treatises, Traditional chinese medicine.

## INTRODUCTION

The history of neurological disorders is as old as human history itself, with evidence of various conditions and their manifestations dating back to ancient civilizations. Here's an overview of the historical progression:

**Ancient Civilizations:** Ancient texts from civilizations such as Mesopotamia, Egypt, Greece, and China contain descriptions of symptoms that are now recognized as neurological disorders. Conditions like epilepsy, stroke, and paralysis were observed and often attributed to supernatural causes. Neuropathy,

**Sumaira Kanwal & Shazia Perveen**

or peripheral neuropathy, refers to damage or dysfunction of the PN, leading to indications such as pain, numbness as well as tingling, and weakness. While the ancient civilizations did not have a comprehensive understanding of neuropathy as a medical condition, there is evidence to suggest that they were aware of symptoms similar to those associated with neuropathy and may have attempted various treatments [1].

**Mesopotamia:** Ancient Mesopotamian medical texts, such as the "Diagnostic Handbook" and the "Therapeutic Treatises," offer valuable insights into the medical practices of the time. These texts contain descriptions of symptoms such as pain and weakness, which could potentially be related to neuropathic conditions. Treatments mentioned in these texts include herbal remedies, incantations, and rituals aimed at appeasing gods or warding off evil spirits, reflecting the religious and supernatural beliefs of the time [2].

**Ancient Egypt:** Egyptian medical texts, including the Ebers Papyrus and the Edwin Smith Papyrus, document various medical conditions and treatments practiced in ancient Egypt. While neuropathy is not explicitly mentioned, symptoms such as pain and numbness are described in these texts, often in the context of injuries or diseases affecting the limbs. Treatments included herbal remedies, massage, and incantations, highlighting the blend of empirical observations and magical beliefs characteristic of ancient Egyptian medicine.

**Ancient Greece:** In ancient Greece, physicians, such as Hippocrates and Galen made significant contributions to medical knowledge, including the understanding of neurological disorders. While their writings do not specifically address neuropathy as a distinct condition, they describe symptoms such as paralysis, tremors, and seizures, which could be indicative of underlying nerve dysfunction. Treatments recommended by these physicians included dietary interventions, exercise, and medicinal herbs, based on the principles of balancing bodily humors and restoring bodily harmony.

**Ancient China:** Traditional Chinese Medicine (TCM) dates back thousands of years and includes a rich repository of knowledge about various medical conditions and their treatments. While there is no direct evidence of neuropathy in ancient Chinese texts, TCM does recognize the concept of "bi" syndrome, which encompasses symptoms such as pain, stiffness, and numbness in the limbs. Treatments for "bi" syndrome typically involve acupuncture, herbal medicine, and therapeutic exercises aimed at restoring the flow of qi (vital energy) and blood through the affected areas.

In ancient China, while there is no direct mention of neuropathy as understood in modern medicine, Traditional Chinese Medicine (TCM) did recognize and treat symptoms that could be associated with nerve dysfunction. Ancient Chinese medical texts, such as the Huangdi Neijing (Yellow Emperor's Inner Canon) and the Shennong Ben Cao Jing (Divine Farmer's Materia Medica), provide insights into how ancient Chinese physicians understood and addressed conditions that may have included neuropathic symptoms. Here's how ancient China approached health and potential connections to neuropathy:

**Qi and Meridian Theory**: Traditional Chinese medicine is based on the concept of qi (vital energy) and its flow through meridians, which are energy pathways in the body. Imbalances or blockages in the flow of qi are believed to lead to disease and dysfunction. While there is no direct translation of "neuropathy" in TCM, conditions causing numbness, tingling, or pain in the extremities may be viewed as disruptions in the flow of qi along the associated meridians [3].

**Bi Syndrome:** TCM recognizes a condition known as "Bi syndrome," which encompasses symptoms such as pain, stiffness, and numbness in the joints and muscles. While not equivalent to neuropathy, Bi syndrome shares some similarities with neuropathic conditions, particularly in terms of sensory disturbances and discomfort in the extremities.

**Acupuncture and Moxibustion:** Acupuncture and moxibustion, techniques involving the insertion of fine needles or the application of heat to specific points on the body, are fundamental treatments in TCM. These therapies are believed to regulate the flow of qi and blood, alleviate pain, and restore balance to the body. While not directly targeting neuropathy, acupuncture and moxibustion may have been used to address symptoms associated with nerve dysfunction.

### Treatment Options for Neuropathy in the Elderly

**Herbal Remedies:** Many ancient civilizations relied on medicinal plants and herbs to treat a wide range of ailments. Herbal remedies with analgesic, anti-inflammatory, and nerve-calming properties might have been used to alleviate pain, numbness, and tingling associated with neuropathy. For example, plants such as willow bark (a natural source of salicylic acid, similar to aspirin) or valerian root (known for its sedative properties) could have been employed for pain relief.

**Massage and Manual Therapy:** Massage and manual therapy techniques have a long history in traditional medicine systems worldwide. Ancient healers may have employed massage to enhance circulation, alleviate muscle tension, and mitigate symptoms of neuropathy.

**Acupressure or Reflexology**, which involves applying pressure to specific points on the body believed to correspond to different organs and systems, might also have been employed.

**Heat Therapy:** Heat therapy, including techniques such as hot baths, steam baths, or the application of heated compresses, was commonly used in ancient healing traditions to relieve pain and promote relaxation. Heat can help dilate blood vessels, improve circulation, and reduce muscle tension, potentially offering relief from neuropathic symptoms.

**Dietary Interventions:** Ancient healers recognized the importance of diet and nutrition in maintaining health and treating illness. Certain foods and nutritional practices might have been recommended to support nerve health and alleviate symptoms of neuropathy. For example, foods rich in antioxidants, vitamins, and minerals could have been encouraged to reduce oxidative stress and inflammation.

**Mind-Body Practices:** Ancient healing systems often incorporated mind-body practices such as meditation, yoga, or tai chi to promote relaxation, reduce stress, and enhance overall well-being. These practices may have been used to complement other treatments for neuropathy by addressing underlying emotional and psychological factors contributing to symptoms.

**Spiritual and Ritualistic Approaches:** In many ancient civilizations, illness was often attributed to spiritual or supernatural causes. Rituals, prayers, and offerings to gods or spirits might have been performed to seek divine intervention and healing. While not directly targeting the physiological mechanisms of neuropathy, these spiritual practices may have provided psychological comfort and a sense of hope to individuals experiencing symptoms.

Overall, treatment options for neuropathy in old age were often based on empirical observations, cultural beliefs, and the resources available within each civilization. While these ancient approaches may not have directly addressed the underlying causes of neuropathy as understood in modern medicine, they likely provided some relief from symptoms. They contributed to the overall well-being of individuals affected by nerve dysfunction.

**Herbal Medicine:** Traditional Chinese herbal medicine encompasses a vast array of medicinal plants and herbal formulations designed to treat various ailments. Certain herbs and herbal combinations were prescribed to address pain, numbness, and other symptoms potentially related to nerve disorders. For example, herbs with analgesic, anti-inflammatory, and nerve-calming properties might have been used to alleviate neuropathic pain or discomfort [4].

**Qi Gong and Tai Chi**: Qi Gong and Tai Chi are ancient Chinese practices that combine breath control, gentle movements, and meditation to promote health and well-being. These mind-body exercises are believed to regulate the flow of qi and enhance the body's natural healing mechanisms. While no specific treatments for neuropathy have been recommended, Qi Gong and Tai Chi may be suggested to improve overall health and alleviate symptoms associated with nerve dysfunction.

Overall, while ancient Chinese medicine did not conceptualize neuropathy in the same way as modern Western medicine, it addressed symptoms and conditions that may have overlapped with neuropathic presentations. The emphasis on restoring balance, promoting circulation, and regulating the flow of qi remains foundational to traditional Chinese approaches to health and healing [5].

In summary, while the ancient civilizations did not have a specific understanding of neuropathy as a medical condition, they were aware of symptoms suggestive of nerve dysfunction. They likely attempted various treatments based on their cultural and medical beliefs. These early observations and treatments laid the groundwork for the development of modern medical approaches to neuropathy.

## CONCLUSION

In conclusion, the history of neuropathy is a fascinating journey that spans millennia, from ancient civilizations to the present day. Throughout history, humanity's understanding of neuropathies has evolved significantly, shaped by cultural beliefs, medical discoveries, and technological advancements. From early theories rooted in mysticism and folklore to the systematic study of nerve disorders in contemporary medicine, the trajectory of neuropathy research reflects the relentless pursuit of knowledge and the human spirit's resilience. While many mysteries remain, the historical narrative of neuropathies serves as a testament to human ingenuity and our ongoing quest to alleviate suffering and improve the quality of life for all.

## REFERENCES

[1] Sherlock ME, Baquero Galvis L, Vicens Q, Kieft JS, Jagannathan S. Principles, mechanisms, and biological implications of translation termination–reinitiation. RNA 2023; 29(7): 865-84. [http://dx.doi.org/10.1261/rna.079375.122] [PMID: 37024263]

[2] Vij N, Kaley HN, Robinson CL, *et al.* Clinical results following conservative management of tarsal tunnel syndrome compared with surgical treatment: a systematic review. Orthop Rev (Pavia) 2022; 14(3): 37539. [http://dx.doi.org/10.52965/001c.37539] [PMID: 36072502]

[3] Aaij R, Abdelmotteleb ASW, Abellan Beteta C, *et al.* Measurement of forward charged hadron flow harmonics in peripheral PbPb collisions at s N N = 5.02 TeV with the LHCb detector. Phys Rev C 2024; 109(5): 054908. [http://dx.doi.org/10.1103/PhysRevC.109.054908]

[4] Long J, Tang M, Zuo M, Xu W, Meng S, Liu Z. The antianxiety effects of koumine and gelsemine, two main active components in the traditional Chinese herbal medicine *Gelsemium* : A comprehensive review. Brain-X 2023; 1(4): e46.
[http://dx.doi.org/10.1002/brx2.46]

[5] Serri O, Meunier A, Bouet PE, El Hachem H, Liu B, May-Panloup P. The use of complementary practices by patients undergoing medically assisted reproduction: The place of Chinese medicine and related practices. medRxiv 2024.

## CHAPTER 6

# Epidemiology of Neuropathies

**Abstract:** The epidemiology of neuropathies encompasses the study of the distribution, risk factors, and patterns of these conditions within populations. Neuropathies can be characterized as a varied group of disorders affecting the peripheral nervous system, and their epidemiology can vary depending on factors such as the type of neuropathy, geographic location, demographic characteristics, primary risk factors, topographical variations, and gender. Epidemiological research plays a vital role in identifying trends, disparities, risk factors, and unmet needs related to neuropathies, ultimately contributing to improved outcomes and quality of life for affected individuals.

**Keywords:** Disparities, Demographic characteristics, Epidemiology, Geographic location, Risk factors.

## INTRODUCTION

Neuropathies may exist in several different forms depending on location, level or types of neurons or Schwann cells that are affected, rate of advancement, harshness, etiology, and many other factors [1].

### Epidemiology of Peripheral Neuropathies

Peripheral neuropathy results from an imbalance in function and structure of peripheral motor, sensory, and autonomic neurons, which are involved either in the entire neuron or at designated levels of it [1].

Mostly, peripheral neuropathics can bc characterized as:

- Immune neuropathies
- Poly neuropathies

### Epidemiology of Diabetic Neuropathies

Diabetic peripheral neuropathy disturbs up to 50% of patients with diabetes and is known as a chief cause of morbidity and increased mortality. Its clinical manifestations include painful neuropathic symptoms and insensitivity, which

**Sumaira Kanwal & Shazia Perveen**

results in an increased risk for burns, foot ulceration, and injuries [2]. Although neuropathy has long been documented as an impediment to diabetes, the influence of this illness has not been effectively recognized [3]. Diabetic peripheral neuropathy is connected with significant morbidity, mortality, as well as diminished quality of life [2].

## Epidemiology of Neuropathic Pain

Neuropathic pain is a particularly severe form of chronic pain, arising as a direct consequence of a lesion or disease affecting the somatosensory nervous system. Examples of common causes of NeuP include diabetes, HIV, and chemotherapy treatment for cancer (causing painful peripheral neuropathies), herpes zoster (causing post-herpetic neuralgia), multiple sclerosis, surgery, stroke, and spinal cord injury. NeuP is likely to be a major contributor to the global burden of chronic pain [4].

## Prevalence of Neuropathic Pain after the COVID-19 Pandemic

COVID-19 most commonly manifests with acute respiratory symptoms; one very common symptom of the disease is pain. Viral infections may have a direct impact on the peripheral nervous system or the Central Nervous System (CNS), or induce post-viral immune syndrome. The most common peripheral lesions responsible for neuropathic pain include acute or chronic polyneuropathy, acute polyradiculoneuritis (Guillain–Barré syndrome), chronic inflammatory demyelinating polyneuropathy, or ganglionopathy. Guillain–Barré syndrome and chronic inflammatory demyelinating polyneuropathy, in particular, have been associated with a large number of viral agents, including coronaviruses, Epstein–Barr virus, HIV, hepatitis viruses, cytomegalovirus, influenza A virus, and Zika.[53] Central nervous system lesions responsible for neuropathic pain after viral infections include transverse myelitis, encephalomyelitis, and stroke [5].

Here are some key aspects of the epidemiology of neuropathies:

- **Prevalence:** Neuropathies are relatively common, with certain types, such as peripheral neuropathy, diabetic neuropathy, and carpal tunnel syndrome, being particularly prevalent. The prevalence of neuropathies varies widely depending on the specific type of neuropathy and the population being studied. For example, peripheral neuropathy has been estimated to affect around 2.4% to 8% of the general population, while diabetic neuropathy affects up to 50% of individuals with diabetes [6].
- **Incidence:** The incidence of neuropathies refers to the rate at which new cases of these conditions occur within a given population over a specified period.

Incidence rates can provide insights into the risk of developing neuropathies over time and may be influenced by factors such as age, gender, genetics, lifestyle, and environmental exposures [7].

- **Risk Factors:** Various risk factors are associated with the development of neuropathies. For example, diabetes is a major risk factor for diabetic neuropathy, while alcohol abuse, exposure to toxins, certain medications, infections, autoimmune diseases, and genetic predisposition may increase the risk of developing other types of neuropathies. Understanding these risk factors is essential for identifying high-risk populations and implementing preventive measures [8].
- **Age and Gender:** The prevalence of neuropathies tends to increase with age, with older adults being at higher risk due to factors such as age-related changes in nerve function, comorbidities, and cumulative exposure to risk factors. Additionally, certain types of neuropathies may show gender disparities, with some conditions being more common in men or women [9].
- **Geographic Variation:** The epidemiology of neuropathies may vary across different geographic regions and populations. Environmental factors, socioeconomic status, healthcare access, and cultural practices can influence the prevalence, incidence, and patterns of neuropathies in different parts of the world [10].
- **Burden of Disease:** Neuropathies can impose a significant burden on individuals, families, healthcare systems, and society as a whole. The burden of neuropathies includes direct medical costs, indirect costs related to productivity losses and disability, and intangible costs such as reduced quality of life and psychosocial impacts [8].

Understanding the epidemiology of neuropathies is crucial for informing public health strategies, healthcare policies, and clinical practices that aim to prevent, diagnose, and manage these conditions effectively.

### Classical Era

During the classical era, Greek and Roman physicians made significant contributions to the understanding of neurological disorders. Figures like Hippocrates and Galen described conditions such as epilepsy, headaches, and paralysis and proposed naturalistic explanations for their causes [11].

### Middle Ages

Religious and supernatural beliefs heavily influenced medical knowledge during the Middle Ages. Neurological disorders were often viewed through a spiritual lens, and treatments involved prayers, exorcisms, and other religious rituals. However, Islamic scholars preserved and expanded upon the medical knowledge of ancient civilizations, contributing to the understanding of neurological disorders [11].

## Renaissance

The Renaissance saw a revival of interest in science and medicine in Europe. Anatomists like Andreas Vesalius made important discoveries about the structure of the human body, including the nervous system. However, neurological disorders were still poorly understood, and effective treatments were lacking [12].

## $18^{th}$ and $19^{th}$ Centuries

The $18^{th}$ and $19^{th}$ centuries experienced significant advancements in understanding neurological disorders, particularly with the rise of experimental physiology and pathology. Figures like Franz Joseph Gall and Jean-Martin Charcot made significant contributions to the study of neuroanatomy and the classification of neurological disorders. The development of the microscope also allowed for the observation of neurological tissues and abnormalities [12].

## $20^{th}$ Century

The $20^{th}$ century witnessed rapid improvements in the understanding and treatment of neurological disorders. The discovery of nerve growth factor by Rita Levi-Montalcini and Stanley Cohen in the 1950s revolutionized the understanding of nerve [13].

## Development and Regeneration

The development of neuroimaging techniques, such as CT scans and MRI, enabled clinicians to visualize the organization of the brain in unprecedented detail. Additionally, advancements in genetics led to the identification of genes associated with various neurological disorders [13].

## Contemporary Period

In recent decades, research into neurological disorders has expanded rapidly. Advances in molecular biology, genetics, and neuroscience have deepened our understanding of the underlying mechanisms of neurological diseases. This has led to the development of targeted therapies for conditions rather as Alzheimer's syndrome, Parkinson's disease, multiple sclerosis, and epilepsy. Additionally, advancements in neurotechnology, including deep brain stimulation and neuroprosthetics, offer new possibilities for treating neurological disorders [14].

Overall, the history of neurological disorders reflects the gradual progression of medical knowledge and technological advancements, from ancient beliefs in supernatural causes to modern scientific understanding and evidence-based treatments. While much progress has been made, neurological disorders remain a significant challenge, and ongoing research is needed to develop better therapies and improve outcomes for patients.

## CONCLUSION

In ancient times, treatment options for neuropathy would have varied depending on the cultural and medical beliefs of the civilization and the availability of resources. While there was no specific understanding of neuropathy as a medical condition, ancient healing systems often addressed symptoms that could be associated with nerve dysfunction. Here are some treatment options that might have been used in the old ages.

## REFERENCES

[1] Bouhy D, Timmerman V. [Animal models of Charcot-Marie-Tooth disease and their relevance for understanding the disease in humans]. Rev Neurol (Paris) 2013; 169(12): 971-7. [http://dx.doi.org/10.1016/j.neurol.2013.07.027] [PMID: 24238786]

[2] Oh J, Vidal-Jordana A, Montalban X. Multiple sclerosis: clinical aspects. Curr Opin Neurol 2018; 31(6): 752-9. [http://dx.doi.org/10.1097/WCO.0000000000000622] [PMID: 30300239]

[3] Beghi E, Giussani G, Sander JW. The natural history and prognosis of epilepsy. Epileptic disorders: international epilepsy journal with videotape. 2015; 17(3): 243-53. [http://dx.doi.org/10.1684/epd.2015.0751]

[4] Kim LG, Johnson TL, Marson AG, Chadwick DW. Prediction of risk of seizure recurrence after a single seizure and early epilepsy: further results from the MESS trial. Lancet Neurol 2006; 5(4): 317-22. [http://dx.doi.org/10.1016/S1474-4422(06)70383-0] [PMID: 16545748]

[5] FitzPatrick L, Bird A. Genetic therapies for neurological disorders. Hum Genet 2022; 141(5): 1085-91. [http://dx.doi.org/10.1007/s00439-021-02399-5] [PMID: 34807307]

[6] Robertson LT. Memory and the Brain. J Dent Educ 2002; 66(1): 30-42. [http://dx.doi.org/10.1002/j.0022-0337.2002.66.1.tb03506.x] [PMID: 12358099]

[7] Ding Q, Zhao H. Long-term effects of SARS-CoV-2 infection on human brain and memory. Cell Death Discov 2023; 9(1): 196. [http://dx.doi.org/10.1038/s41420-023-01512-z] [PMID: 37380640]

[8] Pena SA, Iyengar R, Eshraghi RS, *et al.* Gene therapy for neurological disorders: challenges and recent advancements. J Drug Target 2020; 28(2): 111-28. [http://dx.doi.org/10.1080/1061186X.2019.1630415] [PMID: 31195838]

[9] Hanewinckel R, Ikram MA, Van Doorn PA. Peripheral neuropathies. Handb Clin Neurol 2016; 138: 263-82. [http://dx.doi.org/10.1016/B978-0-12-802973-2.00015-X] [PMID: 27637963]

[10] Drukarch B, Holland HA, Velichkov M, *et al.* Thinking about the nerve impulse: A critical analysis of the electricity-centered conception of nerve excitability. Prog Neurobiol 2018; 169: 172-85. [http://dx.doi.org/10.1016/j.pneurobio.2018.06.009] [PMID: 29981394]

[11] Monje M. Myelin plasticity and nervous system function. Annu Rev Neurosci 2018; 41(1): 61-76. [http://dx.doi.org/10.1146/annurev-neuro-080317-061853] [PMID: 29986163]

[12] Gibson EM, Geraghty AC, Monje M. Bad wrap: Myelin and myelin plasticity in health and disease. Dev Neurobiol 2018; 78(2): 123-35. [http://dx.doi.org/10.1002/dneu.22541] [PMID: 28986960]

[13] Kondiles BR, Horner PJ. Myelin plasticity, neural activity, and traumatic neural injury. Dev Neurobiol 2018; 78(2): 108-22. [http://dx.doi.org/10.1002/dneu.22540] [PMID: 28925069]

[14] Tavee J. Nerve conduction studies: Basic concepts. Handb Clin Neurol 2019; 160: 217-24. [http://dx.doi.org/10.1016/B978-0-444-64032-1.00014-X] [PMID: 31277849]

## CHAPTER 7

# Causes of Neuropathies

**Abstract:** Neuropathy, a condition causing damage to peripheral nerves, can be caused by diabetes, trauma, or infections. Diabetes, particularly when blood sugar levels are high, can damage nerves, while injuries from accidents or surgeries can also cause neuropathy. Neuropathy can occur as a result of autoimmune diseases, toxins, nutritional deficiencies, alcohol abuse, and genetic factors. Autoimmune diseases, such as Guillain-Barré syndrome, lupus, and CIDP, can result from the body's resistance to certain substances. Toxins, nutritional deficiencies, and alcohol abuse can also damage nerves, while genetic predispositions can increase susceptibility. Neuropathy can be associated with various medical conditions, including kidney disease, liver disease, hypothyroidism, certain cancers, vascular disorders, and connective tissue disorders. Idiopathic neuropathy, where the cause is unknown, is a rare condition. Understanding the underlying cause is crucial for appropriate management and treatment.

**Keywords:** Autonomic symptoms, CIDP, Guillain-barré syndrome, Hypothyroidism, Idiopathic neuropathy, Lupus, Neuropathy, Nutritional deficiencies, Peripheral nerves, Peripheral neuropathy.

## INTRODUCTION

Neuropathy is a broad term encompassing any nerve disease or dysfunction affecting peripheral nerves and the central nervous system. Peripheral neuropathy, on the other hand, is characterized by damage or dysfunction of peripheral nerves, presenting symptoms like numbness, tingling, pain, and weakness. Neuropathy is a condition characterized by a range of symptoms, including numbness, pain, sensitivity to touch, muscle weakness, coordination loss, sensation changes, autonomic symptoms, loss of reflexes, foot problems, and sexual dysfunction. Common symptoms include numbness, tingling, pain, heightened sensitivity to touch, muscle weakness, paralysis, loss of coordination, changes in sensation, autonomic symptoms, and loss of reflexes. In severe cases, neuropathy can impair proprioception and balance, increasing the risk of falls. It can also cause foot problems, infections, and deformities. In some cases, it can lead to sexual dysfunction. Neuropathy symptoms vary based on individual factors, underlying

**Sumaira Kanwal & Shazia Perveen**

causes, nerve damage, and health. Neuropathy is a condition affecting nerves outside the brain and spinal cord, categorized into peripheral neuropathy, sensory neuropathy, motor neuropathy, and autonomic neuropathy.

## Causes of Neuropathy

Neuropathy, or damage to the peripheral nerves, can have various causes. Some of the common causes include:

**Diabetes:** Diabetic neuropathy is a common complication of diabetes, particularly when blood sugar levels are poorly controlled over time. High blood sugar levels can damage the nerves, leading to neuropathic symptoms [1] (Fig. **1**).

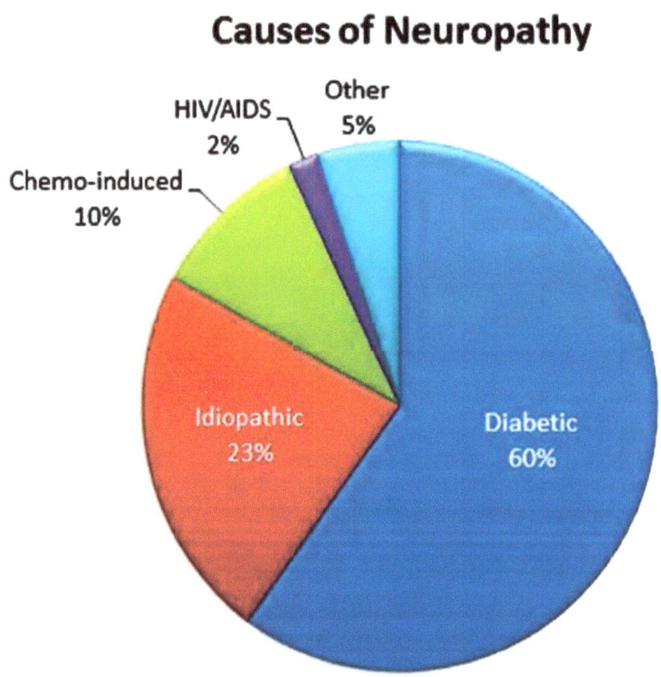


**Fig. (1).** Most common causes of neuropathies.

**Trauma or Injury:** Physical trauma, such as from accidents, falls, sports injuries, or surgical procedures, can result in nerve damage and neuropathy.

**Infections:** Certain infections can directly affect the peripheral nerves, leading to neuropathy. Examples include Lyme disease, shingles (herpes zoster), HIV/AIDS, hepatitis C, and leprosy.

**Autoimmune Disease:** In certain environments, the accumulation of materials in the body due to a malfunctioning resistance system can lead to neuropathy. Examples include Guillain-Barré syndrome, lupus, rheumatoid arthritis, and Chronic Inflammatory Demyelinating Polyneuropathy (CIDP) [2].

**Toxins:** Exposure to certain toxins or chemicals can damage nerves and cause neuropathy. These may include heavy metals (such as lead, mercury, and arsenic), industrial solvents, pesticides, and certain medications (like chemotherapy drugs, antiretroviral drugs, and certain antibiotics).

**Nutritional Deficiencies:** Lack of essential nutrients, such as vitamins B1 (thiamine), B6 (pyridoxine), B12 (cobalamin), E, and folate, as well as minerals like copper, can lead to neuropathy [3].

**Alcohol Abuse:** Chronic alcohol abuse can lead to alcoholic neuropathy, a type of neuropathy caused by the toxic effects of alcohol on the nerves.

**Genetic Factors:** Some individuals may have genetic predispositions that make them more susceptible to developing neuropathy.

**Other Medical Conditions:** Various medical conditions and diseases can be associated with neuropathy, including kidney disease, liver disease, hypothyroidism, certain cancers, vascular disorders, and connective tissue disorders.

**Idiopathic Neuropathy**: Idiopathic neuropathy, now designated as Chronic Idiopathic Axonal Polyneuropathy (CIAP), is a major public health problem in the United States. In some cases, the cause of neuropathy may not be identified, and it is referred to as idiopathic neuropathy [4].

## Difference Between Neuropathy and Peripheral Neuropathy

The terms "neuropathy" and "peripheral neuropathy" are often used interchangeably, but there is a slight difference in their meanings.

**Neuropathy:** Neuropathy is a broad term that refers to any disease or dysfunction of the nerves. It can occur anywhere in the body, including the peripheral nerves (those outside the intelligence and the spinal cord) as well as the innermost nervous system (the brain and the spinal cord). Neuropathy can manifest in various ways, including sensory symptoms (such as numbness, tingling, and pain), motor symptoms (such as weakness or muscle atrophy), and autonomic symptoms (such as changes in blood pressure, heart rate, or digestion).

**Peripheral Neuropathy:** Peripheral neuropathy specifically refers to neuropathy that affects the peripheral nerves, which are the nerves outside of the central nervous system. These nerves spread commencing the mind and spinal cord to the other parts of the body, including the limbs, organs, and skin. Peripheral neuropathy is characterized by damage or dysfunction of these peripheral nerves and typically presents with symptoms such as numbness, tingling, pain, and weakness, often in the limbs.

In summary, while all peripheral ies can be categorized under the broader term "neuropathy," not all neuropathies necessarily involve the peripheral nerves. Neuropathy can affect the nervous system, PN, and CNS.

**Symptoms of Neuropathy**

Neuropathy can cause a wide range of symptoms, relay on the type of nerves affected. Common symptoms of neuropathy include:

**Numbness or Tingling:** Many people with neuropathy experience numbness, tingling, or pins-and-needles sensations in the affected area. This sensation may be localized to specific parts of the body or may spread more broadly.

**Pain:** Neuropathic pain can range from mild to severe and may be described as burning, stabbing, shooting, or electric shock-like. The pain may be constant or intermittent and can be exacerbated by touch or temperature changes.

**Sensitivity to Touch:** Some individuals with neuropathy may experience heightened sensitivity to touch (hyperesthesia) or pain from normally non-painful stimuli (allodynia).

**Muscle Weakness or Paralysis**: Damage to motor nerves can lead to muscle weakness, muscle atrophy (shrinking), or even paralysis in severe cases. This can affect mobility and coordination.

**Loss of Coordination:** Neuropathy can impair proprioception (the sense of body position) and balance, leading to difficulties with coordination and an increased risk of falls.

**Changes in Sensation:** Neuropathy can cause changes in sensation, such as a feeling of heaviness, tightness, or swelling in the affected area, even when no physical changes are present.

**Autonomic Symptoms:** In some cases, neuropathy may affect the autonomic nerves, which control involuntary bodily functions. This can lead to symptoms such as changes in blood pressure, heart rate, sweating, digestion, and bladder function.

**Loss of Reflexes:** Damage to sensory or motor nerves can lead to diminished or absent reflexes, such as the knee-jerk reflex (Fig. **2**).

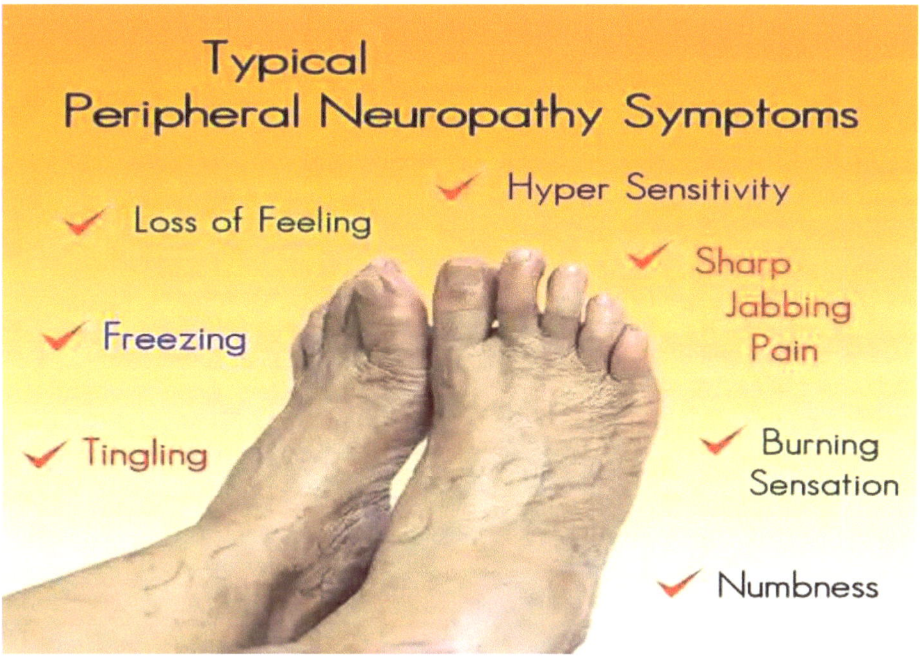


**Fig. (2).** Symptoms of neuropathy.

**Foot Problems:** Neuropathy commonly affects the feet and can lead to complications such as foot ulcers, infections, and deformities (such as Charcot's foot).

**Sexual Dysfunction:** Neuropathy can affect the nerves that control sexual function, leading to symptoms such as erectile dysfunction in men and decreased libido or difficulty achieving orgasm in both men and women.

It is important to note that not everyone with neuropathy will experience all of these symptoms, and the severity and combination of symptoms can vary depending on individual factors such as the underlying cause, the extent of nerve damage, and overall health. If you are experiencing symptoms of neuropathy, it is essential to discuss with a doctor for precise detection and suitable control measures.

## Types of Neuropathies

Neuropathy can be classified into several types based on various criteria, including the nerves affected, the underlying cause, and the symptoms. Some common types of neuropathies are included in Fig. (**3**).

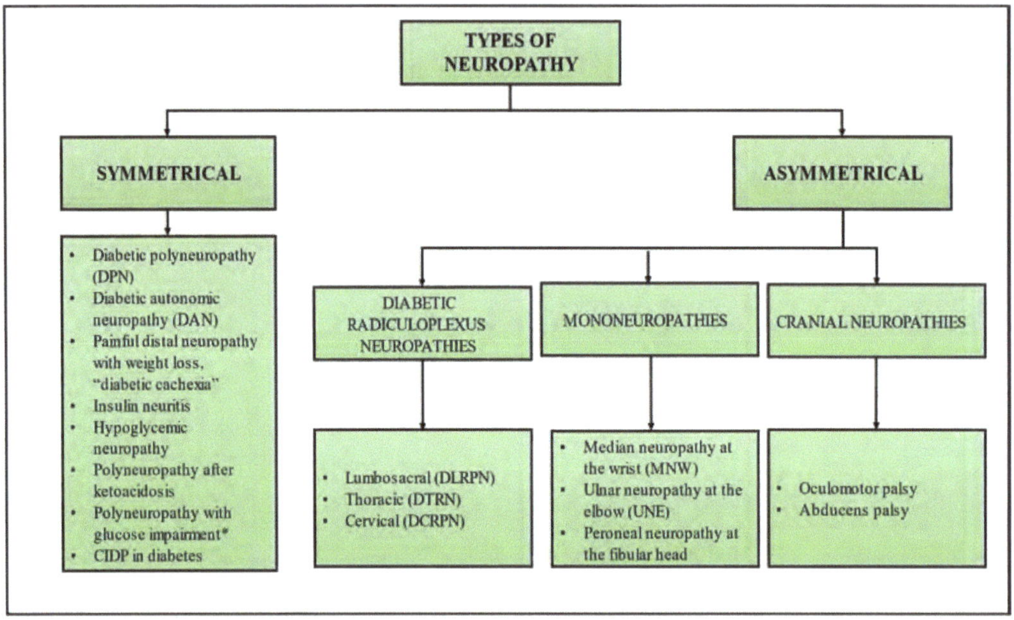


**Fig. (3).** Types of neuropathy.

- **Peripheral Neuropathy:** This is the most common type of neuropathy, affecting the peripheral nerves outside the brain and spinal cord. Peripheral neuropathy can be further categorized based on the type of nerves affected, such as sensory neuropathy (affecting sensory nerves), motor neuropathy (affecting motor nerves), or autonomic neuropathy (affecting autonomic nerves).
- **Diabetic Neuropathy:** Diabetic neuropathy is a form of peripheral neuropathy that arises as a complication of diabetes. It can affect sensory, motor, and autonomic nerves and is caused by prolonged high blood sugar levels damaging the nerves [5] (Fig. **4**).

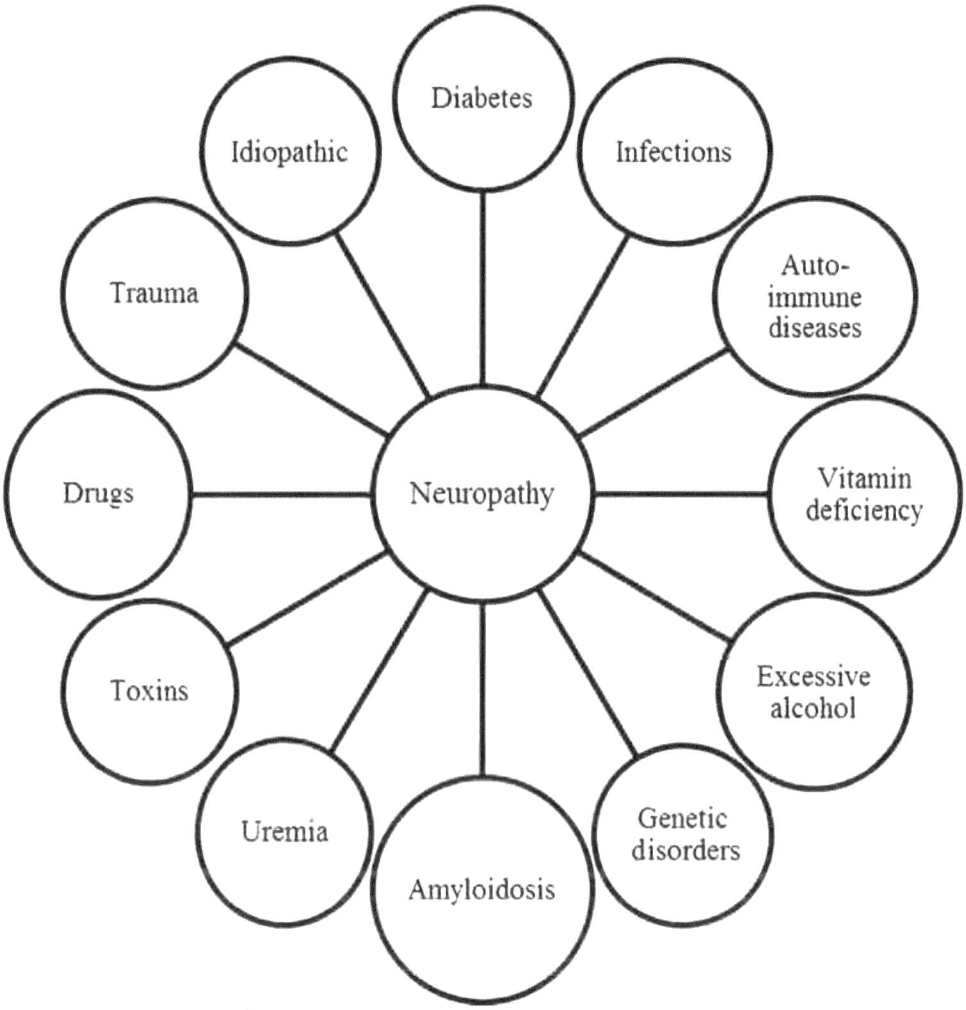


**Fig. (4).** Diabetic peripheral neuropathy: An insight into the pathophysiology,

## CONCLUSION

Understanding the above-mentioned cause of neuropathy is crucial for appropriate management and treatment. Depending on the cause, treatment strategies may include addressing the mentioned conditions, managing symptoms, physical therapy, lifestyle modifications, and medications to alleviate pain and discomfort.

## REFERENCES

[1] Filipovski I, Gabriel RA, Kestenholz R. Ultrasound-guided cryoneurolysis for the treatment of painful Diabetic Neuropathy of the foot: a Case Series. Cureus 2024; 16(3): e56267.

[http://dx.doi.org/10.7759/cureus.56267] [PMID: 38495961]

[2] Mukhtar M, Naseer M, Yasin MM, Luqman F. Atypical presentation of optic neuritis in multiple sclerosis. Cureus 2024; 16(12): e76169.
[http://dx.doi.org/10.7759/cureus.76169] [PMID: 39840190]

[3] Jesie R S, Premi M S G. Nutrient deficiency of paddy leaf classification using hybrid convolutional neural network. International Journal of Electrical and Electronics Research 2024; 12(1): 286-91.
[http://dx.doi.org/10.37391/IJEER.120139]

[4] Kopsky DJ, van Eijk RPA, Warendorf JK, Keppel Hesselink JM, Notermans NC, Vrancken AFJE. Enriched enrollment randomized double-blind placebo-controlled cross-over trial with phenytoin cream in painful chronic idiopathic axonal polyneuropathy (EPHENE): a study protocol. Trials 2022; 23(1): 888.
[http://dx.doi.org/10.1186/s13063-022-06806-8] [PMID: 36273216]

[5] Sunarmi S, Isworo A, Ari D, Sitepu FY, Triredjeki H. The effectiveness of massage therapy on healing of diabetic neuropathy in diabetes mellitus patients. Open Access Macedonian Journal of Medical Sciences, 2022; 10(G): 190-194.

# CHAPTER 8

# Types of Neuropathies

**Abstract:** Autonomic neuropathy is considered to affect involuntary bodily functions, such as blood pressure and digestion, and its causes are diabetes, autoimmune diseases, and certain medications. Cranial neuropathy affects brain-originating cranial nerves, responsible for controlling vision, eye movement, and facial sensation. Hereditary neuropathies are inherited conditions that target the peripheral nervous system functions, while idiopathic neuropathy belongs to a condition of unknown causes. Toxic neuropathy develops due to exposure to toxins or chemicals, whereas nerve inflammation causes inflammatory neuropathy, often due to autoimmune diseases or infections.

Neuropathies' prevalence fluctuates based on type and inhabitants. Peripheral neuropathy, a common type, ranges from 2.4% to 8%, with higher rates in older age groups suffering from diabetes. Diabetic neuropathy, which is considered a common complication of diabetes, affects 50% of people, with prevalence unpredictable based on time interval, severity, and glycemic control as well.

Neuropathy, a condition causing nerve damage, can have various causes and symptoms. Medications, prescription medications, topical treatments, physical therapy, transcutaneous electrical nerve stimulation, acupuncture, lifestyle modifications, alternative therapies, nerve blocks or injections, and surgery are included in common treatment options. Autonomic neuropathy, a complication of conditions like diabetes, autoimmune diseases, and infections, is less common than peripheral neuropathy but can occur as a complication. Cranial neuropathy is comparatively rare but can be predisposed by factors like age, sex, and underlying conditions. Hereditary neuropathies are genetic disorders that disturb peripheral nerves, while toxic neuropathy occurs due to exposure to toxins or chemicals. Inflammatory neuropathies, such as Guillain-Barre syndrome and prolonged inflammatory demyelinating polyneuropathy, are rare but can have noteworthy morbidity and mortality. Approximating the prevalence of neuropathies can be challenging due to underdiagnosis, inconsistency in analytical criteria, and differences in study populations. Furthermore, the prevalence of neuropathies may vary over time due to aging populations, changes in disease patterns, and improvements in diagnostic techniques.

**Keywords:** Autonomic neuropathy, Cranial neuropathy, Inflammatory neuropathy, Neuropathy, Peripheral neuropathy.

**Sumaira Kanwal & Shazia Perveen**

## INTRODUCTION

**Autonomic Neuropathy:** Autonomic neuropathy affects the autonomic nerves that control involuntary bodily functions such as blood pressure, digestion, and bladder function. Major factors involved include diabetes, autoimmune diseases, and certain medications [1].

**Cranial Neuropathy:** Cranial neuropathy involves the destruction of the cranial nerves, which originate from the brain and control functions such as vision, eye movement, facial sensation and movement, hearing, and taste. Cranial neuropathy can result from various causes, including trauma, infections, tumors, and autoimmune diseases [2].

**Hereditary Neuropathy:** Hereditary neuropathies are inherited conditions caused by mutations that affect the major functions of PN; examples include Charcot-Marie-Tooth disease and familial amyloid polyneuropathy [3].

**Idiopathic Neuropathy:** Idiopathic neuropathy refers to neuropathy of unknown cause, where no underlying condition or trigger can be identified. It may be classified based on the specific symptoms or nerves affected, such as idiopathic sensory neuropathy or idiopathic autonomic neuropathy [4].

**Toxic Neuropathy:** Toxic neuropathy occurs as a result of exposure to toxins or chemicals that damage the nerves. Common toxins associated with toxic neuropathy include heavy metals (such as lead, mercury, and arsenic), industrial solvents, pesticides, and certain medications (such as chemotherapy drugs and antiretroviral drugs) [5].

**Inflammatory Neuropathy:** Inflammatory neuropathies are caused by inflammation of the nerves, often as a result of autoimmune diseases or infections. Examples include Guillain-Barre syndrome, Chronic Inflammatory Demyelinating Polyneuropathy (CIDP), and multifocal motor neuropathy [6].

These are just a few examples of the many types of neuropathies that can occur. Each type may present with distinct symptoms, require different diagnostic approaches, and have specific treatment considerations.

### Prevalence of Neuropathies

The prevalence of neuropathies varies depending on the specific type of neuropathy and the population being studied. Here are some estimates for the prevalence of common types of neuropathies (Fig. **1**).

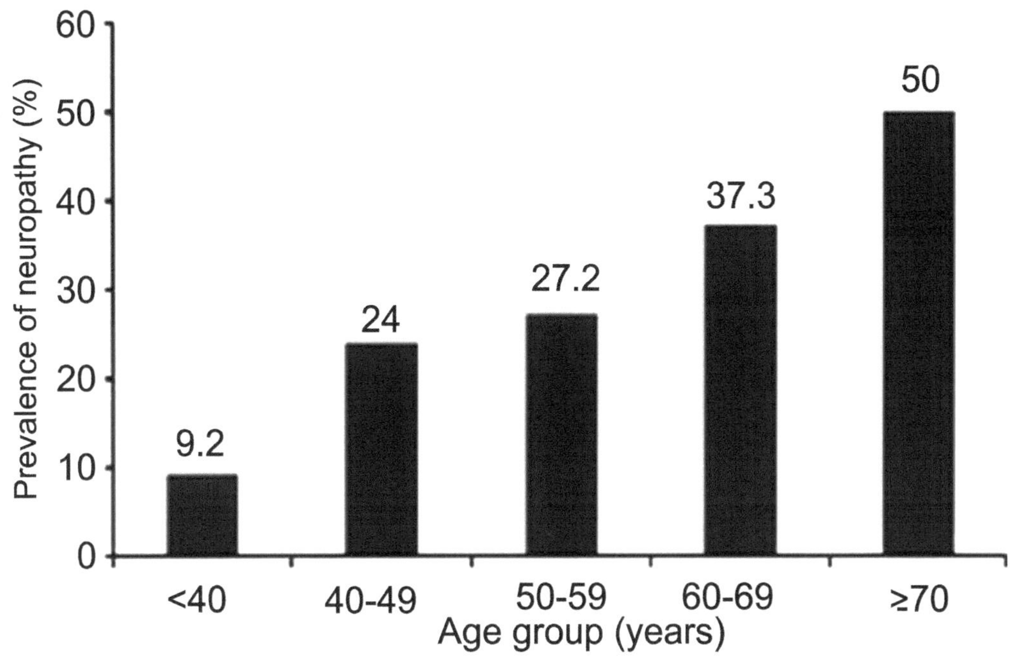


**Fig. (1).** Prevalence of neuropathy according to age groups.

**Peripheral Neuropathy:** Peripheral neuropathy is one of the most common types of neuropathies. Studies suggest that the prevalence of peripheral neuropathy in the general population ranges from 2.4% to 8%, with higher rates observed in older age groups and individuals with conditions such as diabetes [7].

**Diabetic Neuropathy:** Diabetic neuropathy is a common complication of diabetes. It is estimated that approximately 50% of people with diabetes will develop some form of diabetic neuropathy during their lifetime. The prevalence of diabetic neuropathy varies depending on factors such as the duration and severity of diabctcs and glyccmic control [8].

## Treatment Options for Neuropathy

Neuropathy, or nerve damage, can have various causes and symptoms, so the treatment options depend on the various factors and the specific symptoms experienced by the individual. Here are some common treatment approaches:

- **Medications:** Pain relievers: The pain can be managed by the use of a few drugs, such as acetaminophen or nonsteroidal, (NSAIDs) may help alleviate mild neuropathic pain.

- **Prescription Medications:** Antidepressants (such as amitriptyline, duloxetine, or venlafaxine) and gabapentin or pregabalin) are mostly prescribed for neuropathic pain [9].
- **Topical Treatments:** Creams, gels, or patches containing lidocaine, capsaicin, or other medications may provide relief for localized neuropathic pain [10].
- **Physical Therapy:** Exercises and techniques to improve strength, flexibility, and balance, and can protect the nerves from damage [11].
- **Transcutaneous Electrical Nerve Stimulation:** This therapy applies a mild electrical current to the skin, which can help to relieve neuropathic pain for some individuals [12].
- **Acupuncture:** Some people find relief from neuropathic pain through acupuncture, although the evidence for its effectiveness is mixed [13].
- **Lifestyle Modifications:** Making changes such as maintaining a healthy diet, quitting smoking, moderating alcohol consumption, and managing underlying conditions like diabetes can help slow the progression of neuropathy and reduce symptoms [14].
- **Alternative Therapies:** Some people explore alternative treatments such as herbal supplements, vitamins (such as B-complex vitamins), and alpha-lipid acid, or omega-3 fatty acids. However, evidence supporting the effectiveness of these treatments is limited [15].
- **Nerve Blocks or Injections:** In some cases, injecting medications directly into the affected nerves or performing nerve blocks can provide temporary relief from neuropathic pain [16].
- **Surgery:** In extreme cases of neuropathy, surgery is mostly recommended to remove tumors or alleviate compression on nerves.

Individuals with neuropathy need to be in contact with the concerned doctor and design the proper treatment according to the circumstances [17].

## CONCLUSION

It is important to note that estimating the prevalence of neuropathies can be challenging due to factors such as underdiagnosis, variability in diagnostic criteria, and differences in study populations. Additionally, the prevalence of neuropathies may change over time due to factors such as aging populations, changes in disease patterns, and improvements in diagnostic techniques.

## REFERENCES

[1] Bouhy D, Timmerman V. [Animal models of Charcot-Marie-Tooth disease and their relevance for understanding the disease in humans]. Rev Neurol (Paris) 2013; 169(12): 971-7. [http://dx.doi.org/10.1016/j.neurol.2013.07.027] [PMID: 24238786]

[2] Oh J, Vidal-Jordana A, Montalban X. Multiple sclerosis: clinical aspects. Curr Opin Neurol 2018; 31(6): 752-9.

[http://dx.doi.org/10.1097/WCO.0000000000000622] [PMID: 30300239]

[3] Beghi E, Giussani G, Sander JW. The natural history and prognosis of epilepsy. Epileptic disorders: international epilepsy journal with videotape. 2015; 17(3): 243-53. [http://dx.doi.org/10.1684/epd.2015.0751]

[4] Kim LG, Johnson TL, Marson AG, Chadwick DW. Prediction of risk of seizure recurrence after a single seizure and early epilepsy: further results from the MESS trial. Lancet Neurol 2006; 5(4): 317-22. [http://dx.doi.org/10.1016/S1474-4422(06)70383-0] [PMID: 16545748]

[5] FitzPatrick L, Bird A. Genetic therapies for neurological disorders. Hum Genet 2022; 141(5): 1085-91. [http://dx.doi.org/10.1007/s00439-021-02399-5] [PMID: 34807307]

[6] Robertson LT. Memory and the Brain. J Dent Educ 2002; 66(1): 30-42. [http://dx.doi.org/10.1002/j.0022-0337.2002.66.1.tb03506.x] [PMID: 12358099]

[7] Ding Q, Zhao H. Long-term effects of SARS-CoV-2 infection on human brain and memory. Cell Death Discov 2023; 9(1): 196. [http://dx.doi.org/10.1038/s41420-023-01512-z] [PMID: 37380640]

[8] Pena SA, Iyengar R, Eshraghi RS, *et al.* Gene therapy for neurological disorders: challenges and recent advancements. J Drug Target 2020; 28(2): 111-28. [http://dx.doi.org/10.1080/1061186X.2019.1630415] [PMID: 31195838]

[9] Hanewinckel R, Ikram MA, Van Doorn PA. Peripheral neuropathies. Handb Clin Neurol 2016; 138: 263-82. [http://dx.doi.org/10.1016/B978-0-12-802973-2.00015-X] [PMID: 27637963]

[10] Drukarch B, Holland HA, Velichkov M, *et al.* Thinking about the nerve impulse: A critical analysis of the electricity-centered conception of nerve excitability. Prog Neurobiol 2018; 169: 172-85. [http://dx.doi.org/10.1016/j.pneurobio.2018.06.009] [PMID: 29981394]

[11] Monje M. Myelin plasticity and nervous system function. Annu Rev Neurosci 2018; 41(1): 61-76. [http://dx.doi.org/10.1146/annurev-neuro-080317-061853] [PMID: 29986163]

[12] Gibson EM, Geraghty AC, Monje M. Bad wrap: Myelin and myelin plasticity in health and disease. Dev Neurobiol 2018; 78(2): 123-35. [http://dx.doi.org/10.1002/dneu.22541] [PMID: 28986960]

[13] Kondiles BR, Horner PJ. Myelin plasticity, neural activity, and traumatic neural injury. Dev Neurobiol 2018; 78(2): 108-22. [http://dx.doi.org/10.1002/dneu.22540] [PMID: 28925069]

[14] Tavee J. Nerve conduction studies: Basic concepts. Handb Clin Neurol 2019; 160: 217-24. [http://dx.doi.org/10.1016/B978-0-444-64032-1.00014-X] [PMID: 31277849]

[15] Khodorov BI, Timin EN. Nerve impulse propagation along nonuniform fibres. Prog Biophys Mol Biol 1975; 30(2-3): 145-84. [PMID: 792950]

[16] Barnett MW, Larkman PM. The action potential. Pract Neurol 2007; 7(3): 192-7. [PMID: 17515599]

[17] Patel K, Horak H, Tiryaki E. Diabetic neuropathies. Muscle Nerve 2021; 63(1): 22-30. [http://dx.doi.org/10.1002/mus.27014] [PMID: 32589300]

# CHAPTER 9

# Clinical Symptoms of Neuropathies

**Abstract:** Neuropathies affect peripheral neurological structures and exhibit varying clinical symptoms, including motor, sensory, and autonomic, depending on the type of neuropathy and the nerves involved. However, common symptoms may be present in various types, including syndromic, idiopathic, and hereditary neuropathies. This chapter aims to discuss the clinical symptoms of neuropathies.

**Keywords:** Clinical neuropathy, Idiopathic neuropathy, Motor symptoms, Sensory symptoms, Syndromic neuropathies.

## INTRODUCTION

Neuropathies involve damage to the peripheral nervous system and can present with a wide range of clinical signs, motor, sensory, or autonomic, based on the specific type and the nerves affected. Despite this variability, certain symptoms often overlap across different forms, whether they are syndromic, idiopathic, or hereditary in origin.

A few of the common symptoms, such as paresthesia, involve numbness, tingling, loss of sensation, hypersensitivity to touch or pain, burning or shooting pain, reduced temperature sense, and a "pins and needles" sensation [1].

### Motor Symptoms

Motor neuropathy develops when motor neurons, which regulate muscular movement, are damaged. This can lead to various motor dysfunctions. The primary motor symptoms of neuropathy include **muscle weakness**, which involves progressive weakening, typically beginning in the hands or feet, as well as **difficulty with fine motor skills**, such as challenges with tasks like buttoning a shirt or writing; **leg weakness**, which may cause difficulty walking or climbing stairs; **muscle cramps and spasms**, particularly at night, and spasticity (involuntary muscle contractions); **fasciculations**, which are small, involuntary muscle twitches visible under the skin, caused by damaged motor neurons firing spontaneously; **loss of reflexes**, in which deep tendon reflexes, such as knee and

**Sumaira Kanwal & Shazia Perveen**

ankle jerks, may be reduced or absent, leading to poor coordination and balance issues; **foot drop**, whih is characterized by inability to lift the front part of the foot, resulting in dragging while walking and a characteristic high-stepping gait; and **paralysis** and in severe cases, complete loss of voluntary muscle control [2].

These symptoms may affect specific muscle groups or be more generalized, depending on the extent of nerve involvement. Conditions that can cause motor neuropathy include diabetic neuropathy, Guillain-Barré syndrome, motor neuron disease, Chronic Inflammatory Demyelinating Polyneuropathy (CIDP), and toxic neuropathy [3].

**Sensory Symptoms**

Sensory neuropathy develops when the nerves that transmit sensory information from the body to the brain become damaged. This can lead to a range of symptoms that impair a person's ability to perceive pain, temperature, touch, and body position. Sensory symptoms typically appear gradually and may be mild at first, progressing over time if the underlying condition is not properly managed [4].

One of the most common sensory complaints is numbness and tingling, often described as a "pins and needles" sensation. This typically starts in the toes and fingers, gradually spreading upward in a "glove and stocking" distribution. As the condition progresses, the numbness may become permanent, making it difficult for individuals to sense textures, temperatures, or injuries, significantly increasing the risk of unnoticed wounds, particularly in cases of diabetic neuropathy [5].

Another frequent symptom is burning or severe pain, which may occur spontaneously or be triggered by external stimuli. This pain is often more intense at night, disrupting sleep and significantly reducing quality of life. It may be described as stabbing, shooting, or electric shock-like. In severe cases, even light touch, such as from clothing or bed sheets, can become unbearable, a condition known as allodynia.

Conversely, some individuals experience reduced sensitivity to pain and temperature, which can also be dangerous.

Overall, sensory neuropathy can have a major impact on daily life, complicating routine activities and increasing the risk of injury. Identifying the underlying cause, such as diabetes, vitamin deficiencies, autoimmune disorders, or toxic exposures, is essential for effective treatment and prevention of further nerve damage. Treatment may include medications, physical therapy, and lifestyle modifications to relieve symptoms, address the root cause, and support nerve function [6].

**Autonomic Symptoms**

Autonomic neuropathy develops when the nerves that control involuntary physiological functions become damaged. These nerves regulate vital processes, such as heart rate, blood pressure, digestion, temperature control, and bladder function. Their impairment can lead to a wide range of symptoms affecting multiple organ systems. The severity of these symptoms depends on the extent of nerve damage, with underlying causes including diabetes, autoimmune disorders, infections, or certain medications.

One of the most common autonomic symptoms is impaired blood pressure regulation, leading to orthostatic hypotension, a drop in blood pressure upon standing that causes dizziness or fainting [7]. Individuals with autonomic neuropathy may also experience blood pressure fluctuations throughout the day, increasing the risk of falls and injury. Additionally, damage to autonomic nerves can result in an irregular heart rate, causing palpitations, rapid heartbeat, or an inability to properly adjust heart rate during physical activity.

Digestive issues are another major concern in autonomic neuropathy. Damage to the nerves controlling the gastrointestinal tract can lead to gastroparesis, a condition where the stomach empties slowly. Symptoms may include nausea, vomiting, bloating, loss of appetite, and severe constipation. Some individuals may also experience spontaneous episodes of diarrhea or fecal incontinence, particularly at night, due to impaired nerve control of bowel movements. These symptoms can significantly affect nutrition, hydration, and overall quality of life.

Autonomic neuropathy frequently leads to bladder and sexual dysfunction. Nerve damage affecting bladder control can result in urinary retention, while others may suffer from urinary incontinence, leading to involuntary leakage. In men, autonomic neuropathy can cause erectile dysfunction, and in women, it may lead to vaginal dryness and reduced libido, both of which contribute to sexual difficulties [8].

Sweating abnormalities are also common signs of autonomic nerve damage. Some individuals may experience excessive sweating (hyperhidrosis), especially at night or after eating, while others may sweat very little or not at all (anhidrosis), impairing the body's ability to regulate temperature. Anhidrosis can be hazardous, as it increases the risk of heat intolerance and heatstroke, especially in hot environments or during intense physical activity.

Symptoms of autonomic neuropathy can be debilitating and, in some cases, life-threatening, especially when vital functions like heart rate and digestion are affected. Accurate diagnosis and comprehensive management are essential. Treatment focuses on addressing the underlying cause, relieving symptoms, and improving quality of life through medications, dietary changes, and lifestyle modifications [9].

## Syndromic Neuropathies

Syndromic neuropathies are neuropathic conditions that occur as part of broader syndromes or diseases, where neuropathy is a key feature. Examples include Charcot-Marie-Tooth Disease (CMT), Friedreich's Ataxia, Hereditary Neuropathy with Liability to Pressure Palsies (HNPP), mitochondrial disorders, Refsum Disease, Alpers Syndrome, and Fabry Disease [10].

CMT is a group of inherited neuropathies characterized by progressive muscle weakness and wasting, primarily affecting the feet, ankles, and hands. Friedreich's Ataxia is a rare genetic disorder that affects both the nervous system and the heart, leading to muscle weakness, loss of coordination, sensory loss, and cardiac complications. HNPP is a genetic condition marked by recurrent episodes of focal peripheral nerve dysfunction, often triggered by minor trauma or pressure on nerves. Refsum disease is a rare inherited disorder caused by a deficiency in the enzyme responsible for breaking down phytanic acid, leading to its accumulation [11].

Treatment for syndromic neuropathies typically focuses on symptom management, physical therapy, genetic counseling, and supportive care tailored to the individual's needs. Common symptoms include muscle wasting, loss of muscle control, and autonomic dysfunction, such as abnormal sweating, heat intolerance, digestive issues, heart rate or blood pressure irregularities, bladder and sexual dysfunction, balance and coordination problems, frequent falls, fatigue, changes in skin, hair, or nail texture, and neuropathic pain [12].

## Idiopathic Neuropathy

Idiopathic peripheral neuropathy refers to peripheral neuropathy with an unknown cause. Symptoms include sensory signs, such as tingling, reduced touch sensation, hyperalgesia, burning pain, and altered temperature perception. Motor symptoms may involve muscle weakness, difficulty with fine motor skills, muscle cramps, loss of muscle control, and muscle wasting [13].

Autonomic symptoms can include abnormal sweating patterns, heat intolerance, digestive problems, changes in heart rate or blood pressure, bladder dysfunction, sexual dysfunction, balance and coordination difficulties, and fatigue.

Treatment primarily aims to manage symptoms and improve quality of life through medications to relieve pain, physical therapy to enhance mobility and strength, and lifestyle modifications tailored to address specific symptoms or complications [14].

### Hereditary Neuropathies

Genetic disorders affecting the Peripheral Nervous System (PNS) commonly present with clinical symptoms, including altered sensory perceptions, motor weakness, difficulties with fine motor skills, muscle cramps, and muscle wasting. As discussed previously, autonomic symptoms may include abnormal sweating patterns, digestive problems, bladder dysfunction, blood pressure fluctuations, and sexual dysfunction [15].

Balance and coordination difficulties manifest as problems with walking, increased risk of falls, and loss of proprioception. Additional symptoms include fatigue, generalized weakness, changes in skin texture, heightened susceptibility to injuries, and neuropathic pain.

The severity and specific symptoms vary depending on the disorder subtype, the genes involved, and individual differences. Management typically focuses on symptom relief, physical therapy, the use of assistive devices, and genetic counseling for affected individuals and their families [16].

## CONCLUSION

Clinical symptoms are observed in various syndromic neuropathies, including Charcot-Marie-Tooth Disease (CMT), Friedreich's Ataxia, Hereditary Neuropathy with Liability to Pressure Palsies (HNPP), mitochondrial disorders, Refsum disease, Alpers syndrome, and Fabry disease. Treatment typically involves symptom management, physical therapy, genetic counseling, and supportive care tailored to the individual's needs. Common manifestations include muscle wasting and loss of muscle control.

## REFERENCES

[1] Ang L, Mizokami-Stout K, Eid SA, *et al.* The conundrum of diabetic neuropathies—Past, present, and future. J Diabetes Complications 2022; 36(11): 108334. [http://dx.doi.org/10.1016/j.jdiacomp.2022.108334] [PMID: 36306721]

[2] Gentile F, Bertini A, Priori A, Bocci T. Movement disorders and neuropathies: overlaps and mimics in clinical practice. J Neurol 2022; 269(9): 4646-62.

[http://dx.doi.org/10.1007/s00415-022-11200-0] [PMID: 35657406]

[3] Sloan G, Selvarajah D, Tesfaye S. Pathogenesis, diagnosis and clinical management of diabetic sensorimotor peripheral neuropathy. Nat Rev Endocrinol 2021; 17(7): 400-20. [http://dx.doi.org/10.1038/s41574-021-00496-z] [PMID: 34050323]

[4] Jajeh H, Lee A, Charls R, Coffin M, Sood A, Elgafy H. A clinical review of hand manifestations of cervical myelopathy, cervical radiculopathy, radial, ulnar, and median nerve neuropathies. J Spine Surg 2024; 10(1): 120-34. [http://dx.doi.org/10.21037/jss-23-39] [PMID: 38567008]

[5] Jensen TS, Karlsson P, Gylfadottir SS, *et al.* Painful and non-painful diabetic neuropathy, diagnostic challenges and implications for future management. Brain 2021; 144(6): 1632-45. [http://dx.doi.org/10.1093/brain/awab079] [PMID: 33711103]

[6] Kang L, Tian Y, Xu S, Chen H. Oxaliplatin-induced peripheral neuropathy: clinical features, mechanisms, prevention and treatment. J Neurol 2021; 268(9): 3269-82. [http://dx.doi.org/10.1007/s00415-020-09942-w] [PMID: 32474658]

[7] Kaur D, Tiwana H, Stino A, Sandroni P. Autonomic neuropathies. Muscle Nerve 2021; 63(1): 10-21. [http://dx.doi.org/10.1002/mus.27048] [PMID: 32926436]

[8] Duque A, Mediano MFF, De Lorenzo A, Rodrigues LF Jr. Cardiovascular autonomic neuropathy in diabetes: Pathophysiology, clinical assessment and implications. World J Diabetes 2021; 12(6): 855-67. [http://dx.doi.org/10.4239/wjd.v12.i6.855] [PMID: 34168733]

[9] Eleftheriadou A, Spallone V, Tahrani AA, Alam U. Cardiovascular autonomic neuropathy in diabetes: an update with a focus on management. Diabetologia 2024; 67(12): 2611-25. [http://dx.doi.org/10.1007/s00125-024-06242-0] [PMID: 39120767]

[10] Kazamel M, Stino AM, Smith AG. Metabolic syndrome and peripheral neuropathy. Muscle Nerve 2021; 63(3): 285-93. [http://dx.doi.org/10.1002/mus.27086] [PMID: 33098165]

[11] Finsterer J, Löscher WN, Wanschitz J, Iglseder S. Orphan peripheral neuropathies. J Neuromuscul Dis 2020; 8(1): 1-23. [http://dx.doi.org/10.3233/JND-200518] [PMID: 32986679]

[12] Newman NJ, Yu-Wai-Man P, Biousse V, Carelli V. Understanding the molecular basis and pathogenesis of hereditary optic neuropathies: towards improved diagnosis and management. Lancet Neurol 2023; 22(2): 172-88. [http://dx.doi.org/10.1016/S1474-4422(22)00174-0] [PMID: 36155660]

[13] Haroutounian S, Todorovic MS, Leinders M, *et al.* Diagnostic criteria for idiopathic small fiber neuropathy: A systematic review. Muscle Nerve 2021; 63(2): 170-7. [http://dx.doi.org/10.1002/mus.27070] [PMID: 32989823]

[14] Currò R, Salvalaggio A, Tozza S, *et al. RFC1* expansions are a common cause of idiopathic sensory neuropathy. Brain 2021; 144(5): 1542-50. [http://dx.doi.org/10.1093/brain/awab072] [PMID: 33969391]

[15] Pisciotta C, Shy ME. Hereditary neuropathy. Handb Clin Neurol 2023; 195: 609-17. [http://dx.doi.org/10.1016/B978-0-323-98818-6.00009-1] [PMID: 37562889]

[16] Kramarz C, Rossor AM. Neurological update: hereditary neuropathies. J Neurol 2022; 269(9): 5187-91. [http://dx.doi.org/10.1007/s00415-022-11164-1] [PMID: 35596796]

# CHAPTER 10

# Diagnosis of Neuropathies

**Abstract:** The diagnosis of neuropathies involves a comprehensive evaluation, including a detailed medical history, physical examination, and various diagnostic tests. The process starts with a detailed medical history, family history of neurological disorders, and exposure to toxins or medications. The examination assesses motor strength, sensation, reflexes, coordination, and gait. Neuropathy is a condition characterized by abnormalities in the electrical activity and function of nerves and muscles. Common diagnostic tests include electromyography (EMG), Nerve Conduction Studies (NCS), nerve biopsy, imaging studies, blood tests, genetic testing, and specialized testing. Blood tests are used to screen for underlying medical conditions, while genetic testing is used to identify specific genetic mutations. Specialized testing may include autonomic function tests, skin biopsy, or cerebrospinal fluid analysis. In complex cases, a multidisciplinary team of healthcare professionals may be involved. A thorough evaluation, including clinical assessment and diagnostic tests, is crucial for an accurate diagnosis and effective management.

Toxic neuropathies result from exposure to substances, such as alcohol, chemotherapy drugs, heavy metals, and industrial chemicals, which can damage peripheral nerves. Autoimmune disorders, such as Guillain-Barré syndrome and Chronic Inflammatory Demyelinating Polyneuropathy (CIDP), involve the immune system attacking peripheral nerves, resulting in weakness and neurological symptoms. Infectious neuropathies caused by viral, bacterial, or parasitic infections can lead to nerve damage either directly or through immune-mediated mechanisms. Genetic disorders, including Charcot-Marie-Tooth disease and other hereditary neuropathies, cause progressive weakness and muscle atrophy.

**Keywords:** Diagnosis, Electromyography, Guillain-barré syndrome, Hereditary neuropathy, Nerve conduction studies, Neuropathies.

## INTRODUCTION

The diagnosis of neuropathies involves a comprehensive evaluation that includes medical history, physical examination, and various diagnostic tests [1]. This chapter provides an overview of the diagnostic process for neuropathies [2 - 4]. The processes involved are as follows:

**Sumaira Kanwal & Shazia Perveen**

**Medical History:** The healthcare provider typically begins by taking a detailed medical history, including a family history of neurological disorders and exposure to toxins or medications that may contribute to neuropathy [5].

**Physical Examination:** A thorough neurological examination is performed to assess motor strength, sensation (including light touch, pinprick, vibration, and proprioception), reflexes, coordination, and gait. Specific attention is paid to the distribution and pattern of symptoms, as well as any signs of muscle weakness, sensory loss, or autonomic dysfunction [6, 7].

**Diagnostic Tests**

**Electrodiagnostic Studies:** Electromyography (EMG) and Nerve Conduction Studies (NCS) are commonly used to assess the electrical activity and function of nerves and muscles. EMG involves the insertion of needle electrodes into muscles to record electrical activity, while NCS measures the speed and amplitude of nerve impulses along peripheral nerves [8, 9].

**Nerve Biopsy:** A nerve biopsy is a specialized diagnostic procedure used to evaluate specific peripheral neuropathies when other procedures, such as nerve conduction studies and blood tests, do not yield a conclusive result. It entails surgically cutting a tiny piece of a nerve, typically the sural nerve around the ankle, while under local anesthesia. The sample is then examined under a microscope for abnormalities, such as inflammation, axonal degeneration, demyelination, amyloid deposits, or granulomas, which aid in the diagnosis of vasculitis neuropathy, amyloidosis, leprosy, and Chronic Inflammatory Demyelinating Polyneuropathy (CIDP) [10]. Although this treatment can help identify certain causes of neuropathy, it is not commonly used due to risks, such as persistent numbness, pain, infection, and scarring. When possible, less intrusive options, such as skin biopsy for tiny fiber neuropathy or genetic testing for hereditary disorders, are preferable. Despite its limitations, nerve biopsy is nevertheless a useful technique for detecting complex neuropathies when other diagnostic procedures have failed [11].

**Imaging Studies:** Magnetic Resonance Imaging (MRI) or Computed Tomography (CT) scans are used to visualize the nerves and surrounding structures, ruling out other potential causes of symptoms (such as tumors or structural abnormalities) and identifying specific patterns of nerve involvement.

**Blood Tests:** Blood tests are crucial in detecting neuropathies because they reveal underlying diseases that may cause nerve injury. These tests can assist in identifying metabolic, autoimmune, viral, nutritional, and toxic causes of neuropathy. Blood glucose and HbA1c testing are required to diagnose diabetic neuropathy, whereas vitamin B12, B6, and folate levels aid in determining nutritional deficiencies that can cause nerve damage. Thyroid function tests (TSH, T4) are used to assess hypothyroidism, which is a possible cause of neuropathy [12]. Autoimmune indicators, including Antinuclear Antibodies (ANA), Rheumatoid Factor (RF), and Anti-Neutrophil Cytoplasmic Antibodies (ANCA), aid in the diagnosis of autoimmune neuropathies, such as vasculitis or lupus neuropathy. Screening for kidney and liver function is critical because organ disease can lead to toxin accumulation, which impairs nerve function. In addition, infectious disease testing for HIV, syphilis, Lyme disease, and hepatitis B/C helps rule out illnesses that might cause neuropathy. Serum Protein Electrophoresis (SPEP), Immunofixation Electrophoresis (IFE), and anti-Hu antibodies can all be helpful in diagnosing suspected paraneoplastic or monoclonal gammopathy-related neuropathy. Blood tests are a critical step in the diagnosis of neuropathies because they identify the underlying cause and guide proper treatment and care measures [13].

**Genetic Testing:** This is an effective method for detecting hereditary neuropathies, particularly when there is a family history of nerve problems or clinical and electrophysiological data suggest a genetic explanation. It aids in the identification of mutations linked to inherited illnesses, such as Charcot-Mari--Tooth disease (CMT), Hereditary Sensory and Autonomic Neuropathies (HSAN), Hereditary Neuropathy with Pressure Palsies (HNPP), and Familial Amyloid Polyneuropathy (FAP). Genetic testing involves examining DNA from a blood or saliva sample to identify mutations in specific genes that regulate nerve function and structure. This test is especially effective when electrophysiological studies, nerve biopsies, and blood tests do not yield a definitive diagnosis. While genetic testing can identify hereditary neuropathy, it cannot consistently predict the severity or progression of the disease. Furthermore, due to the complexity of genetic variants, results should be evaluated in conjunction with clinical data. As genetic and personalized medicine advance, genetic testing plays an increasingly important role in guiding treatment decisions and offering vital information for family planning and disease management in individuals with inherited neuropathies [14, 15].

**Nerve Biopsy:** In certain cases, a biopsy of peripheral nerves may be performed to examine nerve tissue under a microscope, assess the degree of myelination, and identify any abnormalities or pathological changes.

**Specialized Testing:** Depending on the suspected cause of neuropathy, additional tests may include autonomic function assessments, skin biopsies to evaluate small fiber neuropathy, or cerebrospinal fluid analysis for suspected inflammatory or infectious neuropathies [16].

**Multidisciplinary Evaluation:** In complex cases or when the diagnosis is uncertain, a multidisciplinary team of healthcare professionals, including neurologists, physiatrists, neuromuscular specialists, and other specialists, may be involved in the evaluation and management of neuropathies.

The diagnosis of neuropathies can be challenging due to the diverse range of underlying causes and the overlap of symptoms with other neurological conditions. A thorough evaluation, encompassing a combination of clinical assessments and diagnostic tests, is crucial for accurate diagnosis and effective management [17].

**Differential Diagnosis of Neuropathies**

The differential diagnosis of neuropathies involves considering various possible causes of nerve dysfunction and ruling out other conditions that may present with similar symptoms. Here are some common conditions that may be considered in the differential diagnosis of neuropathies:

**Diabetic Neuropathy:** Neuropathy is a common complication of diabetes mellitus, resulting from prolonged exposure to high blood sugar levels. It typically presents with symmetric sensory loss, pain, and paresthesia in the distal extremities.

**Vitamin Deficiencies:** Deficiencies in vitamins, such as B12, B1 (thiamine), B6, and E, can cause neuropathies. Symptoms may include sensory disturbances, weakness, and gait abnormalities.

**Toxic Neuropathies:** Exposure to certain toxins, chemicals, or medications can damage peripheral nerves and lead to neuropathies. Common examples include alcohol (alcoholic neuropathy), chemotherapy drugs, heavy metals (lead, arsenic), and industrial chemicals.

**Autoimmune Neuropathies:** Autoimmune disorders, such as Guillain-Barre syndrome (acute inflammatory demyelinating polyneuropathy) and Chronic Inflammatory Demyelinating Polyneuropathy (CIDP), involve the immune system attacking the peripheral nerves, resulting in weakness, sensory loss, and other neurological symptoms.

**Infectious Neuropathies:** Certain infections, including viral (*e.g.*, herpes zoster, HIV), bacterial (*e.g.*, Lyme disease), and parasitic (*e.g.*, leprosy) infections, can cause neuropathies either through direct nerve damage or as a result of the body's immune response.

**Hereditary Neuropathies:** Genetic disorders, such as Charcot-Marie-Tooth disease (CMT) and hereditary neuropathy with liability to pressure palsies (HNPP), are inherited conditions that affect peripheral nerves and can cause progressive weakness, sensory loss, and muscle atrophy.

**Compression Neuropathies:** The compression or entrapment of peripheral nerves, such as carpal tunnel syndrome (compression of the median nerve at the wrist) or ulnar nerve entrapment at the elbow, can lead to neuropathic symptoms, including pain, numbness, and weakness.

**Metabolic Neuropathies:** Metabolic disorders, such as uremia (due to kidney failure), liver disease, and amyloidosis, can cause neuropathies due to metabolic imbalances or deposition of abnormal substances in peripheral nerves.

**Idiopathic Neuropathies:** Some cases of neuropathy have no identifiable cause and are referred to as idiopathic neuropathies. These may include conditions, such as idiopathic small fiber neuropathy, where only small-diameter nerve fibers are affected.

**Neurological Disorders:** Certain neurological conditions, such as Multiple Sclerosis (MS), Parkinson's disease, and Amyotrophic Lateral Sclerosis (ALS), may involve peripheral nerve dysfunction as part of their clinical presentation.

**Traumatic Neuropathies:** Traumatic injuries, such as nerve lacerations, crush injuries, or blunt trauma, can damage peripheral nerves and result in neuropathic symptoms [18].

## CONCLUSION

A thorough differential diagnosis, including a detailed medical history, physical examination, and appropriate diagnostic testing, is necessary to identify the underlying cause and guide treatment decisions. Collaboration with neurologists, physiatrists, and other specialists may be necessary to achieve an accurate diagnosis and develop a comprehensive management plan.

## REFERENCES

[1] Ferdousi M, Kalteniece A, Azmi S, *et al.* Diagnosis of neuropathy and risk factors for corneal nerve loss in type 1 and type 2 diabetes: a corneal confocal microscopy study. Diabetes Care 2021; 44(1): 150-6.
[http://dx.doi.org/10.2337/dc20-1482] [PMID: 33144353]

[2] Telleman JA, Herraets IJT, Goedee HS, van Asseldonk JT, Visser LH. Ultrasound scanning in the diagnosis of peripheral neuropathies. Pract Neurol 2021; 21(3): 186-95.
[http://dx.doi.org/10.1136/practneurol-2020-002645] [PMID: 33541914]

[3] Hobson-Webb, L.D. and V.C. Juel, Common Entrapment Neuropathies. Continuum (Minneap Minn),

2017. 23(2, Selected Topics in Outpatient Neurology): p. 487-511.
[http://dx.doi.org/10.1212/CON.0000000000000452]

[4] Murthy JM, Meena AK. Entrapment neuropathies. J Assoc Physicians India 1995; 43(10): 673-5.
[PMID: 8773001]

[5] Reddy MP. Peripheral nerve entrapment syndromes. Am Fam Physician 1983; 28(5): 133-43.
[PMID: 6637744]

[6] Muhammed N, Campbell P, Smith IS. Peripheral nerve entrapment syndromes: diagnosis and management. Br J Hosp Med 1995; 53(4): 141-6.
[PMID: 7735662]

[7] Cantero J. [Compressive syndromes of the peripheral nerves of the arms and legs]. Rev Med Suisse Romande 1974; 94(1): 27-47. [Compressive syndromes of the peripheral nerves of the arms and legs].
[PMID: 4841567]

[8] Pugdahl K, Tankisi H, Fuglsang-Frederiksen A. Electrodiagnostic testing of entrapment neuropathies: A review of existing guidelines. J Clin Neurophysiol 2020; 37(4): 299-305.
[http://dx.doi.org/10.1097/WNP.0000000000000668] [PMID: 33151661]

[9] Colbert SH, Mackinnon SE. Nerve compressions in the upper extremity. Mo Med 2008; 105(6): 527-35.
[PMID: 19052017]

[10] Nathani D, Spies J, Barnett MH, *et al.* Nerve biopsy: Current indications and decision tools. Muscle Nerve 2021; 64(2): 125-39.
[http://dx.doi.org/10.1002/mus.27201] [PMID: 33629393]

[11] Sommer C, Carroll AS, Koike H, *et al.* Nerve biopsy in acquired neuropathies. J Peripher Nerv Syst 2021; 26(S2) (Suppl. 2): S21-41.
[http://dx.doi.org/10.1111/jns.12464] [PMID: 34523188]

[12] Fundaun J, Kolski M, Molina-Álvarez M, Baskozos G, Schmid AB. Types and concentrations of blood-based biomarkers in adults with peripheral neuropathies: A systematic review and meta-analysis. JAMA Netw Open 2022; 5(12): e2248593.
[http://dx.doi.org/10.1001/jamanetworkopen.2022.48593] [PMID: 36574244]

[13] Carmichael J, Fadavi H, Ishibashi F, Shore AC, Tavakoli M. Advances in screening, early diagnosis and accurate staging of diabetic neuropathy. Front Endocrinol (Lausanne) 2021; 12: 671257.
[http://dx.doi.org/10.3389/fendo.2021.671257] [PMID: 34122344]

[14] Korinthenberg R, Trollmann R, Plecko B, *et al.* Differential diagnosis of acquired and hereditary neuropathies in children and adolescents—consensus-based practice guidelines. Children (Basel) 2021; 8(8): 687.
[http://dx.doi.org/10.3390/children8080687] [PMID: 34438578]

[15] Kaur D, Tiwana H, Stino A, Sandroni P. Autonomic neuropathies. Muscle Nerve 2021; 63(1): 10-21.
[http://dx.doi.org/10.1002/mus.27048] [PMID: 32926436]

[16] Younger DS. Diabetic lumbosacral radiculoplexus neuropathy: a postmortem studied patient and review of the literature. J Neurol 2011; 258(7): 1364-7.
[http://dx.doi.org/10.1007/s00415-011-5938-8] [PMID: 21327851]

[17] Valls-Solé J. Challenges in the diagnosis and treatment of small fiber neuropathies. Arq Neuropsiquiatr 2018; 76(3): 129-30.
[http://dx.doi.org/10.1590/0004-282x20180017] [PMID: 29809233]

[18] Neroev VV, Kiseleva TN, Eliseeva EK, Baeva AV, Lugovkina KV, Ryabina MV, Tankovsky VE. (2023). Ultrasound diagnostic criteria of anterior ischemic optic neuropathy and optic neuritis. Russian Ophthalmological Journal, 41.
[http://dx.doi.org/10.21516/2072-0076-2023-16-2-40-46]

# CHAPTER 11

# Alcohol, Drug and Medication-Associated Neuropathies

**Abstract:** Neuropathies are conditions characterized by neuropathic pain, which can be managed through various treatments. Common treatments include pain medications, topical treatments, antiseizure medications, antidepressants, opioids, physical therapy, occupational therapy, TENS therapy, and acupuncture. Pain relievers like acetaminophen or NSAIDs can alleviate mild to moderate pain, while prescription medications like gabapentin, pregabalin, duloxetine, or tricyclic antidepressants may be prescribed for severe cases. Topical creams or patches can provide localized relief. Opioids may be prescribed cautiously for severe cases. Physical therapy can improve strength, balance, flexibility, and coordination.

Neuropathy can be managed through lifestyle changes, nutritional supplements, pain management techniques, treatment of underlying causes, and surgical intervention. Maintaining a healthy diet, exercising regularly, avoiding alcohol and tobacco, and managing underlying medical conditions can improve symptoms and slow disease progression. In rare cases, surgery may be recommended to relieve pressure on the nerve. Regular follow-up visits are essential for monitoring treatment effectiveness and addressing new or worsening symptoms.

**Keywords:** Lifestyle changes, Pain management, Physical therapy, Neuropathies, Neuropathic pain.

## INTRODUCTION

The treatment of neuropathies aims to manage symptoms, slow their progression, and address underlying causes when possible. Treatment approaches mostly depend on the type and severity of neuropathy, as well as individual patient factors. Here are some common treatment strategies [1]:

### Medications

**Pain Medications:** Over-the-counter pain relievers like acetaminophen or Nonsteroidal Anti-inflammatory Drugs (NSAIDs) may help alleviate mild to moderate neuropathic pain. For more severe pain, prescription medications such

**Sumaira Kanwal & Shazia Perveen**

as gabapentin, pregabalin, duloxetine, or tricyclic antidepressants (*e.g.*, amitriptyline, nortriptyline) may be prescribed. Emerging evidence suggests that cannabidiol (CBD) may be an effective treatment for peripheral neuropathy. It has been reported as a well-tolerated option with minimal adverse effects, making it a potentially beneficial treatment for certain patients [2].

Different pharmacological treatments play a significant role in managing pain associated with neuropathy. These include tricyclic antidepressants, SNRIs, calcium-channel blockers, anticonvulsants, and opioids. Exercise and physiotherapy played a significant role in controlling the pain associated with neuropathy. Physiotherapists and Rehabilitation specialists played a prominent role in the treatment and diagnosis [3].

**Topical Treatments:** Topical creams or patches containing capsaicin or lidocaine can provide localized relief for neuropathic pain. Topical Lidocaine is particularly effective in controlling pain and is used worldwide for the treatment of post-herpetic neuralgia, as well as for the treatment of chronic pain. It works by inhibiting the generation and conduction of nerve impulses and the membrane of a neuron [4].

**Antiseizure Medications:** Certain antiseizure medications, such as gabapentin, pregabalin, and carbamazepine, can help manage neuropathic pain by stabilizing abnormal nerve activity. Epilepsy is correlated with neuropathic pain.

**Antidepressants:** Tricyclic antidepressants (*e.g.*, amitriptyline, nortriptyline) and selective Serotonin and Norepinephrine Reuptake Inhibitors (SNRIs) like duloxetine can help relieve neuropathic pain and improve mood.

**Opioid Medications:** In severe cases of neuropathic pain that do not respond to other treatments, opioids may be prescribed cautiously and for short-term use. The neuropathy pain control grade system is recommended for the treatment of neuropathy, as a first-line treatment option, including serotonin-norepinephrine reuptake inhibitors, gabapentin, tricyclic antidepressants, and transcutaneous electrical nerve stimulation for peripheral neuropathic pain. In the second grade, Pregabalin, tramadol, and combination therapy are used. In the third line of treatment, spinal cord stimulation is additionally recommended, along with psychotherapy, including cognitive behavioral therapy and mindfulness [5].

**Physical Therapy:** Physical therapy can help improve strength, balance, flexibility, and coordination, as well as alleviate symptoms such as muscle weakness, numbness, and tingling. Exercise and manual therapy play a significant role in the treatment of sacroiliac joint dysfunction syndrome. Exercise plays a role in controlling pain [6].

**Occupational Therapy:** Occupational therapy can help adapt daily activities to accommodate functional limitations caused by neuropathy and prevent injuries. The main focus of this therapy is to promote health and improve the standard of life by engaging people in various activities related to physical, cognitive, and emotional challenges. It is also involved with special children and adults who are facing age-related diseases. This therapy plays a crucial role in treating sciatic pain by encouraging lifestyle modifications in patients, enabling them to carry out their routine tasks independently [7].

**Transcutaneous Electrical Nerve Stimulation (TENS):** TENS therapy involves applying low-voltage electrical currents to the skin, which may help relieve neuropathic pain by disrupting pain signals sent to the brain. Transcutaneous Electrical Nerve Stimulation (TENS) uses a mild electrical current with the help of electrodes that stimulate the nerves. It is a battery-powered device that passes the electric current through the intact skin surface. Its effects are not long-lasting, but the patient can administer this impulse when needed. It is not expensive and can be easily used, with no reported side effects [8].

**Acupuncture:** Acupuncture may provide relief from neuropathic pain by stimulating specific points on the body and promoting the release of endorphins, the body's natural painkillers. It has been shown to play a significant role in reducing various kinds of pain and has been widely used to treat multiple diseases. Several studies have highlighted its anti-inflammatory effects and its therapeutic potential in treating various nervous system disorders. For example, acupuncture has been used to reduce the required doses of dopaminergic medications in patients with Parkinson's disease and other neurological disorders. Additionally, it is very effective in modulating hyperglycemia in patients with diabetes mellitus [9].

**Lifestyle Modifications:** Making lifestyle changes, such as maintaining a healthy diet, exercising regularly, avoiding alcohol and tobacco, and managing underlying medical conditions like diabetes or vitamin deficiencies, can help alleviate symptoms and slow the progression of neuropathy.

**Nutritional Supplements:** In cases where neuropathy is associated with vitamin deficiencies (*e.g.*, vitamin B12 deficiency), supplementing the deficient nutrients can be beneficial in supporting nerve function and alleviating symptoms

**Pain Management Techniques:** Techniques such as relaxation therapy, biofeedback, mindfulness meditation, and Cognitive-Behavioral Therapy (CBT) can help patients cope with chronic neuropathic pain and improve quality of life.

**Treatment of Underlying Causes:** When neuropathy is secondary to an underlying medical condition (*e.g.*, diabetes, autoimmune disorder, infection), addressing the underlying cause is crucial to prevent further nerve damage.

**Surgical Intervention:** In rare cases of neuropathy caused by nerve compression (*e.g.*, carpal tunnel syndrome), surgery may be recommended to relieve pressure on the affected nerve.

## CONCLUSION

Individuals with neuropathy need to collaborate closely with healthcare professionals to develop a personalized treatment plan tailored to their specific needs and preferences. Regular follow-up visits are crucial for monitoring treatment effectiveness, adjusting medications as needed, and addressing any new or worsening symptoms.

## REFERENCES

[1] Dimitrova A, Murchison C, Oken B. Acupuncture for the treatment of peripheral neuropathy: A systematic review and meta-analysis. J Altern Complement Med 2017; 23(3): 164-79. [http://dx.doi.org/10.1089/acm.2016.0155] [PMID: 28112552]

[2] Xu DH, Cullen BD, Tang M, Fang Y. The effectiveness of topical cannabidiol oil in symptomatic relief of peripheral neuropathy of the lower extremities. Curr Pharm Biotechnol 2020; 21(5): 390-402. [http://dx.doi.org/10.2174/1389201020666191202111534] [PMID: 31793418]

[3] Bernetti A, Agostini F, de Sire A, *et al.* Neuropathic pain and rehabilitation: A systematic review of international guidelines. Diagnostics (Basel) 2021; 11(1): 74. [http://dx.doi.org/10.3390/diagnostics11010074] [PMID: 33466426]

[4] Voute M, Morel V, Pickering G. Topical lidocaine for chronic pain treatment. Drug Des Devel Ther 2021; 15: 4091-103. [http://dx.doi.org/10.2147/DDDT.S328228] [PMID: 34616143]

[5] Moisset X. Neuropathic pain: Evidence based recommendations. Presse Med 2024; 53(2): 104232. [http://dx.doi.org/10.1016/j.lpm.2024.104232] [PMID: 38641202]

[6] Javadov A, Ketenci A, Aksoy C. The Efficiency of Manual Therapy and Sacroiliac and Lumbar Exercises in Patients with Sacroiliac Joint Dysfunction Syndrome. Pain Physician 2021; 24(3): 223-33. [http://dx.doi.org/10.36076/ppj.2021/24/223] [PMID: 33988941]

[7] Thakur S, Kumar A, Dijkstra A, Thakur A. Occupational therapy-based rehabilitation of sciatic nerve pain. Brain-X 2024; 2(4): e70010. [http://dx.doi.org/10.1002/brx2.70010]

[8] Püsküllüoğlu M, Tomaszewski KA, Grela-Wojewoda A, Pacholczak-Madej R, & Ebner F. Effects of transcutaneous electrical nerve stimulation on pain and chemotherapy-induced peripheral neuropathy in cancer patients: A systematic review. [Review Systematic Review]. Medicina 2022; 58(2).

[9] Cho E, Kim W. Effect of acupuncture on diabetic neuropathy: A narrative review. Int J Mol Sci 2021; 22(16): 8575. [http://dx.doi.org/10.3390/ijms22168575] [PMID: 34445280]

# CHAPTER 12

# Treatment Option for Diabetic Neuropathies

**Abstract:** Diabetic neuropathy is a condition that affects the nerves in the body. Treatment options include blood sugar control, pain management medications, topical treatments, and the use of antioxidants like alpha-lipoic acid. Pain management techniques like TENS, acupuncture, and mindfulness meditation can improve quality of life. Physical therapy can improve strength, flexibility, balance, and coordination. Proper foot care is crucial to prevent complications. Nutritional supplements may improve symptoms. Blood pressure and cholesterol management are essential for managing neuropathy. Quitting smoking is vital to avoid complications. Alternative therapies, such as herbal supplements and massage therapy, may provide relief, but their effectiveness is limited. Individuals must work with healthcare professionals to develop a personalized treatment plan.

**Keywords:** Anticonvulsant, Antidepressants, Blood sugar, Nutritional supplements, Pain management.

## INTRODUCTION

The treatment of diabetic neuropathy aims to alleviate symptoms, slow disease progression, and prevent complications. Here are some treatment options commonly used for diabetic neuropathy. It can be controlled through three different methods, including lifestyle modifications, therapy with medicines, and pain treatment with analgesic compounds [1].

**Blood Sugar Control:** Maintaining tight glycemic control is crucial in managing diabetic neuropathy. Keeping blood sugar levels within recommended ranges can help slow the progression of nerve damage and reduce symptoms.

The control of glucose levels in diabetes patients prevents the development of clinical neuropathy. It decreases the chances of nerve conduction abnormalities and elevated vibration thresholds. In type 2 diabetes mellitus, controlling the high level of glucose reduces the likelihood of clinical neuropathy [2].

**Sumaira Kanwal & Shazia Perveen**

## Medications for Pain Management

**Anticonvulsants:** Medications such as gabapentin and pregabalin are commonly prescribed as first-line treatment to manage neuropathic pain associated with diabetic neuropathy. Capsaicin and isosorbide dinitrate, topical agents, are used as second-line treatments, while some medications in polytherapy form are used as third-line treatments in managing the pain associated with diabetic neuropathy in patients [3].

**Antidepressants:** Tricyclic antidepressants (*e.g.*, amitriptyline, nortriptyline) and selective Serotonin and Norepinephrine Reuptake Inhibitors (SNRIs) like duloxetine can help relieve neuropathic pain and improve mood. Polytherapy involving agents like amitriptyline, duloxetine, and pregabalin has shown significant effectiveness in treating diabetic neuropathy compared to monotherapy. While amitriptyline alone can be used, its therapeutic effect is generally less pronounced than when used in combination therapy [4].

**Topical Treatments:** Creams or patches containing capsaicin or lidocaine can provide localized relief for neuropathic pain. Topical agents, such as Capsaicin, the NitroSense patch, and Citrullus colocynthis, are used as topical medicines for controlling the pain associated with diabetic neuropathy. Placebos, although lacking active therapeutic components, are sometimes used in clinical trials for comparison purposes [5].

**Alpha-Lipoic Acid:** Alpha-lipoic acid, an antioxidant, has shown promise in reducing symptoms of diabetic neuropathy and improving nerve function. It can be taken orally or administered intravenously and is used as a treatment for neuropathic pain in diabetic patients [6].

**Pain Management Techniques:** Neuropathic pain can be effectively managed through various techniques, including Transcutaneous Electrical Nerve Stimulation (TENS), acupuncture, relaxation therapy, biofeedback, and mindfulness. Additionally, Lipoic acid, the thiamine derivative (prodrug), and AGE inhibitors are used for the treatment of diabetic sensorimotor polyneuropathy and peripheral neuropathy [7]. Moreover, meditation can help manage neuropathic pain and improve quality of life.

**Physical Therapy:** Physical therapy can help improve strength, flexibility, balance, and coordination, while also alleviating symptoms such as muscle weakness and numbness.

**Foot Care:** Proper foot care is crucial in preventing foot ulcers, infections, and other complications associated with diabetic neuropathy. This includes daily foot inspections, wearing appropriate footwear, keeping feet clean and dry, and avoiding activities that could cause foot injuries.

**Nutritional Supplements:** Some studies have suggested that certain nutritional supplements, such as alpha-lipoic acid, vitamin B12, vitamin D, and acetyl-L-carnitine, may help improve symptoms of diabetic neuropathy.

**Blood Pressure and Cholesterol Management:** Controlling blood pressure and cholesterol levels is important in managing diabetic neuropathy and reducing the risk of cardiovascular complications.

**Smoking Cessation:** Quitting smoking is crucial, as it can worsen neuropathy and increase the risk of complications.

**Alternative Therapies:** Some people find relief from diabetic neuropathy symptoms with alternative therapies such as herbal supplements (*e.g.*, evening primrose oil), acupuncture, and massage therapy. However, the evidence supporting the effectiveness of these treatments is limited.

## CONCLUSION

Individuals with diabetic neuropathy need to work closely with healthcare professionals to develop a comprehensive treatment plan tailored to their specific needs and preferences. Regular monitoring and adjustments to treatment may be necessary to manage symptoms and prevent complications effectively.

## REFERENCES

[1] Ziegler D, Tesfaye S, Spallone V, *et al.* Screening, diagnosis and management of diabetic sensorimotor polyneuropathy in clinical practice: International expert consensus recommendations. Diabetes Res Clin Pract 2022; 186(109063): 109063. [http://dx.doi.org/10.1016/j.diabres.2021.109063] [PMID: 34547367]

[2] Callaghan BC, Little AA, Feldman EL, Hughes RAC. Enhanced glucose control for preventing and treating diabetic neuropathy. Cochrane Libr 2012; 2012(6): CD007543. [http://dx.doi.org/10.1002/14651858.CD007543.pub2] [PMID: 22696371]

[3] Rafiullah M, Siddiqui K. Pharmacological treatment of diabetic peripheral neuropathy: an update. CNS Neurol Disord Drug Targets 2022; 21(10): 884-900. [http://dx.doi.org/10.2174/1871527320666210303111939] [PMID: 33655879]

[4] Tesfaye S, Sloan G, Petrie J, *et al.* Comparison of amitriptyline supplemented with pregabalin, pregabalin supplemented with amitriptyline, and duloxetine supplemented with pregabalin for the treatment of diabetic peripheral neuropathic pain (OPTION-DM): a multicentre, double-blind, randomised crossover trial. Lancet 2022; 400(10353): 680-90. [http://dx.doi.org/10.1016/S0140-6736(22)01472-6] [PMID: 36007534]

[5] Price R, Smith D, Franklin G, *et al.* Oral and topical treatment of painful diabetic polyneuropathy: practice guideline update summary: report of the AAN guideline subcommittee. Neurology 2022; 98(1): 31-43. [http://dx.doi.org/10.1212/WNL.0000000000013038] [PMID: 34965987]

[6] Abubaker SA, Alonazy AM, Abdulrahman A, Abubaker S, Alonazy A, Albasseet A. Effect of alpha-lipoic acid in the treatment of diabetic neuropathy: A systematic review. Cureus 2022; 14(6): e25750. [http://dx.doi.org/10.7759/cureus.25750] [PMID: 35812639]

[7] Ziegler D, Papanas N, Schnell O, *et al.* Current concepts in the management of diabetic polyneuropathy. J Diabetes Investig 2021; 12(4): 464-75. [http://dx.doi.org/10.1111/jdi.13401] [PMID: 32918837]

# CHAPTER 13

# Treatment for Hereditary Neuropathies

**Abstract:** Genetically diverse inherited neuropathies represent a broad group of disorders that affect both motor and sensory functions. For many years, these conditions remained without effective treatment, as no medications were available to stimulate nerve regeneration. However, recent advancements in molecular tools have transformed the landscape of neuropathy treatment, enabling researchers to develop and explore a variety of promising therapeutic approaches. Future research may make several additional disorders treatable within the approaching years. New therapeutic approaches can be categorized into four main groups: gene therapy, gene expression therapy, protein modification techniques, and Enzyme Replacement Therapy (ERT). Overall, in the case of inherited neuropathy, management is symptom-based chiefly. Over the past few years, a better understanding of the pathogenic mechanisms underlying neuropathies has enabled the development of disease-modifying therapies. The following section offers illustrations pertaining to peripheral neuropathies under each of these approaches. This article thoroughly evaluates advancements in peripheral neuropathy treatment that have emerged over the past five years. A revised list of diseases in which peripheral neuropathy is a clinical manifestation was compiled using gene panels commonly employed in the clinical diagnosis of hereditary neuropathy syndromes. While the use of different scales and scoring systems made comparisons challenging, this analysis identified neuropathy-associated diseases with approved therapies. Therefore, in future trials investigating the efficacy of therapies for neuropathies, it is essential to incorporate objective and reproducible assessment methods. These may include built-in monitoring devices, motor unit indexes, imaging techniques such as MRI or sonography, blood biomarkers, and consistent nerve conduction studies.

**Keywords:** Disease-modifying therapy, Genetic counseling , Inherited neuropathies , Treatment .

## INTRODUCTION

Inherited neuropathies comprise a group of genetic disorders characterized by diverse clinical presentations, typically involving both sensory and motor symptoms. Medical research has delivered critical therapeutic discoveries in these fields during the recent period. The development of breakthrough therapies has been driven by advances in the genetic identification of disease-causing genes,

**Sumaira Kanwal & Shazia Perveen**

deeper insights into pathophysiological mechanisms, and the emergence of innovative drug development technologies [1]. These various domains encompass Charcot-Marie-Tooth (CMT) diseases (over 100 genes), distal hereditary motor neuropathies (over 10 genes), sensory neuropathies (Friedreich, CANVAS, dysautonomic neuropathies, congenital pain insensitivity…), amyloid neuropathies (transthyretin (TTR), gelsolin…), and both mitochondrial neuropathies (SANDO, NARP, MNGIE…) as well as metabolic neuropathies (Fabry, porphyria…) [2]. For many years, medical professionals regarded these conditions as untreatable, as no available therapies could restore nerve regeneration. However, the advent of molecular tools has reshaped this perspective, enabling the successful treatment of various neuropathies. It is anticipated that additional neuropathies will soon become treatable. These emerging therapies are grounded in a target-oriented approach. In this brief analysis, we present several practical examples of treatment strategies for peripheral neuropathies [3].

Hereditary neuropathies are inherited disorders that damage the peripheral nerves. Management strategies may include medications, physical therapy, orthopedic devices, surgery, gene therapy, and lifestyle modifications. Treatment plans should be personalized to specific symptoms, disease progression, and overall health. Regular follow-up with a team of healthcare providers is essential for achieving the best treatment and quality of life. Neuropathic pain should be managed using pain relief techniques such as acupuncture and relaxation techniques. The diverse group of inherited peripheral nerve disorders known as hereditary neuropathies displays progressive motor and sensory deficits that usually lead to disability [4]. The most widespread inherited neuropathy (digits as Charcot-Marie-Tooth disease [CMT]) functions as the exemplar disorder for demonstrating how inheritable neurological diseases vary both clinically and genetically, since researchers have discovered over 100 responsible genes. Parkinson's disease lacked any treatments that altered its progression for many years until medical research advanced to develop disease-modifying interventions [5]. However, modern genetic and molecular aspects of pathophysiology are redefining treatment paradigms. Currently, management options for IPN are minimal. The clinical benefits remain questionable, despite several efforts to reduce or ameliorate the disease phenotype after the efficacy of the animal studies has been validated. For instance, vitamin C was confirmed to be successful using rodent models, but the same results were not seen in clinical trials [6]. Currently, PXT3003, a new combination of baclofen, naltrexone hydrochloride, and D-sorbitol, is being investigated in clinical trials; however, its clinical utility requires further clarification [7]. Eventually, specific unfavorable results in clinical practice may be due to inadequate therapy. So far, therapeutic strategies have targeted the phenotype of the disease, either by indirectly lowering the expression of toxic proteins and/or through the potentiation of myelination and axonal integrity. Moreover, this suggests that direct modification of the mutant gene expression should be considered a valid and efficient therapeutic approach.

## Traditional Supportive Methods

The cornerstones of management remain rehabilitative and symptomatic. Orthotic devices, such as Ankle-Foot Orthoses (AFOs), are commonly used to address foot drop and mobility challenges. These devices are prescribed based on the individual needs of each patient [8].

## Physical Therapy

Physical therapy treatments employed for NP care consist of heat and cold therapy, as well as fluid therapy, whirlpool therapy, massage, ultrasound, short-wave diathermy, low-frequency currents, high-voltage galvanic stimulation, and laser therapy. Both persistent postsurgical pain, spinal cord injury, and radiculopathies have been researched using these techniques, although the results yield no consensus [9]. For NP patients, rehabilitative approaches may consist of graded motor imagery, acupuncture, mirror therapy, relaxation techniques, and visual illusions. Other treatment methods are indicated in the various NP, including NP due to phantom pain, CRPS, forced sinistrality, and NP due to spinal cord injury in addition to central poststroke pain [10]. Exercise training may be effective in patients with peripheral NP [11].

## Surgical Interventions

Corrective surgery for major skeletal deformities (*e.g.*, high arches, scoliosis) and adaptive equipment (*e.g.*, elastic shoelaces) can reduce functional deficits. Surgeons perform peripheral nerve procedures to increase functionality and alleviate pain and disability in patients receiving treatment for peripheral nerve disorders with acute nerve damage, nerve compression conditions, and tumors affecting the nerve sheaths. The surgical approach involves redirecting healthy, functioning nerves to compensate for neural deficits caused by injury, disease, or other conditions. Peripheral nerves act as communication pathways between the brain, spinal cord, and the rest of the body. Disorders affecting these nerves can interrupt the transmission of signals from the brain, impairing one or multiple nerve functions and leading to a range of sensory or motor deficits [12].

## New Research Novelties in Relapse Preventive Therapy

Here, we discuss recent advances that demonstrate the transition into precision medicine for CMT1A, such as the utilization of antisense oligonucleotides

(ASOs) and small interfering ribonucleic acid (siRNA) nanoparticles directed towards the PMP22 protein overexpression observed in pre-clinical models, but face challenges associated with delivery and dosage. Sorbitol dehydrogenase (SORD) mutations, which are biallelic, lead to axonal CMT2, and aldose reductase inhibitors (*e.g.*, epalrestat) attenuate toxic sorbitol accumulation, with clinical trials ongoing. Gene editing has shown early success in treating hereditary neuropathies, particularly in conditions such as transthyretin (ATTR) amyloidosis. These advancements highlight the potential of genomic editing as a promising therapeutic strategy for inherited peripheral nerve disorders [13].

With the advent of CRISPR-Cas9 genome editing technology, researchers are increasingly optimizing strategies to treat hereditary neuropathies by correcting genetic defects at the DNA sequence level. Unlike current therapies that primarily manage symptoms, genome editing offers the potential for long-lasting or curative outcomes by directly targeting the root cause of disease—abnormal gene expression. One notable example is the genomic treatment for Charcot-Marie-Tooth disease type 1A (CMT1A), which focuses on reducing the expression of the PMP22 gene. This approach targets the common duplication of the PMP22 gene, either on one chromosome or both, using precise genome editing techniques. CRISPR Cas9 functions as a molecular scissors, cutting DNA at specific locations within the genome. This allows scientists to remove the defective gene segment and replace it with a typical DNA sequence, thereby correcting the genetic abnormality that causes neuropathy. Depending on the type of neuropathy, the researchers are attempting to edit the DNA inside important nerve cells, such as motor neurons or Schwann cells, which generate myelin and are therefore primarily found in the peripheral nervous system. Genome editing, in contrast to current symptomatic treatments, can target the underlying cause of the disease and may stop or reduce disease progression. Once a single gene-editing step is successfully performed, ongoing medication may no longer be necessary, as the body can maintain the corrected state on its own. A major challenge lies in delivering the CRISPR Cas9 components accurately to the appropriate nerve cells in the body. The editing must be highly precise, as unintended modifications to other genes could result in harmful side effects. At present, genome editing therapy for hereditary neuropathies remains in the preclinical stage and requires extensive research before it can be considered for use in humans. Potential application example: This common heritable neuropathy is often associated with a duplication of the PMP22 gene [14].

The second gene, PMP22, exists in two copies in the affected individual and is being investigated using CRISPR-based methods to specifically delete one copy. Such an approach may help alleviate the symptoms associated with the condition.

## Mesenchymal Stem Cells as an Alternative Therapy

Mesenchymal Stem Cells (MSCs) hold promise for the treatment of neuropathy due to their ability to secrete a wide range of cytoprotective and anti-inflammatory factors. These cells are found in bone marrow, umbilical cord blood, and adipose tissue. Multiple studies have demonstrated the therapeutic potential of MSCs in treating neuropathy in both animal models and clinical trials. The research demonstrated that MSC administration decreased pain symptoms by managing the redox environment and mitochondrial balance in pain-related primary afferent neurons during peripheral neuropathy induced by oxaliplatin exposure. Another study indicated that MSC therapy could be a potentially innovative strategy for treating Chemotherapy-Induced Peripheral Neuropathy (CIPN) by alleviating oxidative stress, neuroinflammation, and apoptosis, and regulating axon regeneration after nerve injury [15].

### Metabolic Interventions

In clinical trials, L-serine supplementation for SPTLC1-related hereditary sensory neuropathy type I has been shown to reduce levels of neurotoxic deoxysphingolipids, leading to improvement in sensory symptoms. However, its effectiveness in preventing ulcers has yielded mixed results [16].

### Pain Management

Neuropathic pain is managed according to chronic pain guidelines, often using medications such as gabapentin or certain antidepressants. In Phase 3 trials for CMT1A, a combination of baclofen, naltrexone, and sorbitol demonstrated only modest efficacy, suggesting that further investigation into the formulation is necessary. Despite promising preclinical data, high-dose trials in CMT1A patients ultimately failed to show significant clinical benefit, underscoring the critical importance of rigorous trial design [17].

### Challenges and Future Directions

Transformative as these advances may be, several obstacles remain. The rarity and clinical heterogeneity of hereditary neuropathies pose challenges for standardizing outcome measures and recruiting sufficient participants for clinical trials. Emerging technologies, such as wearable devices and molecular biomarkers, offer potential to enhance the precision of data collection in these trials. Additionally, patient-specific induced pluripotent stem cell (iPSC) models are advancing preclinical research by enabling personalized therapeutic testing. Overall, the field is shifting from palliative care toward targeted genetic and metabolic therapies. However, the successful translation of these discoveries into effective and accessible treatments will require continued collaboration in research and thoughtful clinical trial design [18].

## CONCLUSION

In summary, recent advances in molecular tools and therapeutic approaches, such as gene therapy, protein modification, and enzyme replacement, have revolutionized the treatment of inherited neurological disorders by shifting the focus from symptom management to disease-modifying strategies. Future research aims to develop precise and reproducible methods for assessing disease progression and expanding the spectrum of treatable conditions.

## REFERENCES

[1] McCray BA, Scherer SS. Axonal Charcot-Marie-Tooth disease: from common pathogenic mechanisms to emerging treatment opportunities. Neurotherapeutics 2021; 18(4): 2269-85. [http://dx.doi.org/10.1007/s13311-021-01099-2] [PMID: 34606075]

[2] Bird, T. D. Charcot-Marie-Tooth hereditary neuropathy overview 2022.

[3] Mendell JR, Al-Zaidy SA, Rodino-Klapac LR, *et al.* Current clinical applications of *in vivo* gene therapy with AAVs. Mol Ther 2021; 29(2): 464-88. [http://dx.doi.org/10.1016/j.ymthe.2020.12.007] [PMID: 33309881]

[4] Tazir M, Nouioua S. Distal hereditary motor neuropathies. Rev Neurol (Paris) 2024; 180(10): 1031-6. [http://dx.doi.org/10.1016/j.neurol.2023.09.005] [PMID: 38702287]

[5] Goetz LH, Schork NJ. Personalized medicine: motivation, challenges, and progress. Fertil Steril 2018; 109(6): 952-63. [http://dx.doi.org/10.1016/j.fertnstert.2018.05.006] [PMID: 29935653]

[6] Thenmozhi R, Lee JS, Park NY, Choi BO, Hong YB. Gene therapy options as new treatment for inherited peripheral neuropathy. Exp Neurobiol 2020; 29(3): 177-88. [http://dx.doi.org/10.5607/en20004] [PMID: 32624504]

[7] Dong H, Qin B, Zhang H, Lei L, Wu S. Current treatment methods for charcot–marie–tooth diseases. Biomolecules 2024; 14(9): 1138. [http://dx.doi.org/10.3390/biom14091138] [PMID: 39334903]

[8] Nevisipour M, Honeycutt CF. The impact of ankle-foot-orthosis (AFO) use on the compensatory stepping response required to avoid a fall during trip-like perturbations in young adults: Implications for AFO prescription and design. J Biomech 2020; 103: 109703. [http://dx.doi.org/10.1016/j.jbiomech.2020.109703] [PMID: 32197789]

[9] Szok D, Tajti J, Nyári A, Vécsei L, Trojano L. Therapeutic approaches for peripheral and central neuropathic pain. Behav Neurol 2019; 2019: 1-13. [http://dx.doi.org/10.1155/2019/8685954] [PMID: 31871494]

[10] St John Smith E. Advances in understanding nociception and neuropathic pain. J Neurol 2018; 265(2): 231-8. [http://dx.doi.org/10.1007/s00415-017-8641-6] [PMID: 29032407]

[11] Fornasari D. Pain pharmacology: focus on opioids. Clin Cases Miner Bone Metab 2014; 11(3): 165-8. [PMID: 25568646]

[12] Breivik H, Collett B, Ventafridda V, Cohen R, Gallacher D. Survey of chronic pain in Europe: Prevalence, impact on daily life, and treatment. Eur J Pain 2006; 10(4): 287-333. [http://dx.doi.org/10.1016/j.ejpain.2005.06.009] [PMID: 16095934]

[13] Li YZ, Ji RR. Gene therapy for chronic pain management. Cell Reports Medicine 2024 Oct 15;5(10).

[14] Abdelnour SA, Xie L, Hassanin AA, Zuo E, Lu Y. The potential of CRISPR/Cas9 gene editing as a treatment strategy for inherited diseases. Front Cell Dev Biol 2021; 9: 699597. [http://dx.doi.org/10.3389/fcell.2021.699597] [PMID: 34977000]

[15] Lavorato A, Raimondo S, Boido M, *et al.* Mesenchymal stem cell treatment perspectives in peripheral nerve regeneration: Systematic review. Int J Mol Sci 2021; 22(2): 572. [http://dx.doi.org/10.3390/ijms22020572] [PMID: 33430035]

[16] Fiorillo C, Capodivento G, Geroldi A, *et al.* The *SPTLC1* p.S331 mutation bridges sensory neuropathy and motor neuron disease and has implications for treatment. Neuropathol Appl Neurobiol 2022; 48(7): e12842. [http://dx.doi.org/10.1111/nan.12842] [PMID: 35904184]

[17] Hirst M, Bending MW, Baio G, Yesufu-Udechuku A, Dunlop WCN. Cost-effectiveness modeling for neuropathic pain treatments: investigating the relative importance of parameters using an open-source model. J Med Econ 2018; 21(9): 930-5. [http://dx.doi.org/10.1080/13696998.2018.1486845] [PMID: 29882452]

[18] Knapik E, Brandimarte L, Usher M. Maintenance in sustainable stormwater management: issues, barriers and challenges. J Environ Plann Manage 2024; 1-27.

# CHAPTER 14

# Treatment Options for CMT1A

**Abstract:** CMT1A, a subtype of Charcot-Marie-Tooth disease, is caused by a duplication of the PMP22 gene. Treatment options include physical therapy, orthotic devices, and occupational therapy. Physical therapy focuses on improving muscle strength, mobility, and addressing gait abnormalities, while orthotic devices provide support and enhance hand function. Occupational therapy helps develop independent daily living strategies.

Individuals with CMT1A may benefit from bracing, medications, surgery, genetic counseling, clinical trials, pain management techniques, and regular visits to a healthcare team. Bracing stabilizes joints, corrects deformities, and prevents injuries. Medications manage symptoms like neuropathic pain and muscle cramps. Surgery may be considered to correct skeletal abnormalities. Genetic counseling provides information about CMT1A inheritance patterns and recurrence risk. Pain management techniques, such as TENS, acupuncture, and relaxation techniques, can help manage neuropathic pain.

**Keywords:** Acupuncture, CMT1A, Medication , Relaxation techniques, TENS.

## INTRODUCTION

CMT1A, the most common subtype of Charcot-Marie-Tooth disease (CMT), is caused by a duplication of the PMP22 gene on chromosome 17. While there is currently no cure for CMT1A, treatment options aim to manage symptoms and improve quality of life [1]. Here are some common approaches:

### Physical Therapy

Physical therapy plays a crucial role in managing Charcot-Marie-Tooth disease type 1A (CMT1A). It focuses on maintaining muscle strength, improving mobility, preventing contractures, and managing gait abnormalities.

### Orthotic Devices

Orthotic devices such as Ankle-Foot Orthoses (AFOs) can provide support, improve stability, and correct foot drop. Hand splints may also be prescribed to improve hand function.

Sumaira Kanwal & Shazia Perveen

## Occupational Therapy

Occupational therapy can help individuals with CMT1A develop strategies to perform activities of daily living more independently. It may involve adaptations to the home environment and training in the use of assistive devices [2].

## Bracing

Bracing may be used to stabilize joints, correct deformities, and prevent injuries. Custom-made braces can provide support and improve function in individuals with CMT1A.

## Medications

Medications may be prescribed to manage symptoms associated with CMT1A, such as neuropathic pain, muscle cramps, and muscle spasms. These may include pain relievers, muscle relaxants, and medications to improve nerve conduction [3].

## Surgery

In some cases, surgical interventions may be considered to address severe deformities, correct skeletal abnormalities, or release compressed nerves.

## Genetic Counseling

Genetic counseling can provide information about the inheritance pattern of CMT1A, recurrence risk, and available genetic testing options for family planning.

## Clinical Trials

Participation in clinical trials investigating potential therapies for CMT1A may be an option for individuals interested in experimental treatments. These trials may explore approaches such as gene therapy or novel drug interventions.

## Pain Management Techniques

Techniques such as Transcutaneous Electrical Nerve Stimulation (TENS), acupuncture, and relaxation techniques may help manage neuropathic pain associated with CMT1A.

### Regular Monitoring and Follow-Up

Regular visits with a healthcare team familiar with CMT1A are essential for monitoring disease progression, managing symptoms, and adjusting treatment as needed.

## CONCLUSION

Individuals with CMT1A need to work closely with a multidisciplinary team of healthcare professionals, including neurologists, physical therapists, occupational therapists, orthopedic specialists, and genetic counselors, to develop a comprehensive treatment plan tailored to their specific needs and goals.

## REFERENCES

[1] Lind J, Stensson N, Gerdle B, Ghafouri N. Levels of bioactive endogenous lipids and health-related quality of life in Chronic Idiopathic Axonal Polyneuropathy. Ups J Med Sci 2022; 127: 10-48101. [http://dx.doi.org/10.48101/ujms.v127.8577] [PMID: 37621890]

[2] Zhang X. A study of occupational therapy strategies and psychological regulation of students' internet addiction in the mobile social media environment. Occup Ther Int 2022; 2022(1): 1-10. [http://dx.doi.org/10.1155/2022/7598471] [PMID: 36176490]

[3] Strawn JR, Mills JA, Poweleit EA, Ramsey LB, Croarkin PE. Adverse effects of antidepressant medications and their management in children and adolescents. Pharmacotherapy 2023; 43(7): 675-90. [http://dx.doi.org/10.1002/phar.2767] [PMID: 36651686]

# CHAPTER 15

# Global Burden of Neuropathies

**Abstract:** The global burden of neuropathies, including peripheral neuropathy, diabetic neuropathy, and other forms, is significant and continues to grow due to various factors, such as aging populations, increasing rates of diabetes, and other chronic conditions. Diabetic neuropathy, a common complication of diabetes, contributes significantly to the burden of neuropathies globally. The burden of neuropathies extends beyond the direct health impacts, including economic costs related to medical care, loss of productivity, and decreased quality of life for affected individuals. Additionally, neuropathies can lead to various complications, including falls, injuries, and disabilities, further adding to the burden on healthcare systems and society as a whole. Efforts to address the global burden of neuropathies include early diagnosis and management of underlying conditions, lifestyle interventions to prevent neuropathy progression, and research into novel treatment modalities aimed at alleviating symptoms and improving outcomes for affected individuals.

**Keywords:** Aging, Diabetic neuropathy, Economic conditions, Global burden, Health care symptoms, Neuropathy, Progression.

## INTRODUCTION

The global encumbrance of neuropathies, including peripheral neuropathy, diabetic neuropathy, and other forms, is significant and continues to grow due to various factors, such as aging populations, increasing rates of diabetes, and other chronic conditions [1, 2].

Peripheral neuropathy alone affects millions of people globally, with estimates varying based on geographic location, diagnostic criteria, and population demographics. It is particularly prevalent in regions with high rates of diabetes and conditions such as HIV/AIDS.

Diabetic neuropathy, a common complication of diabetes, contributes significantly to the burden of neuropathies globally. With the increasing incidence of diabetes worldwide, particularly in low- and middle-income countries, the prevalence of diabetic neuropathy is expected to increase.

**Sumaira Kanwal & Shazia Perveen**

The burden of neuropathies extends on the far side the direct health impacts, including economic costs related to medical care, loss of productiveness, and reduced quality of life for affected people. In addition, neuropathies can lead to several complications, including falls, injuries, and inabilities, further adding to the burden on healthcare systems and society as entire.

1. Key Aspects of the Global Burden of Neuropathies

2. Types of Neuropathies

3. Economic Burden

4. Disability and Quality of Life

5. Geographical Variability

The geographical unevenness of neuropathies refers to the divergence in the number, form, causes, and occurrence of neuropathies across various parts of the world. These variations are influenced by factors like socioeconomic status, healthcare approach, cultural practices, prevalence of underlying diseases, environmental exposures, and genetic factors. Here's a look at how neuropathies vary across different regions:

**Diabetic Neuropathy**

Industrial Countries: In parts with high rates of diabetes, such as North America, Europe, and parts of Asia, diabetic neuropathy is a major cause of peripheral neuropathy. Approximately 50% of people with diabetes are affected by diabetic neuropathy. The advanced ratio of type 2 diabetes in these areas adds up to a momentous burden of neuropathic conditions.

Developing Countries: In countries with rapidly growing rates of diabetes, such as China, India, and parts of Latin America, there is also a rising incidence of diabetic neuropathy, though these countries may have lower rates of diagnosis and treatment due to limited healthcare infrastructure. The lack of regular diabetes management often exacerbates the development of neuropathy [3].

**Infectious Neuropathies**

Tropical and Subtropical Regions: Some neuropathies are more prevalent in tropical and subtropical regions, particularly those originating from infections, such as:

Leprosy: Leprosy-related neuropathy remains frequent in nations like India, Brazil, Indonesia, and Nepal, where leprosy is still endemic. Contempt a global decrease in leprosy numbers, neuropathy remains a major complication, and untreated infections can lead to long-term nerve damage.

HIV-Related Neuropathy: In regions with a high prevalence of HIV, such as Sub-Saharan Africa, Latin America, and parts of Asia, neuropathy caused by HIV and its treatments is more common. HIV-associated neuropathy affects 30-50% of individuals living with HIV and can worsen with antiretroviral treatment.

Malaria and Other Tropical Infections: In countries with endemic malaria, malaria-induced neuropathy has been reported, particularly in cases of severe or cerebral malaria. Chagas disease (endemic in Latin America) can also cause neuropathy due to the involvement of peripheral nerves by the Trypanosoma parasite [4].

### Hereditary Neuropathies (*e.g.*, Charcot-Marie-Tooth Disease)

Global Prevalence: Charcot-Marie-Tooth (CMT) disease, a hereditary neuropathy, affects about 1 in 2,500 people worldwide. However, the detection and diagnosis of hereditary neuropathies may be more common in developed countries where genetic testing and specialized neurological care are more accessible.

Undiagnosed Cases in Low-Income Areas: In low-income or rural areas, especially in parts of Africa and Asia, cases of hereditary neuropathies like CMT may go undiagnosed or misdiagnosed due to a lack of healthcare infrastructure, education, and access to genetic testing [5].

### Chemotherapy-Induced Neuropathy (CIPN)

Developed Countries: In high-income countries with advanced cancer treatments, Chemotherapy-Induced Neuropathy (CIPN) is a common side effect of cancer treatments such as taxanes, platinum-based drugs, and vincristine. Around 30-40% of cancer patients may develop CIPN, especially those treated with neurotoxic chemotherapy regimens.

Developing Countries: In low- and middle-income countries, where cancer treatments may be less accessible, chemotherapy-induced neuropathy may be less commonly recognized or less prevalent due to limited access to cancer care or delayed cancer diagnosis [6].

## Toxic Neuropathy

Global Toxic Exposures: Toxic neuropathies can result from exposure to industrial chemicals, heavy metals, or alcohol abuse. The number of these conditions may differ. In industrialized regions, such as Europe and North America, neuropathies inception from exposure to toxic chemicals (*e.g.*, solvents, pesticides, and heavy metals) may be more frequent, particularly in activity settings.

Alcohol-related neuropathy is prevailing in Western countries, where alcohol ingestion rates are higher. Chronic alcohol use can lead to alcoholic neuropathy, which affects 10-30% of persons with alcohol use disorder.

In regions with high levels of arsenic contamination, such as parts of India, Bangladesh, and Cambodia, arsenic-induced neuropathy can be a significant concern [7].

## Geographic and Socioeconomic Factors

Access to Healthcare: Geographical disparities in access to diagnostic services and treatment options contribute to the prevalence of neuropathies. In regions with limited healthcare resources, such as sub-Saharan Africa, South Asia, and parts of Latin America, many individuals with neuropathy may go undiagnosed or untreated, leading to an increased risk of complications like amputations (*e.g.*, in diabetic neuropathy) or irreversible nerve damage.

Rural *vs.* Urban Populations: In rural areas of low-income countries, access to specialized healthcare for neuropathies is often limited, while urban areas may have better access to diagnostic and therapeutic options. Additionally, urban environments may have higher rates of diseases like diabetes, which contributes to neuropathies.

Cultural Practices and Lifestyle: Dietary habits, physical activity levels, and other lifestyle factors can also affect the prevalence of neuropathies. For example, regions with high levels of processed food consumption, such as North America, may have higher rates of diabetes and thus higher rates of diabetic neuropathy.

## Geographical Distribution of Hereditary and Environmental Factors

Genetic Factors: Certain hereditary neuropathies, like CMT, may have specific genetic mutations more prevalent in certain populations. For instance, CMT1A (the most common form of Charcot-Marie-Tooth disease) has a relatively higher prevalence in Caucasian populations, whereas other forms of inherited neuropathies might be more common in South Asian or African populations.

Environmental and Dietary Factors: In some regions, nutrient deficiencies, particularly vitamin B12 deficiency, may contribute to the development of neuropathy, especially in developing countries where access to a diverse and balanced diet is limited.

Aging Populations

Health Disparities

- **Prevalence and Impact**: The prevalence of neuropathies, or disorders affecting the peripheral nervous system, varies by type, population, and region. Here are some estimates for different types of neuropathies:

Neuropathies have a significant impact on health, affecting not only individuals but also healthcare systems, economies, and quality of life. The effects of neuropathies can be far-reaching, as they often lead to chronic conditions that impair various aspects of daily living. Below are some of the key ways in which neuropathies impact health:

**Chronic Pain and Discomfort**

Many types of neuropathies, such as diabetic neuropathy and chemotherapy-induced neuropathy, lead to chronic pain, often described as burning, tingling, or shooting pain. This constant discomfort can severely affect a person's quality of life.

Sensory loss, including numbness or reduced sensitivity, also contributes to pain and discomfort. For example, diabetic neuropathy can lead to foot ulcers and infections due to reduced sensation, which can progress to severe complications like amputations if not properly managed.

**Loss of Mobility and Muscle Weakness**

Neuropathies such as Charcot-Marie-Tooth disease and other hereditary or acquired motor neuropathies can result in significant muscle weakness and atrophy, especially in the hands, feet, and legs.

Impaired balance and coordination due to sensory loss in the feet increase the risk of falls, which can lead to fractures or other serious injuries.

Progressive muscle weakness can limit a person's ability to perform basic tasks like walking, standing, or climbing stairs, which leads to reduced independence and the need for mobility aids, such as canes or wheelchairs.

## Autonomic Dysfunction

Neuropathies can also affect the autonomic nervous system, which controls involuntary functions, such as heart rate, digestion, and blood pressure. For example, diabetic autonomic neuropathy can lead to cardiovascular problems, including a higher risk of heart attacks and arrhythmias.

Other issues include gastrointestinal problems (*e.g.*, gastroparesis, which slows down digestion) and bladder dysfunction, both of which can result in discomfort and the need for medical intervention.

## Disability and Reduced Quality of Life

As neuropathies can lead to significant physical and functional limitations, they are a major cause of disability. Affected individuals may struggle with everyday activities such as dressing, cooking, and cleaning.

The mental health impact is also considerable, as chronic pain, loss of independence, and the psychological burden of living with a debilitating condition can lead to depression, anxiety, and social isolation.

For individuals with diabetic neuropathy or other chronic neuropathies, managing daily tasks becomes difficult, often resulting in reduced participation in social and work activities.

## Increased Risk of Complications

Neuropathy can lead to serious complications, especially in individuals with chronic conditions like diabetes or HIV. For example, people with diabetic neuropathy are more prone to foot ulcers and infections, which, if not treated promptly, can result in amputations.

People with HIV-related neuropathy or those undergoing chemotherapy are also at risk of secondary infections, delayed recovery, and additional complications due to the impaired nerve function.

## Healthcare Costs and Economic Impact

The healthcare burden of treating neuropathies is significant. This includes the costs of diagnosis, treatment, and long-term care. For instance, managing complications from diabetic neuropathy, such as foot ulcers and amputations, involves costly hospitalizations, surgeries, rehabilitation, and ongoing medical care.

Neuropathies also contribute to lost productivity due to work disability. This affects not only the individual but also their families, employers, and society, as chronic pain or disability may prevent people from working or engaging in full-time employment.

In the case of cancer patients, chemotherapy-induced neuropathy can result in delays or discontinuation of treatment, leading to higher costs and poorer clinical outcomes.

**Psychosocial Impact**

Social isolation is a common outcome of chronic neuropathies. Individuals with severe pain, mobility issues, or other disabilities may withdraw from social interactions and activities, leading to a lack of support and increased mental health challenges.

The emotional toll of living with chronic pain or dysfunction can be profound. People with neuropathies often experience a reduced sense of self-worth, anxiety about the future, and feelings of helplessness.

Neuropathies in children, such as in Charcot-Marie-Tooth disease, can affect developmental milestones, leading to psychological stress for both children and their families.

**Impact on Daily Life and Functional Independence**

People living with neuropathies often face limitations in their ability to perform everyday activities. For example, diabetic neuropathy may lead to difficulty with walking, and hereditary neuropathies may impair the use of hands and feet.

This loss of functional independence means that many individuals with severe neuropathy need help with basic tasks, such as bathing, eating, or dressing. In cases of more advanced neuropathy, individuals may require full-time care or may have to move into assisted living facilities.

**Impact on Families and Caregivers**

Neuropathy not only affects the individual but also places a strain on family members and caregivers. The emotional stress of managing a loved one's chronic condition, along with the physical and financial burden, can take a toll on caregivers' health and well-being. The impact of neuropathies on families and caregivers can be profound, as these conditions often require long-term management and can significantly change the daily lives of those involved [8].

Here's an in-depth look at the various ways neuropathies affect families and caregivers:

**Emotional and Psychological Strain**

Stress and Anxiety: Caring for a loved one with neuropathy can cause significant emotional distress. Families may worry about the physical and mental health of their loved one, and about the long-term outlook of the condition. The unpredictability of some neuropathies, such as Guillain-Barré Syndrome or chemotherapy-induced neuropathy, adds to this stress.

Depression: Caregivers are at a higher risk of depression due to the emotional burden of managing a chronic condition. Feelings of helplessness, isolation, or concern for the future can take a mental toll.

Guilt and Frustration: Family members may feel guilty if they are unable to alleviate their loved one's pain or suffering. This can be compounded by frustration from witnessing the gradual decline of their loved one's health and independence [9].

**Physical and Financial Burden**

Physical Strain: Caring for someone with neuropathy often involves assisting with daily activities, which can be physically demanding. Tasks such as helping the person with mobility, personal care, or administering medications can be exhausting. Caregivers may experience musculoskeletal strain, especially if the person being cared for is immobile or requires frequent transfers.

Financial Impact: The financial burden of caring for someone with neuropathy can be substantial. There may be costs for medical treatments, medications, specialized equipment (such as wheelchairs or mobility aids), and even home modifications. Additionally, caregivers may need to reduce their work hours or even quit their jobs to provide full-time care, resulting in lost wages and economic strain on the family.

Health Costs: Managing the complications of neuropathy, such as foot ulcers in diabetic neuropathy or gastrointestinal issues in autonomic neuropathy, can require frequent doctor visits, hospitalizations, and therapies, which may not always be fully covered by insurance.

**Impact on Family Relationships**

Increased Caregiver Role: In many families, a single person often takes on the primary caregiving role. This can place stress on the caregiver's relationships with other family members, especially if they feel unsupported or overwhelmed. Additionally, caregiving can sometimes lead to resentment or tension among family members, especially if the burden is not shared equitably.

Disruption of Family Dynamics: The time and energy required for caregiving can reduce the caregiver's ability to participate in family activities, leading to feelings of isolation and disconnection. Family holidays, social events, or routine activities may need to be canceled or adjusted to accommodate the needs of the person with neuropathy.

Impact on Children and Spouses: In cases where a spouse or parent is affected by neuropathy, children or other family members may take on roles beyond their capacity, leading to emotional stress and potential role confusion within the family. Young children may struggle with seeing a parent or caregiver in pain or losing their independence, while adult children may feel torn between work, personal life, and caregiving duties [10].

**Social Isolation**

Caregivers of individuals with neuropathy often experience social isolation, as the demands of caregiving limit their ability to engage in social activities, friendships, or leisure pursuits. The person receiving care may also withdraw socially, particularly if their symptoms, such as pain or mobility issues, make it difficult to participate in family or community events.

In some cases, the caregiver's isolation can lead to a sense of loneliness or alienation, especially if they feel there is no one to talk to about their struggles.

**Physical Health Impact on Caregivers**

Burnout: Caregiver burnout is a significant risk, as the constant physical and emotional demands of providing care can lead to exhaustion, sleep disturbances, and diminished physical health. Many caregivers neglect their own health in the process, often missing medical appointments or not taking proper care of themselves due to the demands placed on them.

Increased Risk of Health Problems: Caregivers are at a higher risk of developing chronic conditions like hypertension, cardiovascular disease, and depression due to the constant stress and physical strain. This can be exacerbated if they are not receiving sufficient support or respite care.

## Impact on Daily Life and Routines

Disrupted Work and Career: The caregiving role often requires flexibility, which can lead to absenteeism from work or a complete inability to maintain full-time employment. This disruption affects both the caregiver's career development and the family's financial stability.

Changes to Family Routines: Caregivers must often adjust their daily routines to accommodate medical treatments, therapy sessions, or regular caregiving duties (such as feeding, bathing, or mobility assistance). This often leads to disruption of the family's day-to-day functioning, making it harder to keep up with household tasks and responsibilities.

## Impact on Mental Health of Children

Children growing up with a family member suffering from neuropathy can experience feelings of anxiety, sadness, or confusion about the illness and changes in the family structure. They may become caregivers themselves, prematurely taking on responsibilities that affect their own development.

This may also contribute to behavioral problems or academic challenges as children struggle with the emotional burden of caregiving or the uncertainty surrounding the condition of the affected loved one.

## Need for Support Systems

Support Networks: Family members and caregivers often need external support, such as from other family members, friends, or professional caregivers. Respite care services, social worker support, or community-based resources can help ease the load by offering temporary relief and guidance on how to manage the challenges of caregiving.

Counseling and Therapy: Many caregivers benefit from counseling or support groups, where they can share experiences with others in similar situations and learn coping strategies. Therapy can help caregivers manage stress and improve mental well-being.

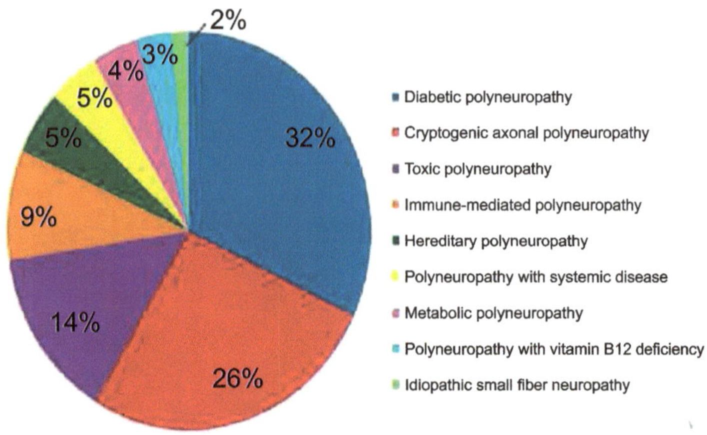


**Fig. (1).** Estimated prevalence of common Neuropathies.

Family members often have to take on caregiving roles, providing assistance with daily activities and medical care. This can limit the caregiver's ability to work and pursue personal goals, which can impact family finances and dynamics [11].

## CONCLUSION

Neuropathies have a multidimensional impact on health, affecting physical, emotional, social, and economic aspects of life. The chronic pain, disability, and functional impairments associated with neuropathies lead to reduced quality of life, increased healthcare costs, and a significant burden on families and caregivers. Effective management, early diagnosis, and access to appropriate healthcare services are essential to mitigate the impact of these conditions and improve outcomes for affected individuals.

Global Prevalence: The global prevalence of peripheral neuropathies is estimated to be around 2-8% of the population. This includes a wide range of causes and types of neuropathies affecting sensory, motor, and autonomic nerves. The estimated prevalence of neuropathy is illustrated in Fig. (**1**).

Efforts to address the global burden of neuropathies include early diagnosis and management of underlying conditions, lifestyle interventions to prevent neuropathy progression, and research into novel treatment modalities aimed at alleviating symptoms and improving outcomes for affected individuals.

## REFERENCES

[1] Dal Canto E, Ceriello A, Rydén L, *et al.* Diabetes as a cardiovascular risk factor: An overview of global trends of macro and micro vascular complications. Eur J Prev Cardiol 2019; 26(2_suppl) (Suppl.): 25-32.

[http://dx.doi.org/10.1177/2047487319878371] [PMID: 31722562]

[2] Goyal R, Singhal M, Jialal I. Type 2 Diabetes. StatPearls. Treasure Island (FL) ineligible companies. Disclosure: Mayank Singhal declares no relevant financial relationships with ineligible companies. Disclosure: Ishwarlal Jialal declares no relevant financial relationships with ineligible companies: StatPearls Publishing. Copyright © 2024, StatPearls Publishing LLC.; 2024.

[3] Kumar S, Gokulakrishnan S, Narasimman P. Effect of electroacupuncture on sensory peripheral nerve function in diabetic peripheral neuropathy: A randomized controlled trial protocol. SSRN 2024; 4942746.

[4] Cho Y, Kim BS, Yoo WS, Seo SW, Chung IY. Antiphospholipid syndrome of bilateral nonarteritic anterior ischemic optic neuropathy patient deteriorating over time. Korean J Ophthalmol 2021; 35(2): 168-70.
[http://dx.doi.org/10.3341/kjo.2020.0100] [PMID: 33596624]

[5] Rudnik-Schöneborn S, Auer-Grumbach M, Senderek J. Charcot-Marie-Tooth disease and hereditary motor neuropathies – Update 2020. Med Genetik 2020; 32(3): 207-19.
[http://dx.doi.org/10.1515/medgen-2020-2038]

[6] Kim E. Chemotherapy-induced peripheral neuropathy: bench to clinical practice. Korean J Pain 2020; 33(4): 291-3.
[http://dx.doi.org/10.3344/kjp.2020.33.4.291] [PMID: 32989193]

[7] Kavanagh S, Pallin JA, Doherty AS, Lazzarini P, O'Keeffe L, Buckley CM. Prevalence and incidence of peripheral neuropathy, peripheral artery disease, foot disease, and lower extremity amputation in people with diabetes in Ireland; a systematic review protocol. HRB Open Res 2024; 7: 1.
[http://dx.doi.org/10.12688/hrbopenres.13823.2] [PMID: 39544222]

[8] Ledda C, Montanaro E, Imbalzano G, *et al.* Burden of caregiving for cardiovascular dysautonomia in Parkinson's disease. Clin Auton Res 2022; 32(6): 455-61.
[http://dx.doi.org/10.1007/s10286-022-00888-9] [PMID: 36030471]

[9] De Padova S, Casadei C, Berardi A, *et al.* Caregiver emotional burden in testicular cancer patients: from patient to caregiver support. Front Endocrinol (Lausanne) 2019; 10: 318.
[http://dx.doi.org/10.3389/fendo.2019.00318] [PMID: 31191451]

[10] Solan LG, Beck AF, Shardo SA, *et al.* Caregiver perspectives on communication during hospitalization at an academic pediatric institution: a qualitative study. J Hosp Med 2018; 13(5): 304-10.
[http://dx.doi.org/10.12788/jhm.2919] [PMID: 29345256]

[11] Zúñiga ML, Mulholland K, Lewin-Fischer P, Martinez San Román I, Toledo L, Urada L. Examining the effects of parental migration on youth mental health and substance use: a qualitative study in rural Yucatán, México. Front Psychiatry 2024; 15: 1368619.
[http://dx.doi.org/10.3389/fpsyt.2024.1368619] [PMID: 38807689]

# CHAPTER 16

# Impact of Neuropathies on the Economy

**Abstract:** The impact of neuropathies on the economy can be significant, affecting various aspects, including healthcare costs, workforce productivity, and quality of life. This chapter provides a breakdown of how neuropathies impact the economy. Neuropathies require extensive medical care, including diagnosis, treatment, and ongoing management. Depending on the type of neuropathy, affected individuals may experience limitations in mobility and sensory function. Neuropathic symptoms, such as pain, numbness, and weakness, can result in increased absenteeism from work as individuals struggle to manage their condition or undergo treatments. Addressing the economic impact of neuropathies requires comprehensive strategies aimed at improving prevention, early detection, and management of these conditions. Investing in research, healthcare infrastructure, and policies that promote timely diagnosis and effective treatment can help mitigate the economic burden of neuropathies while enhancing the well-being of affected individuals and society as a whole.

**Keywords:** Economy, Management of neuropathy, Neuropathy, Policies, Strategies.

## INTRODUCTION

Neuropathies can have a significant impact on the economy, affecting various aspects, such as healthcare costs, workforce productivity, and quality of life. Here's a breakdown of how neuropathies impact the economy:

### Healthcare Costs

Neuropathies require extensive medical care, including diagnosis, treatment, and ongoing management. This encompasses expenses related to doctor visits, medications, diagnostic tests (*e.g.*, nerve conduction studies, imaging), physical therapy, and in some cases, surgical interventions. The cumulative healthcare costs associated with neuropathies can strain healthcare systems and lead to substantial financial burdens for individuals, families, and society as a whole [1].

The healthcare costs of neuropathies can have significant, far-reaching impacts on the economy at multiple levels, from individuals and families to governments and healthcare systems. Here's a detailed look at how these costs affect the broader economy:

**Sumaira Kanwal & Shazia Perveen**

## Direct Medical Costs

**Diagnosis and Treatment:** The healthcare costs associated with diagnosing and managing neuropathies (which often involve expensive tests, consultations with specialists, and long-term treatment regimens) contribute to rising healthcare expenditures. Treatments may include medications (*e.g.*, pain relievers, anticonvulsants), physical therapy, and surgeries, all of which can be costly [2].

**Hospitalizations and Emergency Care:** Severe forms of neuropathy or complications (such as diabetic neuropathy leading to foot ulcers or infections) may require frequent hospital visits, prolonged stays, or emergency care, leading to significant costs in the healthcare system.

**Specialized Services**: Neuropathy often requires specialized care, which may include consultations with neurologists, pain management clinics, or rehabilitation services. These services tend to be more expensive compared to routine healthcare.

## Long-Term Healthcare Cost

**Chronic Condition Management:** Neuropathy is often a chronic condition, meaning patients may require ongoing healthcare interventions over their lifetime. The cumulative cost of long-term treatment, including medication for pain management or disease progression (*e.g.*, for diabetic neuropathy), puts continuous pressure on healthcare resources [3].

**Complications and Comorbidities:** Neuropathy can cause additional health issues such as falls, infections, and cardiovascular problems. For example, diabetic neuropathy can lead to amputations, which in turn require additional healthcare services and rehabilitation. These complications significantly increase healthcare expenditures.

## Increased Burden on Public Health Systems

**Medicare and Medicaid:** For elderly populations or those with lower incomes, neuropathy-related treatments are often covered by public health programs like Medicare or Medicaid. This places a heavy financial burden on public health systems, especially considering that neuropathies are common among older adults.

**Rising Demand for Services**: As the population ages and the prevalence of diseases like diabetes rises, so does the demand for neuropathy-related healthcare services. This demand could overwhelm existing healthcare infrastructure, leading to higher overall costs and possible strain on resources [4].

**Insurance Costs**

**Increased Premiums**: Neuropathy-related claims lead to higher medical insurance costs for both individuals and businesses. Insurance premiums may increase for everyone as the overall costs of treating neuropathies grow. The cost of managing neuropathy may also impact employer-sponsored insurance plans, leading to higher premiums for employers, which in turn can affect the economy as a whole by reducing disposable income.

**Uninsured and Underinsured Populations**: Individuals without adequate insurance may struggle to afford the cost of neuropathy care, leading to delayed treatment or worsened health outcomes, which can ultimately drive up overall healthcare spending due to complications and emergency care.

**Productivity Losses**

**Workplace Absenteeism**: Neuropathy-related pain and disability can cause affected individuals to take more sick days, reducing their productivity at work. This lost productivity impacts not only the individual but also the company and the broader economy [5].

**Presentism**

Even when individuals with neuropathy continue to work, their condition may affect their ability to function at full capacity. Chronic pain and fatigue can reduce work efficiency and performance, leading to a decline in productivity and lower economic output.

**Early Retirement or Disability**

For severe cases of neuropathy, individuals may need to retire early or apply for disability benefits. This removes skilled workers from the labor force, leading to both personal financial hardship and economic losses due to reduced workforce participation.

**Indirect Economic Costs: Caregiver Burden**

Family members often provide care for individuals with neuropathies, resulting in indirect costs, such as lost wages from caregiving responsibilities. This can be especially significant in the case of chronic, disabling neuropathies, where the need for long-term care is high.

### Social and Emotional Impact

The emotional toll of living with chronic neuropathy can lead to increased mental health care costs, including therapy and psychiatric treatments for depression and anxiety, which are common among people with chronic pain conditions. This further adds to the economic burden on healthcare systems.

### Impact on Healthcare System Resources

**Overburdened Healthcare Providers**: The increasing prevalence of neuropathy, especially with conditions like diabetes and aging populations, results in an overburdened healthcare system. Healthcare providers must dedicate more resources to managing neuropathy cases, which may strain existing healthcare infrastructure and lead to higher operating costs for medical institutions.

**Inefficiencies in Care Delivery:** Poorly managed or delayed treatment for neuropathy can lead to inefficient care, such as emergency room visits for preventable complications, which are more expensive than regular outpatient care or preventative treatment [6].

### Long-Term Economic Impact

**Healthcare Inflation**: The rising costs of neuropathy treatments contribute to the broader trend of healthcare inflation. As more people develop chronic conditions like neuropathy, the overall cost of healthcare increases, impacting the economy at large by raising insurance premiums, government spending on public health programs, and out-of-pocket expenses for individuals.

**Health Inequities:** Low-income populations and communities with limited access to healthcare may face higher rates of untreated neuropathy, leading to worsened health outcomes and more expensive emergency care in the future. This can further perpetuate health disparities and create a cycle of increasing economic inequality.

### Potential for Preventive Measures

**Early Intervention and Prevention:** Investing in early diagnosis and preventive measures (such as lifestyle interventions for diabetic neuropathy or screening for neuropathy in high-risk populations) can reduce long-term healthcare costs by preventing or mitigating the severity of the condition. However, current systems may lack sufficient funding or focus on preventive healthcare, resulting in avoidable higher costs later.

### How Neuropathies Affect Productivity and Economic Growth

Neuropathies can have a profound effect on productivity, both at an individual level and within broader economic systems [7]. Here's how neuropathies impact productivity:

#### Workplace Absenteeism

**Frequent Sick Days**: People with neuropathies, especially those experiencing chronic pain or mobility issues, may need to take frequent sick days to manage their symptoms, attend medical appointments, or deal with complications.

**Extended Leave**: Severe cases of neuropathy may necessitate extended medical leave or even long-term disability, removing workers from the workforce for prolonged periods, further reducing productivity.

#### Presentism (Reduced Work Performance)

**Chronic Pain and Fatigue:** Even when individuals with neuropathy are physically present at work, the condition often leads to presentism, where employees are working at reduced efficiency. Chronic pain, fatigue, and discomfort can hinder concentration, slow down task completion, and reduce cognitive performance, impacting overall productivity.

**Difficulty Performing Tasks:** Neuropathy can affect fine motor skills (*e.g.*, typing, handling tools) and make it difficult to perform manual or repetitive tasks that require dexterity. Employees with sensory or motor deficits may take longer to complete tasks, leading to inefficiency.

**Cognitive Impairments**: Some neuropathies, especially those related to conditions like diabetes or chemotherapy-induced neuropathy, can cause cognitive issues, such as difficulty concentrating, memory problems, or processing information quickly. These challenges can hinder decision-making and problem-solving, further reducing productivity.

#### Increased Error Rates

**Reduced Focus and Attention**: The discomfort caused by neuropathy may reduce an individual's ability to focus for long periods, increasing the likelihood of errors in their work. Whether in healthcare, manufacturing, or office settings, mistakes can be costly in terms of time, resources, and safety.

**Safety Concerns:** Neuropathy that affects sensation in the hands or feet may increase the risk of accidents or workplace injuries. For example, workers with reduced foot sensation may be more likely to trip, fall, or injure themselves, leading to more time off and additional safety measures.

## Impact on Job Performance

**Difficulty in Physical Tasks**: Neuropathies that affect motor function (*e.g.*, in the hands, feet, or legs) can make it hard for individuals to perform physically demanding jobs. Employees may struggle with tasks that require lifting, walking, or standing for extended periods, which can impact performance in sectors like construction, healthcare, and manufacturing.

**Reduced Productivity in Cognitive Roles**: Neuropathy-related fatigue or cognitive impairment can reduce efficiency and speed for employees in intellectual or knowledge-based roles, such as in offices or technical fields. This can lead to delays in project timelines, lower output, and missed deadlines.

## Increased Healthcare Appointments and Treatment Time

**Time Spent on Medical Care**: Individuals with neuropathy often require regular medical appointments for check-ups, medication management, and physical therapy. Taking time off work for these appointments can further reduce productive work hours, especially for those requiring frequent follow-ups.

**Chronic Pain Management:** Those managing chronic neuropathy pain may need additional time for rest, medication, or other pain-relief activities during the workday. This can disrupt the workflow and reduce overall performance.

## Long-Term Disability and Early Retirement

**Inability to Perform Work**: As neuropathies worsen, they can lead to more significant disability, making it impossible for affected workers to continue in their current roles. This could result in early retirement or the need for workers to transition to lower-paying, less demanding positions.

**Early Exit from the Workforce**: Neuropathy-related disability may also prompt individuals to take early retirement or apply for disability benefits, removing experienced workers from the workforce and causing long-term productivity losses. The loss of skilled labor impacts industries and organizations in terms of knowledge, expertise, and output [8].

**Economic Costs Due to Productivity Loss**

**Impact on Employers:** Employers face financial losses due to absenteeism, presentism, and long-term disability claims related to neuropathy. They may need to hire temporary workers or offer accommodations for affected employees, which can further increase costs and reduce overall workplace productivity.

**Sector-Specific Impacts:** Certain industries are more susceptible to productivity losses from neuropathies. For example, in sectors like manufacturing or healthcare, where manual labor and physical tasks are essential, even a small reduction in workforce performance can have a substantial impact on output.

**Impact on Team Dynamics**

**Decreased Collaboration:** If an employee is struggling with neuropathy symptoms, they may be less able to fully engage in team activities, which can reduce collaboration and overall team performance. This can be particularly impactful in creative or team-driven environments where effective communication and contribution from all members are crucial.

**Increased Workload for Co-Workers**: When employees with neuropathy are unable to contribute at their usual level, coworkers may need to take on additional responsibilities, leading to potential burnout, dissatisfaction, and further reductions in overall team productivity.

**Disability and Loss of Productivity:** Neuropathies can cause significant disability, impairing individuals' ability to work and perform daily activities. Depending on the severity and type of neuropathy, affected individuals may experience limitations in mobility, sensory function, or motor skills, which can impact their employment prospects and earning potential. Consequently, there may be a loss of productivity both at the individual level and within the broader workforce, leading to economic repercussions.

**Workplace Absenteeism and Presentism:** Neuropathic symptoms, such as pain, numbness, and weakness, can result in increased absenteeism from work as individuals struggle to manage their condition or undergo treatments. Moreover, even when individuals remain at work, their productivity may be compromised due to pain, fatigue, or other neuropathy-related symptoms, a phenomenon known as presentism. These issues contribute to decreased efficiency and effectiveness in the workplace, translating into economic losses for employers and the economy as a whole.

**Social Security and Disability Benefits:** Severe cases of neuropathies may render individuals unable to work, leading to reliance on social security disability benefits or other forms of financial assistance. The provision of disability benefits places a financial strain on government resources and social insurance programs, impacting public expenditure and fiscal policies.

**Indirect Costs and Secondary Effects:** Neuropathies can also lead to indirect costs and secondary effects that impact the economy. For instance, individuals may require additional support services, such as home care assistance or assistive devices, to manage their condition and maintain independence. Additionally, neuropathies can contribute to comorbidities and complications, necessitating further medical interventions and increasing overall healthcare expenditures [9].

## How Can Economic Loss Be Minimized While Having Neuropathies?

### *Early Diagnosis and Preventive Care*

**Early Detection**: Early diagnosis of neuropathy allows for more effective treatment and can prevent the condition from progressing to more severe stages. For example, regular screening for diabetic neuropathy can help detect the condition before it causes irreversible damage.

**Preventive Measures**: For conditions like diabetes, managing blood sugar levels, engaging in regular exercise, and making dietary changes can reduce the risk of developing neuropathy. Early intervention can prevent costly medical treatments and improve long-term health outcomes.

**Public Health Initiatives**: Encouraging regular check-ups and providing education on lifestyle changes to prevent neuropathy, especially in high-risk populations (*e.g.*, those with diabetes or cancer), can reduce the incidence of the disease and the subsequent economic burden.

### *Improved Medical Management*

**Comprehensive Pain Management**: Implementing effective pain management strategies, such as the use of medications (*e.g.*, anticonvulsants, antidepressants, or topical treatments) or alternative therapies (*e.g.*, acupuncture, physical therapy), can help individuals with neuropathy manage their symptoms and maintain a higher level of productivity at work.

**Access to Rehabilitation Services**: Physical therapy and occupational therapy can help individuals maintain mobility, strength, and dexterity, reducing the severity of functional impairments and allowing them to continue working in their current roles or maintain a higher level of independence.

**Telemedicine and Remote Monitoring:** Telemedicine enables individuals to consult with specialists without needing to travel, saving both time and money. Remote monitoring for conditions like diabetic neuropathy can also help patients better manage their health at home, reducing the need for frequent in-person visits and the associated costs.

### *Workplace Accommodations*

**Flexible Work Schedules:** Employers can reduce absenteeism and presentism by offering flexible work schedules or remote work options. This flexibility allows employees with neuropathies to manage their condition more effectively while continuing to work, thus minimizing lost productivity.

**Ergonomic Adjustments:** For individuals whose neuropathy affects mobility or dexterity, making adjustments to the workplace (*e.g.*, ergonomic desks, chairs, or keyboards) can improve comfort and functionality, thereby reducing strain on affected areas and allowing employees to work more efficiently.

**Task Modification:** Adjusting job responsibilities to align with the abilities of employees with neuropathy can help them maintain their productivity. For example, workers with neuropathy affecting their hands may be reassigned to less physically demanding tasks that still use their skills.

**Supportive Work Environments**: Creating a supportive work environment that includes awareness and understanding of neuropathy can help reduce the stigma surrounding the condition, leading to better employee morale and retention.

### *Access to Disability Benefits and Financial Support*

**Social Safety Nets:** Providing workers with access to disability benefits or other financial support systems (*e.g.*, workers' compensation) can reduce the financial stress associated with neuropathy. These safety nets allow individuals to prioritize their health while maintaining financial stability, thereby reducing the risk of economic hardship.

**Short-Term Disability Programs**: Short-term disability programs can help employees with neuropathy manage income loss during periods of acute illness or flare-ups, allowing them to take the necessary time off to recover without compromising their financial security.

### *Encouraging Return-to-Work Programs*

**Vocational Rehabilitation:** For individuals with severe neuropathies, vocational rehabilitation programs can help them transition back into the workforce or retrain for roles that accommodate their physical limitations. This may involve reassessing their skills and providing training for less physically demanding roles or jobs in industries that require cognitive rather than physical labor.

**Gradual Return-to-Work Policies**: Employers can offer graduated return-to-work policies for employees with neuropathy, allowing them to gradually increase their hours or work intensity as they adjust to the demands of their jobs [10].

### *Reducing the Burden on Healthcare Systems*

**Integrated Care Models:** Integrating healthcare services (*e.g.*, primary care, neurology, pain management, and rehabilitation) can reduce fragmented care and ensure that individuals with neuropathy receive comprehensive, coordinated treatment. This could lead to more efficient use of healthcare resources, potentially reducing overall treatment costs.

**Outpatient Care Options**: Focusing on outpatient treatments instead of inpatient care can help lower the costs associated with treating neuropathy. Programs like pain management clinics and outpatient rehabilitation can be more cost-effective while still providing effective care.

**Insurance Coverage**: Expanding insurance coverage to include neuropathy-specific treatments and therapies can help alleviate financial strain on patients. This may include covering medication, therapy, and specialist consultations that improve outcomes and reduce long-term healthcare costs.

### *Promoting Work-Life Balance and Mental Health Support*

**Mental Health Services**: Addressing the psychological impact of neuropathies, such as depression and anxiety, is essential. Providing access to mental health support through therapy or counseling can improve well-being, reduce absenteeism, and enhance overall productivity.

**Work-Life Balance Programs**: Offering programs that support work-life balance, such as wellness initiatives or stress management workshops, can help individuals with neuropathy manage both their health and work responsibilities more effectively.

### *Public Awareness and Education*

**Raising Awareness:** Educating the public, employers, and healthcare providers about neuropathies and their economic impact can help reduce stigma and encourage early intervention. Greater awareness can lead to more proactive management, improved outcomes, and long-term cost savings.

**Workplace Training Programs**: Employers can train managers and HR personnel to better understand the needs of employees with neuropathies. This knowledge can help ensure that employees are properly accommodated, thereby reducing workplace friction and improving overall productivity.

### *Advances in Research and Treatment*

**Investing in Research:** Continued investment in neuropathy research can lead to better treatments, cures, and more efficient management strategies, which could reduce the long-term economic impact. For example, advancements in treatments for diabetic neuropathy could prevent the condition from progressing to more debilitating stages, leading to lower healthcare costs.

**Faster Approval of Medications**: Streamlining the approval process for effective neuropathy treatments could help patients access medications and therapies sooner, potentially preventing complications that could drive up treatment costs [11].

## CONCLUSION

Neuropathies impact productivity in various ways, including increased absenteeism, reduced cognitive and physical performance, higher error rates, and safety concerns. These impacts can lead to both direct losses for employers (in terms of time, wages, and output) and indirect losses for the economy, as skilled workers may need to leave the workforce or retire early. Addressing these issues through proper medical care, workplace accommodations, and support systems can help mitigate the impact on productivity, but the economic consequences of neuropathies remain significant.

By focusing on early diagnosis, effective medical management, workplace accommodations, financial support systems, and public education, the economic losses associated with neuropathies can be minimized. A multi-faceted approach involving healthcare systems, employers, and government policies is key to reducing both the direct and indirect costs of neuropathies, allowing individuals to maintain their productivity and well-being while also alleviating the financial burden on society.

Addressing the economic impact of neuropathies requires comprehensive strategies aimed at improving prevention, early detection, and management of these conditions. Investing in research, healthcare infrastructure, and policies that promote timely diagnosis and effective treatment can help mitigate the economic burden of neuropathies while enhancing the well-being of affected individuals and society as a whole. Minimizing the economic loss associated with neuropathies involves a combination of medical, workplace, and societal interventions aimed at improving the quality of life for affected individuals, maintaining productivity, and reducing healthcare costs. Here are several strategies that can help reduce the economic impact of neuropathies: By focusing on early diagnosis, effective medical management, workplace accommodations, financial support systems, and public education, the economic losses associated with neuropathies can be minimized. A multi-faceted approach involving healthcare systems, employers, and government policies is key to reducing both the direct and indirect costs of neuropathies, allowing individuals to maintain their productivity and well-being while also alleviating the financial burden on society.

## REFERENCES

[1] de Siqueira Filha NT, Li J, Phillips-Howard PA, *et al.* The economics of healthcare access: a scoping review on the economic impact of healthcare access for vulnerable urban populations in low- and middle-income countries. Int J Equity Health 2022; 21(1): 191. [http://dx.doi.org/10.1186/s12939-022-01804-3] [PMID: 36585704]

[2] Boulanger L, Zhao Y, Bao Y, Russell MW. A retrospective study on the impact of comorbid depression or anxiety on healthcare resource use and costs among diabetic neuropathy patients. BMC Health Serv Res 2009; 9(1): 111. [http://dx.doi.org/10.1186/1472-6963-9-111] [PMID: 19566952]

[3] Athanasakis K, Petrakis I, Karampli E, Vitsou E, Lyras L, Kyriopoulos J. Pregabalin *versus* gabapentin in the management of peripheral neuropathic pain associated with post-herpetic neuralgia and diabetic neuropathy: a cost effectiveness analysis for the Greek healthcare setting. BMC Neurol 2013; 13(1): 56. [http://dx.doi.org/10.1186/1471-2377-13-56] [PMID: 23731598]

[4] Song X, Wilson KL, Kagan J, Panjabi S. Cost of peripheral neuropathy in patients receiving treatment for multiple myeloma: a US administrative claims analysis. Ther Adv Hematol 2019; 10: 2040620719839025. [http://dx.doi.org/10.1177/2040620719839025] [PMID: 30967926]

[5] Ko CM, Tai R. 2019; Corporate governance and climate change risk management: A case study of transport industry in Hong Kong. SSRN 3506543. [http://dx.doi.org/10.2139/ssrn.3506543]

[6] Neira-Vera GDJ, Silva-Idrovo RR, Andrade-Garófalo C, Carrillo-Pérez FX, Avilés-Almeida PA, Poveda-Burgos GH. Benefit and economic impact of food security in ecuador. Russian Law Journal 2023; 11(11S): 322-33.

[7] Roquelaure Y, Fouquet N, Chazelle E, *et al.* Theoretical impact of simulated workplace-based primary prevention of carpal tunnel syndrome in a French region. BMC Public Health 2018; 18(1): 426.

[http://dx.doi.org/10.1186/s12889-018-5328-6] [PMID: 29606118]

[8] Bromberg T, Gasquet NC, Ricker CN, Wu C. Healthcare costs and medical utilization patterns associated with painful and severe painful diabetic peripheral neuropathy. Endocrine 2024; 86(3): 1014-24.
[http://dx.doi.org/10.1007/s12020-024-03954-6] [PMID: 39001927]

[9] Sakai F, Igarashi H, Yokoyama M, et al. Diagnosis, knowledge, perception, and productivity impact of headache education and clinical evaluation program in the workplace at an information technology company of more than 70,000 employees. Cephalalgia 2023; 43(4).
[http://dx.doi.org/10.1177/03331024231165682] [PMID: 36967710]

[10] Juba OO. Impact of workplace safety, health, and wellness programs on employee engagement and productivity. *International Journal of Health.* Medicine and Nursing Practice 2024; 6(4): 12-27.

[11] Xu Y. Investigating the impact of sleep quality on workplace productivity: An analysis of influencing factors and improvement strategies. Advances in Economics, Management and Political Sciences 2024; 113(1): 61-8.
[http://dx.doi.org/10.54254/2754-1169/2024.LD18181]

# CHAPTER 17

# Challenges in Neuropathies in Developing Nations

**Abstract:** Neuropathies in developing nations are exacerbated by limited healthcare resources, restricted access to diagnostic tools, and socioeconomic disparities. These conditions are prevalent due to infectious diseases, nutritional deficiencies, and environmental toxins. Limited healthcare access, particularly in rural areas, leads to undiagnosed or suboptimal care. Diagnostic tools like nerve conduction studies and electromyography are scarce or unavailable, causing delays in treatment and increased complications.

Neuropathies in developing nations can be challenging due to treatment accessibility and affordability issues, as essential medications may be excessively expensive or inaccessible. These diseases can exacerbate existing socioeconomic disparities, limiting opportunities for economic advancement and social integration. Addressing neuropathies requires comprehensive public health strategies, including improving access to healthcare services, strengthening healthcare infrastructure, and raising awareness about risk factors. Integrating neuropathy prevention strategies into global health initiatives can maximize resources and improve outcomes. For this purpose, collaboration between governments, healthcare organizations, NGOs, and international partners is essential.

**Keywords:** Developing nations, Healthcare access, Neuropathies, Public health strategies, Socioeconomic disparities.

## INTRODUCTION

Neuropathies pose unique challenges in developing nations, where factors such as limited healthcare resources, inadequate access to diagnostic tools and treatments, and socioeconomic disparities exacerbate the burden of these conditions. Here is an overview of neuropathies in developing nations:

1. **Prevalence and Epidemiological Trends:** Neuropathies are prevalent in developing nations, often driven by factors such as infectious diseases (*e.g.*, leprosy), nutritional deficiencies (*e.g.*, vitamin B12 deficiency), and exposure to environmental toxins (*e.g.*, pesticides). Additionally, the rising prevalence of chronic conditions like diabetes and HIV/AIDS further contributes to the burden of neuropathies in these regions [1].

**Sumaira Kanwal & Shazia Perveen**

2. **Limited Access to Healthcare:** Developing nations often face challenges in delivering comprehensive healthcare services, including neurological care. Rural areas, in particular, may lack specialized healthcare facilities and trained personnel capable of diagnosing and managing neuropathic disorders. As a result, many individuals with neuropathies in these regions may go undiagnosed or receive suboptimal care.
3. **Diagnostic Limitations:** Diagnostic tools such as nerve conduction studies, electromyography, and advanced imaging modalities may be scarce or unavailable in many developing nations. This hampers the accurate diagnosis and monitoring of neuropathies, leading to delays in treatment initiation and increased risk of complications.
4. **Treatment Accessibility and Affordability:** Even when treatments for neuropathies are available, they may be prohibitively expensive or inaccessible to individuals in developing nations, particularly those from low-income backgrounds. Essential medications, including pain management drugs and disease-modifying therapies, may be out of reach for many patients, further compromising their quality of life and functional status [2].
5. **Socioeconomic Impact:** Neuropathies can exacerbate existing socioeconomic disparities in developing nations, perpetuating cycles of poverty and inequality. Individuals with neuropathies may face barriers to education, employment, and social participation due to disability and functional limitations, limiting their opportunities for economic advancement and social integration.
6. **Public Health Challenges:** Addressing neuropathies in developing nations requires comprehensive public health strategies aimed at prevention, early detection, and affordable treatment. This includes efforts to improve access to essential healthcare services, strengthen healthcare infrastructure, enhance medical education and training, and raise awareness about risk factors and preventive measures [3].

Public health challenges in poor nations are multifaceted and often interconnected, arising from a combination of socioeconomic, environmental, political, and healthcare system factors. These challenges disproportionately affect vulnerable populations and hinder the overall health and development of these nations. Below are some of the most pressing public health challenges faced by Low- and Middle-Income Countries (LMICs):

### Infectious Diseases

Communicable Diseases: Infectious diseases, such as malaria, tuberculosis (TB), HIV/AIDS, cholera, and other waterborne diseases, remain a major public health threat in underdeveloped nations. Limited access to vaccines, sanitation, and proper healthcare infrastructure exacerbates the spread of these diseases.

Antimicrobial Resistance: In many low-income countries, there is overuse or misuse of antibiotics due to limited regulation, leading to the emergence of Antimicrobial Resistance (AMR), which complicates the treatment of infections.

## Malnutrition

Undernutrition: A significant portion of the population in underdeveloped countries experiences chronic undernutrition. This includes both protein-energy malnutrition and micronutrient deficiencies, which contribute to stunting, wasting, and other long-term health issues, especially among children.

Obesity and Overnutrition: Ironically, underdeveloped countries also face the rising burden of obesity, particularly in urban areas, driven by poor diets, processed foods, and a lack of access to healthy, nutritious food.

Food Insecurity: A lack of consistent access to enough nutritious food is a root cause of malnutrition, leading to poor immune function, stunted growth, and increased vulnerability to diseases.

## Inadequate Healthcare Infrastructure

Limited Access to Healthcare Services: Many underdeveloped countries struggle with inadequate healthcare infrastructure, especially in rural and remote areas. Lack of healthcare facilities, medical supplies, and essential medications prevents timely diagnosis and treatment.

Healthcare Workforce Shortages: The shortage of trained healthcare professionals, such as doctors, nurses, and specialists, is a major barrier to providing quality care. Many healthcare workers are overburdened and underpaid, leading to burnout and lower-quality care.

Lack of Emergency Medical Services: Emergency care systems are often rudimentary or non-existent, leading to poor outcomes in cases of trauma, childbirth complications, or acute medical conditions.

## Maternal and Child Health

High Maternal Mortality: Underdeveloped countries often have limited access to skilled birth attendants, prenatal care, and emergency obstetric services. As a result, maternal mortality rates are high, particularly due to complications like hemorrhage, sepsis, and obstructed labor.

High Child Mortality: Children in underdeveloped countries are more likely to die from preventable causes, such as pneumonia, diarrhea, malnutrition, and malaria.

Lack of immunization, clean water, and adequate nutrition contribute to increased childhood mortality.

Adolescent Health: Adolescents in underdeveloped countries are at risk of early pregnancies, sexually transmitted infections, and mental health challenges, often exacerbated by limited sexual health education and healthcare access.

**Non-Communicable Diseases (NCDs)**

Rising Burden of NCDs: Diseases like cardiovascular diseases, diabetes, cancer, and chronic respiratory diseases are rising in underdeveloped countries as lifestyles change, urbanization increases, and dietary patterns shift. Poor access to screening and early treatment for NCDs exacerbates the problem.

Lack of Preventive Measures: Inadequate awareness and prevention programs for NCDs, coupled with limited resources for treatment, contribute to the growing burden of these diseases [4].

**Environmental Health Issues**

Poor Sanitation and Water Quality: Lack of access to clean drinking water and proper sanitation facilities leads to waterborne diseases like cholera, dysentery, and typhoid fever. Poor waste management practices exacerbate environmental pollution, creating breeding grounds for disease.

Air Pollution: Indoor and outdoor air pollution is a major health risk in many low-income countries. In urban areas, vehicle emissions and industrial pollution lead to respiratory diseases, while in rural areas, the use of solid fuels for cooking (*e.g.*, wood, coal) increases the risk of chronic respiratory conditions.

Climate Change: Climate change can exacerbate existing health problems, leading to more extreme weather events (*e.g.*, floods, heatwaves) and affecting the spread of vector-borne diseases like malaria and dengue fever.

**Inadequate Health Financing**

Limited Government Spending: Health expenditures are often low in underdeveloped countries, which limits the government's ability to provide adequate healthcare services, build infrastructure, and fund essential public health programs.

Out-of-Pocket Expenditure: Many people in underdeveloped countries have to pay for healthcare out of pocket, leading to financial hardship, particularly for those with chronic conditions or in need of expensive treatments.

External Aid Dependence: While international aid plays a crucial role in supporting health systems in underdeveloped countries, the reliance on aid is unsustainable in the long term. Countries may struggle to maintain healthcare services and programs once external funding diminishes or changes priorities [5].

## Mental Health

Stigma and Lack of Awareness: Mental health issues are often stigmatized in underdeveloped countries, and people with mental health conditions may not seek help due to cultural or social barriers. The lack of mental health services and trained professionals further compounds the problem.

Limited Access to Care: Mental health services are often inadequate, with few facilities, resources, or trained providers. Many people with mental health conditions live untreated or are given inadequate care, which affects their quality of life.

Psychosocial Issues: Poverty, violence, displacement (*e.g.*, refugees), and trauma (*e.g.*, war or natural disasters) contribute to high rates of depression, anxiety, and other mental health conditions in low-income countries.

## Health Inequities

Social Determinants of Health: Socioeconomic factors, such as income, education, gender, and access to clean water, significantly impact health outcomes in underdeveloped countries. Discrimination and social exclusion also lead to health inequities, particularly for marginalized groups such as women, ethnic minorities, and people with disabilities.

Gender Inequality: In many underdeveloped countries, gender inequality restricts women's access to healthcare, education, and employment, contributing to poorer health outcomes for women and children.

## Health System Weaknesses

Fragmented Health Systems: Health systems in underdeveloped countries may be fragmented, inefficient, or underfunded, leading to poor coordination between different levels of care (primary, secondary, and tertiary) and lack of comprehensive healthcare coverage.

Corruption and Mismanagement: Corruption and poor governance can divert resources away from essential health services, affecting the quality and accessibility of care. Health systems may also suffer from a lack of accountability and transparency.

Solutions and Strategies: To address these challenges, several strategies are required: Strengthening Healthcare Systems: Investments in healthcare infrastructure, workforce training, and medical supplies are essential for improving healthcare access and quality.

Improving Public Health Education: Public health campaigns to raise awareness about hygiene, vaccinations, nutrition, and disease prevention can significantly reduce the burden of infectious diseases.

Addressing Social Determinants of Health: Efforts to tackle poverty, improve education, and reduce inequality are fundamental to improving overall health outcomes.

International Collaboration and Aid: Collaborating with international organizations and donors can help provide necessary resources, but long-term sustainability must be prioritized.

Community-based Approaches: Empowering communities through health education and local healthcare programs can help address barriers to access and improve health outcomes.

Addressing these challenges requires a comprehensive approach, where health policies are integrated with broader economic, social, and environmental strategies [6].

**Integration with Global Health Initiatives**

Neuropathies are increasingly recognized as important components of global health agendas, with initiatives aimed at addressing neurological disorders gaining momentum. Integration of neuropathy prevention and management strategies into broader health programs, such as those targeting non-communicable diseases or neglected tropical diseases, can help maximize resources and improve outcomes for individuals in developing nations. Neuropathies, or diseases affecting the peripheral nervous system, are a significant health challenge globally, but they pose unique challenges in developing nations. These challenges are often multifaceted, involving limited access to healthcare, lack of awareness, and a lack of resources for diagnosis and treatment. Below are key challenges faced by developing nations in managing neuropathies:

**Limited Access to Healthcare Services**

Rural and Remote Areas: Many people in developing nations live in rural or remote areas, where healthcare infrastructure is minimal. Neuropathy patients often lack access to specialists or diagnostic facilities (*e.g.*, EMG, nerve conduction studies). Shortage of Trained Healthcare Professionals: Neurologists and other specialized healthcare professionals may be in short supply. This can lead to delayed or inaccurate diagnoses.

**Lack of Awareness and Education**

General Public: There is often a lack of awareness among the general population about neuropathy symptoms, leading to delays in seeking medical attention. Conditions like diabetic neuropathy, for instance, may go unrecognized until they cause significant disability. Healthcare Providers: In some cases, primary healthcare providers might lack knowledge about neuropathies or the appropriate management strategies, especially in regions where resources for medical education are limited.

**Inadequate Diagnostic Facilities**

Limited Diagnostic Tools: Diagnostic tests such as nerve conduction studies, MRI, or skin biopsies, which are crucial for the diagnosis of neuropathies, may not be available in many areas due to financial constraints.

Misdiagnosis: Neuropathies are often misdiagnosed as other diseases due to the lack of specialized diagnostic tests. The symptoms may overlap with those of other conditions, such as infections, malnutrition, or metabolic disorders.

**High Treatment Costs**

Many neuropathies, particularly those associated with diabetes or HIV/AIDS, require long-term management and medication, which can be expensive for individuals in developing countries. Even basic pain management may be unaffordable.

**Poor Health Insurance Systems**

In many developing nations, health insurance systems are either underdeveloped or nonexistent, leaving people to bear the full cost of treatment and diagnostic tests.

**Prevalence of Underlying Risk Factors**

Diabetes and Hypertension: Chronic conditions like diabetes, hypertension, and HIV/AIDS are more prevalent in developing nations. These conditions can lead to neuropathies (*e.g.*, diabetic neuropathy), but the management of these diseases is often suboptimal, which worsens the neuropathy.

Malnutrition: Malnutrition, especially a lack of essential vitamins like B12, can contribute to neuropathies. In developing nations, nutritional deficiencies are more common, adding to the incidence of neuropathies.

Infections: In some regions, infections like leprosy and HIV/AIDS are leading causes of neuropathy. Limited access to treatment and preventative care increases the risk of these infections causing long-term nerve damage.

Lack of Preventative Healthcare Limited Health Promotion: Preventative strategies, such as proper management of diabetes, education on foot care for those with neuropathy, or vaccination against infections that cause nerve damage, are often not prioritized in developing nations. Poor Screening Programs: There are limited screening programs for people at risk for neuropathy, such as those with diabetes or a family history of neurological disorders.

**Cultural and Social Factors**

Stigma and Social Isolation: People with neuropathies may experience stigma or social isolation, especially when their symptoms are visible (*e.g.*, foot deformities due to diabetic neuropathy). In some cultures, there may be misconceptions about the nature of the disease, leading to social marginalization.

Traditional Medicine: In many developing nations, traditional medicine practices may be preferred over modern healthcare. While traditional medicine may offer some benefits, it often lacks scientific backing and can delay the effective treatment of neuropathies.

**Limited Research and Data**

Lack of Local Research: There is often insufficient research into neuropathies specific to the socio-economic and environmental context of developing nations. Without local data, it becomes difficult to formulate targeted public health policies or healthcare interventions.

Underreporting: Many cases of neuropathy are not reported, and the true prevalence may be underestimated. The lack of national data hinders efforts to address the public health burden posed by neuropathies.

**Fragmented Healthcare Systems**

Inadequate Coordination: In many developing countries, healthcare systems are fragmented, making it difficult to provide coordinated care for people with complex neuropathies that require multidisciplinary approaches (*e.g.*, neurologists, endocrinologists, physiotherapists).

Urban *vs.* Rural Disparity: Healthcare facilities in urban areas may be better equipped, but rural areas, where many people live, often lack the necessary infrastructure and staff to manage complex conditions like neuropathies [7].

## Environmental and Lifestyle Factors

Poor Working Conditions: Many individuals in developing countries work in environments with exposure to toxins or physical strain that can contribute to neuropathies. For instance, heavy manual labor or exposure to certain chemicals without protective gear can lead to neuropathy over time.

Inadequate Housing and Sanitation: Poor living conditions, including inadequate sanitation and housing, can contribute to conditions like tropical diseases and infections that lead to nerve damage.

## Solutions and Strategies

To address these challenges, the following strategies may be effective:

Strengthening Healthcare Infrastructure: Expanding access to diagnostic facilities, especially in rural areas, and improving the training of healthcare providers in diagnosing and managing neuropathies.

Public Awareness Campaigns: Promoting awareness about neuropathy and its risk factors, encouraging early diagnosis and management, especially for chronic conditions like diabetes.

Affordability and Access to Medications: Reducing the cost of neuropathy medications and ensuring their availability through partnerships with international organizations, governments, and NGOs.

Community-based Programs: Implementing community outreach programs that can provide education, prevent risk factors, and improve the overall management of neuropathies.

# CONCLUSION

Addressing these challenges requires a concerted effort from governments, healthcare organizations, NGOs, and communities to ensure that people in developing nations can access the care and support they need for neuropathy management.

## REFERENCES


[1] Lotfy M, Adeghate J, Kalasz H, Singh J, Adeghate E. Chronic complications of diabetes mellitus: A mini review. Curr Diabetes Rev 2016; 13(1): 3-10. [http://dx.doi.org/10.2174/1573399812666151016101622] [PMID: 26472574]

[2] Engvall K, Gréen H, Fredrikson M, Lagerlund M, Lewin F, Åvall-Lundqvist E. Impact of persistent peripheral neuropathy on health-related quality of life among early-stage breast cancer survivors: a population-based cross-sectional study. Breast Cancer Res Treat 2022; 195(3): 379-91. [http://dx.doi.org/10.1007/s10549-022-06670-9] [PMID: 35941422]

[3] Prasun P. Multiple Acyl-CoA Dehydrogenase Deficiency. 1993.

[4] Iqbal C, Ihsan Kamaruddin M, Ode Novi Angreni W, Asmi AS, Muhammad Nur Q. Communication, education, and information on non-communicable diseases. Abdimas Polsaka 2024; 3(2): 67-74. [http://dx.doi.org/10.35816/abdimaspolsaka.v3i2.74]

[5] Soares RDB, Soares EP, Pimentel RMS, Torquato JHS, Silva TR, Portela AM. Impacts of climate variability on hospitalizations and mortality from waterborne diseases in northern brazil. Revista Políticas Públicas & Cidades 2024; 13(2): e1325. [http://dx.doi.org/10.23900/2359-1552v13n2-326-2024]

[6] Berardi C, Hinwood M, Smith A, Melia A, Paolucci F. Barriers and facilitators to the integration of digital technologies in mental health systems: A protocol for a qualitative systematic review. PLoS One 2021; 16(11): e0259995. [http://dx.doi.org/10.1371/journal.pone.0259995] [PMID: 34807937]

[7] Esteves T A, Atabay G J, Tan E Y. Determinants of dispensing antibiotics without prescription by community pharmacists in developing countries: A review. Journal of Applied Pharmaceutical Science 2023; 13(7): 040-54.

# CHAPTER 18

# Impact of Neuropathy on an Individual

**Abstract:** People with neuropathy face significant challenges to their physical health, emotional well-being, social relationships, and financial stability. Along with physical symptoms such as pain, numbness, tingling, weakness, and sensory irregularities that interfere with daily activities, neuropathy also leads to broader health complications. These symptoms contribute to both physical and emotional distress, significantly reducing overall well-being. By affecting the patient's mental well-being, neuropathy symptoms often lead to severe depression, anxiety, and feelings of helplessness. Neuropathy often leads to social isolation and marital strain, primarily due to the patient's reduced ability to participate in social events or fulfill family responsibilities. The condition also imposes a heavy financial burden, including the high costs of medical bills, medications, diagnostic tests, and rehabilitation therapies. These expenses, combined with the challenges of managing daily living, can make it difficult for patients to meet even their basic needs. Tasks such as driving, cooking, or completing household duties become significant barriers when physical limitations interfere with independence. Neuropathy is associated with multiple complications, including progressive nerve damage, worsening symptoms, declining physical function, and increased healthcare costs and utilization. Managing neuropathy typically involves multiple medications, yet patients frequently encounter challenges such as adverse side effects, financial burdens, and inconsistent access to care. Effective healthcare for neuropathy patients requires a systematic approach that addresses both symptom management and the promotion of overall patient well-being.

**Keywords:** Diagnostic tests, Health promotion, Holistic approach, Neuropathy, Rehabilitation services, Relationship strain, Sensory disturbances, Social isolation.

## INTRODUCTION

Peripheral nerve damage is a manifestation of neuropathy, a condition that can have a significant impact on a person's life in a variety of ways. The impact of neuropathy on an individual can be profound, affecting various aspects of their daily life, physical health, emotional well-being, and social interactions. Here is a breakdown of the impact of neuropathy on an individual [1].

**Sumaira Kanwal & Shazia Perveen**

## Physical Symptoms and Functional Limitations

Neuropathy often manifests with symptoms such as pain, numbness, tingling, weakness, and sensory disturbances. These symptoms can interfere with mobility, balance, and coordination, making it challenging for individuals to perform everyday tasks such as walking, standing or grasping objects. People experiencing neuropathy symptoms often struggle with daily activities, particularly due to reduced mobility. For instance, Chemotherapy-Induced Peripheral Neuropathy (CIPN) results from nerve damage caused by chemotherapy and typically presents in a 'stocking-glove' pattern [2]. This condition can lead to tingling, discomfort, and pain, significantly impairing quality of life. To better understand its impact, the European Organization for Research and Treatment of Cancer (EORTC) developed a questionnaire that evaluates how these symptoms affect functional abilities, revealing a strong correlation between patient-reported experiences and clinical assessments. Moreover, studies indicate that approximately two-thirds of individuals with peripheral neuropathy experience pain [3].

## Decreased Quality of Life

Neuropathic symptoms can significantly impair an individual's quality of life, leading to discomfort, distress, and diminished overall well-being. Chronic pain, in particular, can be debilitating, affecting sleep, appetite, mood, and cognitive function, and contributing to fatigue, irritability, and social withdrawal. Suffering from neuropathy can significantly reduce a person's quality of life, mainly due to persistent symptoms and dysfunction. Studies have shown that neuropathy is often linked to a significant decline in quality of life, especially among cancer survivors affected by CIPN [4]. Unfortunately, the effects of neuropathy often persist long after treatment has ended. For example, studies have shown that about 31% of patients receiving oxaliplatin chemotherapy go on to report neurologically related problems after five years. In addition, coping with constant pain and disability can lead to a stronger feeling of helplessness and frustration, making life more difficult [5].

## Impact on Mental Health

Living with neuropathy can take a toll on an individual's mental health, causing anxiety, depression, and feelings of helplessness or hopelessness. Coping with chronic pain and physical limitations can exacerbate stress and emotional distress, leading to mood disorders and impaired coping mechanisms. Constant anxiety and restrictions can lead to severe emotional distress as individuals may feel disconnected from activities they once enjoyed. Studies have found that individuals with diabetes and neuropathy frequently experience higher levels of depression, and fear of falling often causes them to avoid physical activity, potentially worsening their condition. The relationship between physical symptoms and mental health highlights the importance of an integrative approach that addresses both the physical and emotional aspects of neuropathy [6].

## Social Isolation and Relationship Strain

The effects of neuropathy on daily life are complex and distressing, as individuals often struggle to engage in social activities, maintain friendships, or fulfill family roles. These challenges can lead to social withdrawal due to feelings of discomfort or fear of harm. Feelings of embarrassment, frustration, or inadequacy may emerge from an inability to participate in previously enjoyed activities or meet social expectations, often resulting in social isolation and loneliness [7]. Family and friends might feel stress regarding the patient's withdrawal because they remain unaware of the actual condition their loved one faces. People suffering from neuropathic symptoms may experience worsened feelings of loneliness and inadequacy due to visible signs of their condition. People who have suffered from cancer state that enduring post-treatment neuropathy symptoms isolate them from their social circle and create intensified feelings of anxiety and sadness [8].

## Financial Burden

For patients, the condition of neuropathy brings financial hardship to their lives. Neuropathy treatment costs patients a lot of money, since it requires constant visits from doctors, payment for tests, as well as physical rehabilitation services. Individuals who lose their jobs because of disability or reduced work capacity often encounter serious financial hardship, making it difficult to meet basic needs. Managing neuropathic symptoms adds to this burden, as out-of-pocket spending on medications, diagnostic tests, and rehabilitation quickly escalates. Over time, the combined weight of mounting medical bills, therapy fees, and lost wages places a substantial economic strain on patients and their families. This financial stress, in turn, can heighten anxiety and depression, further compromising overall health [9].

## Challenges in Daily Living

People with neuropathy often find everyday activities—such as driving, cooking, and completing household tasks—challenging, leading to increased dependence on others and making even simple routines feel nearly impossible. Moreover, patients also experience strong pain, along with weakness and unusual sensations. Understanding and performing tasks such as typing and copying written material is challenging, as they require both fine motor coordination and functional skills [10].

## Risk of Complications

Neuropathy complicates the treatment process, as it can lead to serious complications such as infections, progressive nerve deterioration, accidental injuries, and treatment failure—often worsened by inadequate management or lack of care. These complications may further result in disabilities, increasing both healthcare costs and the demand for medical services. As such, neuropathy represents a significant clinical challenge that makes the overall condition more difficult to manage [11]. Diabetic neuropathy is particularly critical because affected individuals often have reduced sensation in their legs, which prevents them from noticing injuries or lesions that might otherwise seem minor. This lack of awareness can lead to serious complications, including infections and, ultimately, amputation. Scientific studies show that foot ulcers occur up to ten times more frequently in individuals with diabetic neuropathy than in those without diabetes. Beyond limb issues, neuropathy also causes functional problems, including nerve damage that leads to symptoms such as orthostatic hypotension, digestive disturbances, and bladder dysfunction. These complications significantly impact daily life and require specialized care. For patients with autonomic neuropathy, symptom management often involves dietary adjustments and the use of compression garments to help control blood pressure and improve quality of life [12].

## Higher Cost of Treatment

Managing neuropathy is challenging both physically and emotionally. Patients must adhere to strict treatment plans that often include medication, physical therapy, and lifestyle changes, including personal wellness activities. However, side effects from medications, financial difficulties, and limited access to healthcare services can make it difficult for patients to maintain consistent treatment. Treatment typically involves a combination of medications, physical therapy, and lifestyle modification programs. The complexity of pain management can further complicate medication schedules, as commonly prescribed drugs like gabapentin and pregabalin may cause side effects. Additionally, frequent medical appointments increase the time and financial burden on both patients and their families. Research also indicates that individuals with diabetic neuropathy often face barriers to care, such as transportation issues and financial constraints, which hinder their ability to manage their treatment effectively [13].

# CONCLUSION

Neuropathy negatively affects every fundamental aspect of a person's life—physical, emotional, social, and financial. Successfully managing neuropathy requires a comprehensive approach that combines symptom-targeted medication with strategies to enhance overall health and improve quality of life.

Patients with neuropathy face a range of challenges that demand appropriate solutions. This chapter analyzed key factors impacting daily life, including physical symptoms, limitations in everyday activities, reduced quality of life, mental health issues, social isolation, relationship stress, financial strain, and complications requiring medical care.

Neuropathy patients often suffer from unaddressed cognitive, emotional, and behavioral difficulties. Pain, numbness, and weakness can severely restrict their ability to perform even basic daily tasks, making a quality life unattainable. Emotional distress, coupled with physical limitations, can deepen negative thoughts and increase suicidal ideation. Anxiety and loneliness are common as individuals withdraw from social interactions and activities.

Work capacity frequently declines, causing income loss and financial hardship. Recovering previous levels of function is challenging, and patients require practical support systems to manage both personal and household responsibilities—struggles shared with others facing similar social and family issues.

Despite effective treatments, diabetic neuropathy remains a serious complication that necessitates preventive efforts to avoid severe outcomes like foot ulcers and infections. Treatment plans combining physical therapy with emotional and physical support are essential, as medication alone is often insufficient.

Given the wide-ranging impact of neuropathy, it is crucial for healthcare providers, caregivers, and policymakers to fully understand its complexities. Studying the interrelated problems associated with neuropathy enables healthcare professionals to develop more effective, patient-centered care strategies.

# REFERENCES

[1] Zaki S, Alam MF, Sharma S, El-Ashker S, Ahsan M, Nuhmani S. Impact of concurrent exercise training on cardiac autonomic modulation, metabolic profile, body composition, cardiorespiratory fitness, and quality of life in type 2 diabetes with cardiac autonomic neuropathy: a randomized controlled trial. J Clin Med 2024; 13(13): 3910. [http://dx.doi.org/10.3390/jcm13133910] [PMID: 38999476]

[2] Johnson NE, Heatwole CR, Ferguson M, Sowden JE, Jeanat S, Herrmann DN. Patient identification of the symptomatic impact of charcot-marie-tooth disease type 1A. J Clin Neuromuscul Dis 2013; 15(1):

19-23.
[http://dx.doi.org/10.1097/CND.0b013e31829e22e3] [PMID: 23965405]

[3] Hamid R, Al-Wasiti E, Jabbar AM. Correlation between human BDNF rs6265 gene polymorphism and type-2 diabetes and diabetic peripheral neuropathy. Anaesth Pain Intensive Care 2024; 28(4): 752-6.
[http://dx.doi.org/10.35975/apic.v28i4.2517]

[4] Maria , Khan A, Rahat A, Haleem F, Khalid Z, Gulalai . Frequency of fall risk in patients with diabetic peripheral neuropathy and its impact on quality of life. Journal of Health and Rehabilitation Research 2024; 4(1): 825-30.
[http://dx.doi.org/10.61919/jhrr.v4i1.504]

[5] Dahl AA, Smeland KB, Eikeland S, *et al.* Distressed personality is associated with late adverse effects in long-term survivors of Hodgkin lymphoma. Acta Oncol 2024; 63: 600-6.
[http://dx.doi.org/10.2340/1651-226X.2024.40312] [PMID: 39099321]

[6] Reina-Bueno M, Palomo-Toucedo IC, Medina-Núñez MÁ, Munuera-Martínez PV, Castro-Méndez A, Vázquez-Bautista MC. Impact on the quality of life and physiological parameters in patients with diabetes mellitus. Appl Sci (Basel) 2021; 11(15): 6829.
[http://dx.doi.org/10.3390/app11156829]

[7] Sudo SZ, Montagnoli TL, Rocha BS, Santos AD, de Sá MPL, Zapata-Sudo G. Diabetes-induced cardiac autonomic neuropathy: impact on heart function and prognosis. Biomedicines 2022; 10(12): 3258.
[http://dx.doi.org/10.3390/biomedicines10123258] [PMID: 36552014]

[8] Alrawaili MS, Abuzinadah AR, AlShareef AA, *et al.* Serum SARM1 levels and diabetic peripheral neuropathy in type 2 diabetes: Correlation with clinical neuropathy scales and nerve conduction studies and impact of COVID-19 vaccination. Vaccines (Basel) 2024; 12(2): 209.
[http://dx.doi.org/10.3390/vaccines12020209] [PMID: 38400192]

[9] Yang C, Zhao X, An X, *et al.* Axonal transport deficits in the pathogenesis of diabetic peripheral neuropathy. Front Endocrinol (Lausanne) 2023; 14: 1136796.
[http://dx.doi.org/10.3389/fendo.2023.1136796] [PMID: 37056668]

[10] Avidos L, Magalhães A, Criado MB, Nogueira A. Severity of peripheral neuropathy, in different domains, in type II diabetic patients. Revista Ibero-Americana De Podologia 2024; 6(1): E0712024.
[http://dx.doi.org/10.36271/iajp.v6i1.71]

[11] Görgülü Ü, Çiftçi S, Polat Ü. Diyabetik nöropatinin yönetiminde güncel tedavi yaklaşımları ve hemşirelik bakımı. Sağlık Bilimlerinde Değer 2022; 12(3): 560-5.

[12] Liang J, Gong X, Hu X, *et al.* Integrated genetic analysis of diabetic complications: Bioinformatics insights into foot ulcers, neuropathy and peripheral artery disease. Int Wound J 2024; 21(2): e14748.
[http://dx.doi.org/10.1111/iwj.14748] [PMID: 38358067]

[13] Preston FG, Riley DR, Azmi S, Alam U. Painful diabetic peripheral neuropathy: practical guidance and challenges for clinical management. Diabetes Metab Syndr Obes 2023; 16: 1595-612.
[http://dx.doi.org/10.2147/DMSO.S370050] [PMID: 37288250]

# CHAPTER 19

# Impact of Neuropathy on Caregivers' Lives

**Abstract:** Caregivers of individuals with neuropathies face various challenges that can impact their physical, emotional, and social well-being. They often have to assist with daily activities, such as bathing and mobility, which can lead to physical strain and injuries. Emotionally, caregivers may experience helplessness, frustration, and anxiety while witnessing their loved ones suffer. Financially, the costs of medical care and assistive devices can strain budgets, especially if caregivers have to reduce their working hours to provide full-time care. Socially, caregivers may become isolated and struggle to maintain relationships and pursue personal interests. The stress of caregiving can also strain relationships and lead to health issues like hypertension and depression. However, seeking support through services like respite care and counseling can help caregivers cope with these challenges and maintain their own well-being.

**Keywords:** Caregivers, Challenges, Counseling, Physical strain, Social well-being.

## INTRODUCTION

The impact of neuropathies on caregivers' lives can be profound, affecting various aspects of their physical, emotional, and social well-being. Here are some ways in which neuropathies can impact caregivers [1]. The everyday responsibilities of caregiving become the primary difficulty that CGs face, requiring excessive time and energy. Individuals who engage in caregiver duties consist mainly of female relatives, including partners, sons and daughters, or daughters-in-law, sons, parents, siblings, friends, and distant relatives [2]. During 1986, the medical literature introduced the concept of caregiver burden, which focused on dementia patient care [3]. Research has shown that younger caregivers commonly abandon their educational studies, which affects their professional advancement in later life [4]. The survey revealed that caregiving duties have caused negative impacts on the professional lives of 51.3% of the participants. When caregivers have both good income and high socioeconomic standing, the impact of their financial constraints decreases.

Science confirms that a close relative's illness leads to significant distress, which causes worse health results in caregivers [5]. Results from the study show that 61.3% of study participants failed to take care of their health while providing care.

Sumaira Kanwal & Shazia Perveen

Research has confirmed that caregivers typically develop health risks due to their caregiving duties, which result in worsened physical status and intensified existing chronic diseases [6]. Dementia care providers experience depressive symptoms more frequently compared to other types of caregivers, according to research [7]. Lack of time during caregiving reduces self-care for family members who end up becoming vulnerable to health problems [8]. The study evidence reveals that caregiving creates general life disruptions because 65% of participants experienced modifications in their sleep patterns and eating behavior. Analysis of caregiver health effects through meta-analysis showed that depression and physical health complications are more prevalent among caregivers than in non-caregivers [9].

Multiple research papers present different findings because they recognize caregiving responsibilities as beneficial experiences. Different research reports indicate that caregivers may occasionally experience improved health conditions due to their caregiving experience. Particular groups of caregivers display pronounced levels of stress and clinical depression symptoms when caring for their family members. The caregiving role presents extensive challenges to caregivers who lack appropriate knowledge, skills, social support, and access to respite care and community services.

The occurrence of Care Burden (CB) depends on factors related to both the patient and the caregiver (CG). Caregiver-related elements include age, sex, health status, quality of sleep, educational background, occupational responsibilities or retirement status, expectations about the disease, and various medical, social, psychological, and legal challenges. Additionally, personal competencies and the level of support received from public health systems and private care institutions also influence the extent of care burden. Family background, together with the relationship between the caregiver and the client, as well as space in the patient's home and CG socioeconomic parameters and resilience, make up essential components for CB [10]. In most diseases, CB increases with disease duration and progression, and with the duration of care. The duration of healthcare, combined with proper comprehensive support systems, allows CB levels to achieve stability during end-stage conditions of dementia. Specific knowledge regarding patient and caregiver requirements, combined with personal support alongside medical assistance, helps caregivers face their daily caregiving obligations and enhances their life satisfaction. Neurological diagnosis together with disease severity and behavioral impairment and psychiatric symptoms increases the likelihood of caregivers falling into mental and somatic health problems while trying to manage their personal needs and occupational and social obligations and financial burden and restricted family life, and leisure. The evaluation of subjective and objective CB should occur immediately, and caregivers should receive personalized support.

**Physical Demands**

The care of patients with neuropathies typically requires assistance in completing daily routines, including bathing and dressing, and feeding, and helping with walking. Proper lifting techniques, together with appropriate assistive devices, should be used because physical strain and musculoskeletal injuries often develop when caregivers lift or transfer the individual. Many caregivers experience negative physical health results because depressive symptoms and poor mental health combine with the physical challenges of caring for someone unable to perform basic activities of daily living, including bathing and grooming tasks. The demanding responsibility of caring for another person typically results in augmented requirements for health treatment for the caregiver. Among caregivers, 11 percent indicate that caregiving made their physical health deteriorate [11]. The subjective well-being, together with the physical health of caregivers, generally falls below that of people who do not provide care [12, 13]. According to research from 2005, a substantial three-fifths of caregivers (60%) declared either poor or average health status, or they had one or more chronic illnesses and disability, while only one-third of non-caregivers reported this status [14]. The rate at which caregivers experienced chronic health issues such as heart attack/heart disease, together with cancer and diabetes, and arthritis, exceeded those of non-caregivers by 81% (45% *vs.* 24%) [15]. Physical medical conditions such as acid reflux and headaches, as well as pain from aching, affect caregivers at enhanced rates [16] while serious illness occurrences are more prevalent among caregivers [17] and they show increased obesity distributions and bodily pain levels [18]. Scientific evidence shows that caregiving reduces immune function, making sufferers more prone to infections and cancer development. Studies show that caregivers experience elevated stress hormone production by 23% and antibody deficiency amounts to 15% [19]. The wound healing process tends to be delayed among caregivers [20]. The physical strain of caregiving leads to health complications for caregivers who must offer care to bed-bound or dependent patients who need hands-on help with movement and bathing activities. The statistics show that ten percent of primary caregivers express physical exhaustion [21]. Stressful situations trigger cardiovascular reactions within caregivers that elevate their risk past noncaregivers for developing heart disease alongside hypertension [22]. Female caregivers who support individuals with neuropathic conditions tend to show increased risks of high blood pressure, along with diabetes and elevated cholesterol levels [23]. At the same time, women dedicating nine or more weekly hours to caring for their ill or disabled spouses witness a twofold enhanced heart disease risk [24].

## Emotional Stress

Caregiving for someone with neuropathies can be emotionally challenging. Witnessing a loved one experience pain, discomfort, or functional limitations due to their condition can evoke feelings of helplessness, frustration, sadness, and anxiety in caregivers. Additionally, the uncertainty surrounding the progression and management of neuropathic symptoms can contribute to caregiver stress and burnout. Family caregivers experience deteriorating psychological well-being because of their caregiving duties. Numerous mental health problems, including stress and anxiety as well as depression, affect family caregivers as they support fragile elderly people.

## Rising Caregiver Depression

Research studies repeatedly detect elevated depressive symptoms, which also lead to mental health issues in caregivers in comparison with individuals who do not provide care. Medical experts predict that between forty to seventy percent of caregivers experience clinical depression symptoms, while major depression affects between twenty-five percent to fifty percent of these persons [25]. When care recipients' functional abilities deteriorate, the amount of care burden experienced by caregivers and their depressive symptoms worsen [26]. People who care for dementia patients demonstrate greater clinical depression symptoms. Medical research indicates depression affects between 30% and 40% of caregivers who take care of individuals with dementia [27, 28]. The placement of patients within nursing homes fails to remedy depression and anxiety disorders, which caregivers already possess, and often these disorders become more severe. The degree of depression symptoms, along with anxiety, stays consistently high among caregivers after placing their relative in a facility [29]. Kingston reports that caregivers with depression tend to have additional anxiety disorders and substance abuse or dependence problems, and chronic medical conditions. Depression stands as one of the major health conditions that leads individuals to attempt suicide [30].

## Nursing Burdens & Caregiver Stress

Research indicates that caregivers experience increased stress than people who do not provide caregiving roles [31] while reporting feelings of frustration and anger, and being drained and guilty, and helpless from their caregiving duties [32]. Seven percent of caregivers have emotional stressors, and 26 percent recognize caregiving as an emotional burden for them. The frustration from inadequate care recipient recovery affects 13% of caregivers, according to a study [33]. Being a caregiver leads people to experience various effects, such as self-identity confusion, along with decreased self-esteem, alongside worry and uncertainty

[34]. Caregivers demonstrate inferior levels of self-acceptance, together with feelings of decreased effectiveness and lower control in their existence in comparison to non-caregiving peers [35, 36]. When caregivers lie down to sleep at night, approximately 22% experience exhaustion because many of them believe they cannot manage their entire caregiving tasks [37]. Persistently stressful situations faced by caregivers produce a higher danger of cognitive impairment, which affects their short-term memory and attention abilities and verbal IQ scores [38].

## Effect of Stress in Caregiving

The elevated stress levels of caregivers trigger them to use more alcohol, along with other substances. Research findings demonstrate that caregivers consume prescription and psychotropic drugs to a greater extent than individuals without caregiving roles [39]. Family members who provide care to others show more hostility compared to people who do not offer such support [40]. A spouse acting as a caregiver for an impaired relative who requires significant physical or cognitive assistance is at greater risk of experiencing depression and may be more likely to engage in harmful behaviors toward their loved one

## Health Consequences

The continuous pressure of caregiving tasks creates health problems that result in high blood pressure, sleep problems, depression, as well as immune system decline among caregivers. Family caregivers who delay their own healthcare needs to focus on their care recipient face higher risks of health deterioration since they either keep their current problems active or are at risk for developing new health conditions. Female caregivers, who make up approximately two-thirds of all unpaid caregivers, tend to experience worse outcomes than male caregivers regarding depressive symptoms and anxiety levels, along with subjective well-being and life satisfaction, and physical health status, according to statistical research. Research indicates that women whose spouse receives care during more than 36-hour weekly periods face significantly elevated risks for mental health problems. Women surveyed at the national level showed that twenty-one percent of these patients received mammograms less frequently [41].

## Financial Burden

People with neuropathies typically need ongoing healthcare that includes medical treatments with medications, together with doctor visits to conduct diagnostic tests, and possibly require assistive devices and house modifications. Caring for a family member with neuropathies often leads to financial pressure on caregivers since they need to pay for associated costs while possibly cutting down their work hours or quitting jobs to be full-time caregivers. The cost of medical care, together with medicine prescriptions and healthcare instruments, and residence redesigns, creates significant financial burdens for caregivers. The cost of care tends to become expensive, particularly when it involves long-term treatment of chronic illnesses or disabilities. The care tasks often force both caregivers and patients into financial hardship because these care responsibilities often lead them to reduce work hours or abandon their jobs to offer full-time care, which causes earnings and retirement savings to decrease. Working caregivers implemented adjustments to their work hours or unpaid absences from work at a rate of 61%, according to the report, leading to adverse effects on their financial situation. Research results revealed that caregivers experience a loss of $303,880 throughout their lives because they take shorter working hours or exit work or retire early for caregiving duties. The economic pressure faced by caregivers intensifies because of their caregiving demands and results in added medical costs experienced by caregivers themselves. This research shows that caregivers typically develop more long-term sicknesses and suffer depression and increased nervousness, thereby generating additional expenses for healthcare. The financial consequences of caregiving responsibilities affect different individuals differently. Those who are low-income, along with women and minority people deal with excessive financial difficulties because of their caregiving duties. The chapter reports that low-income and minority caregivers face greater risks of serious economic issues from fulfilling their caregiving duties.

## Social Isolation

The demands of caregiving create barriers for caregivers who wish to participate in social events and keep social relationships, and follow their personal interests. Group certification as a caregiver often results in social isolation, which causes feelings of loneliness because caregivers find limited time to practice self-care and maintain meaningful outside relationships. Caregiving tends to create stress on both familial and friendship-based relationships and partnerships. The pressures and requirements of tending to someone else can create tensions between caregivers and their families, as well as broken communication channels and growing negative emotions about the situation. Caring responsibilities often cause guilt, together with resentment, because caregivers believe their duties prevent them from reaching their personal life objectives [41].

## Need for Support

People who care for individuals with neuropathies can improve their situation when they receive access to important support services, which include emergency care programs and counseling sessions as well as care provider support networks and education materials. External support systems consisting of healthcare professionals and social services together with other caregivers enable caregivers to face caregiving difficulties while preserving their personal well-being. Lack of financial support and resources exacerbates the burden on caregivers. Caregivers often fail to discover assistance programs or face problems when trying to access the available programs.

## CONCLUSION

The care of individuals with neuropathies produces major positive and negative effects on caregivers across their physical health and emotional state, and their financial situation and social structures, and interpersonal connections. Healthcare providers must identify caregiver needs to build their ability to deliver quality caregiving and preserve their health, along with their well-being. Evidence stemming from this analysis can serve as a foundation to create support systems for caregivers across Australia. Healthcare providers need readiness to support caregivers regarding their psychological well-being, along with their social needs and health status requirements. Health care professionals must emphasize that caregiving includes valuable traits such as feeling proud as well as having purpose and satisfaction from helping dear ones. Caregivers face different financial challenges that stem from healthcare costs and job income loss, as well as expenditures on health services. The solution demands government strategy development alongside business backing and better availability of financial help for care providers. Caring responsibility creates diverse financial difficulties for caregivers, which include direct costs and both financial and health-related costs. Policy changes, together with employer backing alongside financial resource availability improvements, represent what is required to tackle these challenges experienced by caregivers. The resource highlights insufficient access to caregiver financial support programs while demanding policy adjustments to resolve this problem.

## REFERENCES


[1] Schneider J, Murray J, Banerjee S, Mann A. EUROCARE: a cross-national study of co-resident spouse carers for people with Alzheimer's disease: I—factors associated with carer burden. Int J Geriatr Psychiatry 1999; 14(8): 651-61. [http://dx.doi.org/10.1002/(SICI)1099-1166(199908)14:8<651::AID-GPS992>3.0.CO;2-B] [PMID: 10489656]

[2] George LK, Gwyther LP. Caregiver well-being: a multidimensional examination of family caregivers of demented adults. Gerontologist 1986; 26(3): 253-9. [http://dx.doi.org/10.1093/geront/26.3.253] [PMID: 3721232]

[3] Adelman RD, Tmanova LL, Delgado D, Dion S, Lachs MS. Caregiver Burden. JAMA 2014; 311(10): 1052-60. [http://dx.doi.org/10.1001/jama.2014.304] [PMID: 24618967]

[4] Ribeiro AS, de Carvalho BM, Costa AK, *et al.* The impact on the quality of life and burden over

caregivers of young patients with epilepsy in the transition process: an experience report. Arquivos de Neuro-Psiquiatria 2024 Oct;82(S 02): A120.

[5] Acaster S, Lo SH, Nestler-Parr S. A survey exploring caregiver burden and health-related quality of life in hereditary transthyretin amyloidosis. Orphanet Journal of Rare Diseases 2023 Jan 26;18(1): 17.

[6] Adler R, Mehta R. Catalyzing technology to support family caregiving. National Alliance for Caregiving 2014; pp. 1-18.

[7] Deshields TL, Rihanek A, Potter P, *et al.* Psychosocial aspects of caregiving: perceptions of cancer patients and family caregivers. Support Care Cancer 2012; 20(2): 349-56. [http://dx.doi.org/10.1007/s00520-011-1092-1] [PMID: 21298291]

[8] Bakas T, Burgener SC. Predictors of emotional distress, general health, and caregiving outcomes in family caregivers of stroke survivors. Top Stroke Rehabil 2002; 9(1): 34-45. [http://dx.doi.org/10.1310/GN0J-EXVX-KX0B-8X43] [PMID: 14523721]

[9] Roth DL, Fredman L, Haley WE. Informal caregiving and its impact on health: a reappraisal from population-based studies. Gerontologist 2015; 55(2): 309-19. [http://dx.doi.org/10.1093/geront/gnu177] [PMID: 26035608]

[10] Park B, Kim SY, Shin JY, *et al.* Prevalence and predictors of anxiety and depression among family caregivers of cancer patients: a nationwide survey of patient–family caregiver dyads in Korea. Support Care Cancer 2013; 21(10): 2799-807. [http://dx.doi.org/10.1007/s00520-013-1852-1] [PMID: 23729225]

[11] Pinquart M, Sörensen S. Differences between caregivers and noncaregivers in psychological health and physical health: A meta-analysis. Psychol Aging 2003; 18(2): 250-67. [http://dx.doi.org/10.1037/0882-7974.18.2.250] [PMID: 12825775]

[12] Ransmayr G, Hermann P, Sallinger K, *et al.* Caregiving and caregiver burden in dementia home care: results from the prospective dementia registry (PRODEM) of the Austrian alzheimer society. J Alzheimers Dis 2018; 63(1): 103-14. [http://dx.doi.org/10.3233/JAD-170657] [PMID: 29614643]

[13] How Do Family Caregivers Fare? A Closer Look at Their Experiences (Data Profile, Number 3). Washington, DC: Georgetown University 2005.

[14] Schulz R, O'Brien AT, Bookwala J, Fleissner K. Psychiatric and physical morbidity effects of dementia caregiving: prevalence, correlates, and causes. Gerontologist 1995; 35(6): 771-91. [http://dx.doi.org/10.1093/geront/35.6.771] [PMID: 8557205]

[15] Ho A, Collins S, Davis K, Doty M. A look at working-age caregivers roles, health concerns, and need for support (issue brief). New York, NY: The Commonwealth Fund 2005.

[16] Evercare® Study of Caregivers in Decline: A Close-up Look at the Health Risks of Caring for a Loved One Bethesda, MD: National Alliance for Caregiving and Minnetonka. MN: Evercare 2006.

[17] Shaw WS, Patterson TL, Semple SJ, *et al.* Longitudinal analysis of multiple indicators of health decline among spousal caregivers. Ann Behav Med 1997; 19(2): 101-9. [http://dx.doi.org/10.1007/BF02883326] [PMID: 9603684]

[18] Barrow S, Harrison RA. Unsung heroes who put their lives at risk? Informal caring, health and neighbourhood attachment. J Public Health (Oxf) 2005; 27(3): 292-7. [http://dx.doi.org/10.1093/pubmed/fdi038] [PMID: 15985447]

[19] Glaser R, Kiecolt-Glaser JK. Chronic stress modulates the virus-specific immune response to latent herpes simplex virus Type 1. Ann Behav Med 1997; 19(2): 78-82. [http://dx.doi.org/10.1007/BF02883323] [PMID: 9603681]

[20] Vitaliano PP, Zhang J, Scanlan JM. Is caregiving hazardous to one's physical health? A meta-analysis. Psychol Bull 2003; 129(6): 946-72. [http://dx.doi.org/10.1037/0033-2909.129.6.946] [PMID: 14599289]

[21] Kiecolt-Glaser JK, Marucha PT, Mercado AM, Malarkey WB, Glaser R. Slowing of wound healing by psychological stress. Lancet 1995; 346(8984): 1194-6. [http://dx.doi.org/10.1016/S0140-6736(95)92899-5] [PMID: 7475659]

[22] How Do Family Caregivers Fare? A Closer Look at Their Experiences (Data Profile, Number 3). Washington, DC: Georgetown University 2005.

[23] King AC, Oka RK, Young DR. Ambulatory blood pressure and heart rate responses to the stress of work and caregiving in older women. J Gerontol 1994; 49(6): M239-45. [http://dx.doi.org/10.1093/geronj/49.6.M239] [PMID: 7963275]

[24] Lee S, Colditz GA, Berkman LF, Kawachi I. Caregiving and risk of coronary heart disease in U.S. women. Am J Prev Med 2003; 24(2): 113-9. [http://dx.doi.org/10.1016/S0749-3797(02)00582-2] [PMID: 12568816]

[25] Prasad F, Hahn MK, Chintoh AF, *et al.* Depression in caregivers of patients with schizophrenia: a scoping review. Social psychiatry and psychiatric epidemiology 2024 Jan;59(1): 1-23.

[26] How Do Family Caregivers Fare? A Closer Look at Their Experiences (Data Profile, Number 3). Washington, DC: Georgetown University 2005.

[27] Marks NF, Lambert JD, Choi H. Transitions to caregiving, gender, and psychological well-being: A prospective U.S. national study. J Marriage Fam 2002; 64(3): 657-67. [http://dx.doi.org/10.1111/j.1741-3737.2002.00657.x]

[28] How Do Family Caregivers Fare? A Closer Look at Their Experiences (Data Profile, Number 3). Washington, DC: Georgetown University 2005.

[29] Vitaliano PP, Echeverria D, Yi J, Phillips PEM, Young H, Siegler IC. Psychophysiological mediators of caregiver stress and differential cognitive decline. Psychol Aging 2005; 20(3): 402-11. [http://dx.doi.org/10.1037/0882-7974.20.3.402] [PMID: 16248700]

[30] U.S. Department of Health and Human Services. (1998). Informal Caregiving: Compassion in Action. (Based on data from the National Survey of Families and Households [NSFH]), Washington, DC: Author.

[31] Evercare® Study of Caregivers in Decline: A Close-up Look at the Health Risks of Caring for a Loved One Bethesda, MD: National Alliance for Caregiving and Minnetonka. MN: Evercare 2006.

[32] Kantanis A, Pelantaki M, Fountaki ML, *et al.* Stress and quality of life in caregivers of patients with multiple sclerosis. Medicina 2024 Jun 24;60(7): 1033.

[33] Beach SR, Schulz R, Williamson GM, Miller LS, Weiner MF, Lance CE. Risk factors for potentially harmful informal caregiver behavior. J Am Geriatr Soc 2005; 53(2): 255-61. [http://dx.doi.org/10.1111/j.1532-5415.2005.53111.x] [PMID: 15673349]

[34] National Alliance for Caregiving & AARP. Caregiving in the US Washington. DC: Author 2004.

[35] Johnson RW, Wiener JM. A profile of older americans and their caregivers (occasional paper number 8). Washington, DC: The Urban Institute 2006.

[36] Pinquart M, Sörensen S. Gender differences in caregiver stressors, social resources, and health: an updated meta-analysis. J Gerontol B Psychol Sci Soc Sci 2006; 61(1): P33-45. [http://dx.doi.org/10.1093/geronb/61.1.P33] [PMID: 16399940]

[37] Cannuscio CC, Jones C, Kawachi I, Colditz GA, Berkman L, Rimm E. Reverberations of family illness: a longitudinal assessment of informal caregiving and mental health status in the Nurses' Health Study. Am J Public Health 2002; 92(8): 1305-11. [http://dx.doi.org/10.2105/AJPH.92.8.1305] [PMID: 12144989]

[38] Evercare® Study of Caregivers in Decline: A Close-up Look at the Health Risks of Caring for a Loved One Bethesda, MD: National Alliance for Caregiving and Minnetonka. MN: Evercare 2006.

[39] Hajek A, Kretzler B, König HH. Informal caregiving, loneliness and social isolation: A systematic

review. Int J Environ Res Public Health 2021; 18(22): 12101.
[http://dx.doi.org/10.3390/ijerph182212101] [PMID: 34831857]

[40] Stone RI, Keigher SM. Toward an equitable, universal caregiver policy: the potential of financial supports for family caregivers. J Aging Soc Policy 1994; 6(1-2): 57-75.
[http://dx.doi.org/10.1300/J031v06n01_05] [PMID: 10186860]

[41] Keefe, J. (2015) Supporting caregivers and caregiving in Canada. IHSPR Policy Rounds – Caring for Caregivers (Webinar, Feb 26th, 2015).

# CHAPTER 20

# Ongoing Latest Research for Treatment of Inherited Neuropathies

**Abstract:** The medical research community continues to investigate the development of treatments for inherited neuropathies, particularly Charcot-Marie-Tooth disease (CMT), through various strategies aimed at symptom relief, disease progression management, and genetic defect correction. Medical research now focuses on four main directions: gene therapy, along with small molecule therapies and stem cell therapy, nerve growth factors, and combination therapies, as well as precision medicine and symptomatic treatments. The goal of gene therapy is to correct genetic abnormalities, whereas small-molecule drugs target specific cellular processes. Stem cell therapy demonstrates its ability to create new nerve tissue, while nerve growth factors help both nerve cells thrive and operate correctly. The combination therapy method focuses on treating multiple aspects of neuropathy pathology simultaneously, whereas precision medicine delivers treatments based on individual genetic profiles. Research into symptomatic treatments seeks to control both pain and other symptoms that affect patients with inherited neuropathies. The advancement of treatment methods for these conditions remains insufficient, although researchers continue their work together with patients in clinical trials to develop new therapies.

**Keywords:** Neuropathy, Precision medicine, Pathology, Social well-being, Slow disease progression.

## INTRODUCTION

Hereditary sensory and motor neuropathies, Charcot-Marie-Tooth disease, and familial amyloid polyneuropathy are hereditary peripheral neuropathies, genetic conditions that impact the peripheral nervous system. With an incidence of around 1 in 2,500, the most prevalent kind is hereditary sensory and motor neuropathy, commonly referred to as Charcot-Marie-Tooth disease (CMT). One of the most prevalent genetic disorders of the neurological system is inherited peripheral neuropathy. Undoubtedly, the most prevalent inherited neuropathy is Charcot-Marie-Tooth (CMT) disease, which was formerly classified as Hereditary Motor and Sensory Neuropathy (HMSN) [1]. While there are currently no particular treatments for CMT, several treatments have been proposed in recent years. Rehabilitative techniques continue to be the most effective therapy option for these individuals in clinical practice. There is significant disagreement over how

**Sumaira Kanwal & Shazia Perveen**

to rehabilitate CMT sufferers adequately. Genetically diverse conditions affecting the peripheral nerves, inherited neuropathies, commonly referred to as Charcot-Marie-Tooth (CMT) disease, cause severe and gradually worsening impairment in the course of an individual's life. The last three decades have seen the discovery of numerous molecular genetic pathways, which have paved the way for the development of a wide variety of medicines and ushered in an exciting era of medical discovery for this formerly incurable group of conditions. Several therapeutic modalities, including gene replacement and silencing therapies, as well as small-molecule medicines, are currently undergoing preclinical research, and a number of them have progressed to the clinical trial stage. Research into the treatment of inherited neuropathies, including conditions like Charcot-Marie-Tooth disease (CMT), is ongoing, with scientists exploring various approaches to alleviate symptoms, slow disease progression, and potentially reverse the underlying genetic defects [2]. Some of the latest areas of research include:

**Gene Therapy**: Approximately thirty years ago, a process known as "gene therapy" was developed. It helps repair damaged genes by either adding genes to counteract the disease-causing effects of faulty ones or replacing them with healthy genes. As a consequence, some proteins that are essential for the production of receptors, ion channels, neurotransmitters, and biochemical mediators—all of which are crucial for preserving the body's physiological conditions—are expressed more often. It offers several benefits over conventional pharmaceutical therapies, including the ability to identify genetic targets rather than only addressing illness symptoms, which makes it relatively more effective. Gene therapy is the process of introducing gene material into a patient, usually by transmissible viruses. To mediate the delivery of genes to various cell types, a wide variety of viral vectors and vector capsid serotypes have been created. Virus vector gene therapy offers the benefits of being a one-time medication with long-lasting effects and the ability to cross both the Blood-Nerve Barrier (BNB) and the Blood-Brain Barrier (BBB). Gene therapy aims to correct the genetic mutations responsible for inherited neuropathies. This approach involves delivering normal copies of the faulty genes into affected cells to restore their function. Recent advancements in gene editing technologies such as CRISPR/Cas9 hold promise for more precise and efficient gene correction. Types of hereditary peripheral neuropathy treatments include gene therapy. There are three kinds of IPN treatments based on the method of inheritance. The delivery of a functioning gene, known as gene replacement, was used to compensate for the absence of a functional protein in cases of recessively inherited conditions. The illness phenotype of dominantly inherited IPN was improved by using the neuroprotective gene NT-3. The study confirmed that mutant allele-specific techniques successfully decrease gain-of-toxicity mutant proteins in cases of dominantly inherited IPN. The normalization of PMP22 expression for CMT1A requires multiple methods because CMT1A results from the duplication of the PMP22 gene. Researchers have identified two methods to effectively reduce protein levels in living organisms by disrupting the TATA-box, combined with antisense oligonucleotides (ASOs) or miRNAs targeting the 3'-untranslated region (3'-UTR) of PMP22.

- **Small Molecule Therapies**: Researchers are investigating small-molecule drugs that can target specific cellular pathways involved in neuropathy development. These drugs may help improve nerve function, reduce nerve damage, or enhance nerve regeneration. Drug repurposing efforts, where existing drugs approved for other conditions are tested for efficacy in neuropathies, are also ongoing. The last common pathway of axonal degeneration, which is a fundamental mechanism in axonal CMTs and a subsequent consequence in demyelinating CMT forms, is the focus of the majority of pharmacological therapy attempts for CMT neuropathies. It consistently corresponds with impairment and is a useful therapeutic target. Medically targetable pathways are identified when more pathways linked to axonal damage and degeneration are revealed. Preclinical and clinical testing are now underway for several conditions, including CMT1 and CMT2. Common features of CMT neuropathies include deficiencies in axonal transport, changes in mitochondrial dynamics, programmed axon degeneration, and delayed axon regeneration. These conditions provide potential for medication-based treatments, which are covered in the sections that follow for typical CMT types [3].

**Stem Cell Therapy**: Embryonic cells, known as stem cells, possess the capacity to differentiate into mature cells and self-renew. Tissue growth, development, and homeostasis all depend on them. Stem cells may be divided into two subtypes based on their developmental stages: adult stem cells and Embryonic Stem Cells (ESCs). ESCs that originate from the inner cell mass of blastocyst-stage embryos before gastrulation are the best example of pluripotent stem cell therapy because they can become cells of all three germ layers, including ectoderm, mesoderm, and endoderm. Adult stem cells demonstrate both cell differentiation capabilities according to their lineage origins, and they protect neural tissues primarily through hematopoietic stem cells and mesenchymal stem cells. The neuroprotective effect predominantly results from paracrine bystander effects, which consist of three main processes: transmitter reestablishment, neural and synaptic integration, and the formation of new neural connections, while maintaining tissue plasticity and secreting survival-enhancing and neurotrophic factors. Research shows that stem cell therapy has the ability to restore damaged nerves in individuals with inherited neuropathic conditions. Scientists continue to investigate two types of stem cells, namely mesenchymal stem cells and induced pluripotent stem cells, because they possess the capacity to transform into nerve cells while integrating with the nervous system. Though they have several cell types, HSCs (Hematopoietic Stem Cells) exclusively develop into myeloid or lymphoid blood cells. Progenitor cells that are exclusive to a certain tissue are oligopotent stem cells that possess the ability to repair or regenerate in that tissue. Because they need gene insertion procedures and induce oncogenesis, iPSCs (induced Pluripotent Stem Cells), which are pluripotent cells, have limited therapeutic promise. MSCs (mesenchymal stem cells) are capable of differentiating into a wide range of cell types among the several types of stem cells. MSCs can replace or repair fibroblasts, brain cells, photoreceptor cells, and corneal epithelial cells [4].

- **Nerve Growth Factors**: Nerve growth factors are proteins that promote the growth, survival, and function of nerve cells. Studies are investigating the therapeutic potential of delivering nerve growth factors directly to affected nerves to stimulate regeneration and repair. Neurons in the Peripheral Nervous System (PNS) and cholinergic neurons in the Central Nervous System (CNS) depend on nerve growth factors for both development and phenotypic maintenance. The conventional neurotrophic model posits that NGF is generated in target tissues, released, and then bound by specific receptors on nerve terminals. It is then retrogradely carried to the neuron body, where it performs its neurotrophic function. With pro-apoptotic and neurotrophic properties, the mature, active form of NGF is derived from the proteolytic cleavage of a precursor form (ProNGF), which plays significant roles in both development and adult life [5].

**Combination Therapies**: Some researchers are exploring combination therapies that target multiple aspects of neuropathy pathology simultaneously. For example, a combination of drugs may aim to reduce inflammation, improve mitochondrial function, and promote nerve regeneration to achieve synergistic effects. When single treatments are either ineffective or constrained by dose-related side effects, combination therapy is commonly employed in clinical settings. However, it has also been demonstrated in animal models that several central and peripheral processes underpinning NP coexist and may be targets for pharmacological interventions. Therefore, employing medication combinations to target multiple pathways at once may be more beneficial than using a single agent to target this mechanism. Notably, this idea has been validated by numerous medication combination analyses using an animal model of neuropathic pain. Additionally, no one mechanism can be linked to a particular patient's NP condition. Therefore, there is a greater probability of obtaining adequate relief for pain when medication combinations with potential complementary activities are used. Two trials investigated the treatment of CMT1A with PTX3003, a combination therapy comprising sorbitol, baclofen, and naltrexone.

- **Precision Medicine Approaches**: With advances in genetic sequencing and an increasing understanding of disease mechanisms, there is a growing interest in personalized or precision medicine approaches for inherited neuropathies. Tailoring treatments to individual genetic profiles and disease characteristics may lead to more effective therapies. A therapeutic method that takes individual variation into account, precision medicine (also known as customized or stratified medicine) aims to provide a course of therapy that is specifically tailored to each patient. The strategy aims to provide suitable treatments at optimal dosages to the right patients at proper times in order to improve health outcomes while minimizing costs. Through precision medicine, healthcare professionals can mitigate the impact of neurobehavioral diseases by providing targeted treatments, including medications, neuromodulation devices, and behavioral therapies, to patients who are most likely to benefit from them. The US National Institutes of Health's (NIH) Precision Medicine Initiative defines precision medicine as a disease prevention and treatment method that analyzes how genes, environment, and lifestyle variables differ between individuals.
- **Symptomatic Treatments**: Scientists continue their work on disease-modifying therapies while also researching treatments for the symptomatic management of inherited neuropathy symptoms, which include pain, muscle weakness, sensory disturbances, and others. Medical interventions combine drugs with physical therapy and orthopedic treatments, in addition to assistive devices for management. Scientific studies are challenging the former belief that CMT patients do not experience pain by showing that pain often occurs in CMT neuropathy. The pain characteristics in CMT patients include both neuropathic pain and nociceptive pain. The recent practical guidelines from the European Federation of Neurological Societies task force should serve as the basis for pharmacological medications treating neuropathic pain [6].

## CONCLUSION

The development of treatments for inherited neuropathies has made significant progress, although most treatments exist at preclinical or early clinical stages. Research expansion, combined with clinical and scientific cooperation and patient trial participation, will drive field progress and lead to enhanced treatment outcomes for individuals with inherited neuropathy. The world is witnessing evolving times, which lead to significant progress in creating new therapy options for peripheral neurological disorders, being developed steadily. The pharmaceutical industry has developed siRNA and ASO treatments that are now available commercially for treating porphyria and hA-TTR. Research about TTR gene-targeting CRISPR-Cas9 genome editing therapy exists for treating patients with hA-TTR. Novel therapies targeting DNA and mRNA are currently being tested for Charcot-Marie-Tooth disease because of their proven success in treating hA-TTR and porphyria. Hereditary neuropathy treatment probably requires the combined use of gene therapy with expression therapy, along with conventional pharmaceutical interventions.

## REFERENCES

[1] Rudnik-Schöneborn S, Auer-Grumbach M, Senderek J. Charcot-Marie-Tooth disease and hereditary motor neuropathies – Update 2020. Med Genetik 2020; 32(3): 207-19. [http://dx.doi.org/10.1515/medgen-2020-2038]

[2] Kobak J, Tyczyńska M, Forma A, *et al.* Optic nerve neuropathies – causative factors, methods of diagnostics, current and future possibilities of treatment. J Educ Health Sport 2022; 12(4): 44-61. [http://dx.doi.org/10.12775/JEHS.2022.12.04.004]

[3] Hu Y, Girdenytė M, Roest L, *et al.* Analysis of the contributing role of drug transport across biological barriers in the development and treatment of chemotherapy-induced peripheral neuropathy. Fluids Barriers CNS 2024; 21(1): 13. [http://dx.doi.org/10.1186/s12987-024-00519-7] [PMID: 38331886]

[4] Hermans EC, van Gerven CCE, Johnsen L, Tungen JE, Nijboer CH, de Theije CGM. Dietary LPC-bound *n*-3 LCPUFA protects against neonatal brain injury in mice but does not enhance stem cell therapy. Nutrients 2024; 16(14): 2252. [http://dx.doi.org/10.3390/nu16142252] [PMID: 39064695]

[5] Prautsch KM, Degrugillier L, Schaefer DJ, Guzman R, Kalbermatten DF, Madduri S. *Ex-vivo* stimulation of adipose stem cells by growth factors and fibrin-hydrogel assisted delivery strategies for treating nerve gap-injuries. Bioengineering (Basel) 2020; 7(2): 42. [http://dx.doi.org/10.3390/bioengineering7020042] [PMID: 32380789]

[6] Canals PC, Aguilar AG, Carter GT, *et al.* Patient reported outcomes using medical cannabis for managing pain in charcot-marie-tooth disease. Am J Hosp Palliat Care 2023; 40(11): 1163-7. [http://dx.doi.org/10.1177/10499091231158388] [PMID: 36793224]

# CHAPTER 21

# Crispr Technology as A Treatment Option for Inherited Neuropathies

**Abstract:** CRISPR technology holds promise as a potential treatment for inherited neuropathies, such as Charcot-Marie-Tooth disease (CMT), through gene correction, silencing, regulation, and cell therapy. Gene correction involves editing faulty DNA sequences, whereas gene silencing suppresses the expression of disease-causing genes. Gene regulation modulates gene expression levels related to neuropathy pathology. Cell therapy involves transplanting CRISPR-engineered cells to replace damaged cells with healthy ones. However, challenges hinder the widespread application of CRISPR technology in treating inherited neuropathies. These include the need for efficient and safe delivery of CRISPR components, minimizing off-target effects, and addressing ethical and regulatory considerations. Research efforts are underway to overcome these challenges and advance CRISPR technology for clinical applications in neuropathy treatment. Despite these obstacles, CRISPR therapies have the potential to revolutionize the management of debilitating inherited neuropathies.

**Keywords:** Cell therapy, CRISPR, Gene correction, Gene regulation, Gene silencing.

## INTRODUCTION

### CRISPR

"Clustered Regularly Interspaced Short Palindromic Repeats" (CRISPR) technology holds significant promise as a potential treatment option for inherited neuropathies, including conditions such as Charcot-Marie-Tooth disease (CMT). Gene therapy involves the deliberate insertion of a targeted gene into an organism's genome, resulting in changes that lead to therapeutic effects. Advances in genetics and bioengineering have enabled the engineering of vectors, including plasmids, nanoparticles, and viruses, to transfer extrachromosomal material into target cells. This advance has made the practice of gene therapy feasible [1]. There are three distinct forms of gene therapy: *in situ, in vivo,* and *ex vivo*. With *ex vivo* gene therapy, the disease phenotype is corrected by extracting the patient's impacted cells and genetically modifying them using the therapeutic gene or other techniques. The "corrected" cells are then infused back into the patient. However,

Sumaira Kanwal & Shazia Perveen

because the appropriateness of *ex vivo* gene therapy is based on the specific tissue involved, it cannot always be a well-planned strategy [2]. Over the last decades, many research studies have been conducted to study the possibility of applying CRISPR/Cas and nanotechnology in gene therapy. The low toxicity of nanotechnology, along with its controlled release, scalability, and targeted drug administration, makes it an attractive option for medical research. The CRISPR/Cas9 system is a significant tool for genome editing in molecular diagnostics and next-generation therapies. The emphasis of CRISPR technology lies in the field of gene editing, modification of gene regulation, and the cause of specific genetic alterations. The applications of the treatments give rise to possibilities beyond traditional therapy approaches in managing hereditary disorders. Research is currently being conducted on their efficacy for a range of genetic conditions, including Alzheimer's disease, Parkinson's disease, Huntington's disease, Duchenne muscular dystrophy, and cystic fibrosis [3].

## GENE CORRECTION

CRISPR-Cas9 and other CRISPR-based systems can precisely edit the DNA sequence of genes. In the context of inherited neuropathies, where mutations in specific genes lead to disease development, CRISPR technology can potentially correct these mutations by replacing or repairing the faulty gene sequence. For example, in CMT, where mutations in genes such as PMP22, GJB1, and MFN2 are implicated, CRISPR could be used to correct these mutations in the cells of affected individuals. Due to their loose structure and wide range of applications, several viral vectors have been developed to transfer or replace genes efficiently. Several types of viral vectors are used in gene therapy, such as lentiviral, adenoviral, retroviral, and adeno-associated viral vectors [4].

## GENE SILENCING

CRISPR systems can also be used to silence or inhibit the expression of disease-causing genes. In cases where a mutation cannot be corrected directly, suppressing the expression of the faulty gene may still alleviate symptoms or slow disease progression. What stands out is that the CRISPR system allows for targeting multiple sites using several sgRNAs and a single Cas9 enzyme. In addition, it employs one co-promoter to maintain the consistent expression of every sgRNA, thereby amplifying the method's efficiency. Some of the most typical genome editing techniques used include CRISPR/Cas, TALEN, and ZFN. These tools include gene expression changes, transcription, post-translational modification, and cell and nucleus entry [5].

## GENE REGULATION

CRISPR technology can be employed to modulate the expression levels of specific genes involved in neuropathy pathology. By regulating the activity of genes associated with nerve function, regeneration, or myelination, CRISPR-based approaches may promote therapeutic effects in inherited neuropathies. This technique is known as "genome editing" and involves altering specific parts of the genomes of living organisms. Genome editing technologies are founded on engineering endonucleases, which are nucleases that have sequence-specific DNA binding domains [6].

## CELL THERAPY

CRISPR-engineered cells, such as stem cells or other cell types, can be transplanted into affected individuals to deliver therapeutic gene edits or gene-regulatory elements. This approach could potentially replace damaged or dysfunctional cells with healthy, genetically corrected ones, restoring normal nerve function. While CRISPR technology holds great promise, several challenges need to be addressed before it can be widely applied as a treatment for inherited neuropathies. Parvoviruses are small, naked, single-stranded viruses classified under Parvoviridae. Among this family, Adeno-Associated viral Vectors (AAVs) are a prominent genus (or type) widely utilized in gene therapy. AAVs can primarily deliver transgene products to both dividing and non-dividing cells in an episomal form, but they require a helper virus particle, such as the herpes simplex virus, to take effect [7].

## DELIVERY

The efficient and safe delivery of CRISPR components, such as Cas9 protein and guide RNAs, to target cells in the nervous system remains a significant challenge. Strategies for targeted delivery to specific types of nerve cells need to be developed. One of the major challenges in viral vector-based gene therapy is identifying suitable viruses for specific cell types within the body. Over time, viruses may also undergo mutations, leading to the development of further diseases in the body [8]. The three genes that comprise the single-stranded genome of AAVs encode all the viral components needed for their life cycle. These genes, along with their associated regulatory elements like promoters and translation start sites, include rep (for replication), cap (for capsid), and aap (for assembly). These viruses are a better choice for gene transfer because they are less likely to spread illness [9]. Lentivirus Vectors (LV) comprise single-stranded RNA (ssRNA) that can express and transport large transgenes. It can infect cells that divide as well as those that do not. Viral genes, such as gag, pol, and rev, are removed to make lentivirus vectors safer. These are believed to be harmless viruses and serve as a valuable tool for studying gene expression, as they can integrate at random locations [10].

## OFF-TARGET EFFECTS

CRISPR editing may inadvertently modify unintended genomic sites, leading to off-target effects. Minimizing off-target effects and ensuring the specificity of CRISPR edits are critical for the safety and efficacy of therapeutic applications. The CRISPR system has numerous potential applications, including cell imaging, gene expression, genome editing, and epigenetic regulation. In gene-editing techniques, a PAM sequence that consists of NGG or NAG nucleotides is required to bind to the target sequence for the spCas9 protein. The nuclease may interact with the scaffold RNA domain of sgRNAs, which comprises approximately 20 nucleotides that target the gene. The target sequence is guided by sgRNAs to the Cas9 nuclease [11]. In recent years, genome editing techniques have been used to cure diseases. Investigation of gene function and regulatory sequences that will facilitate target locus knockout is enabled through these systems. These systems also enable the construction of models for inherited disorders, which may lead to the development of new treatment modalities. Many of the structures in these systems mediate specific, crucial functional characteristics [12].

## ETHICAL AND REGULATORY CONSIDERATIONS

As with any emerging technology, ethical and regulatory frameworks must be established to govern the use of CRISPR-based therapies, including considerations of informed consent, equitable access, and potential long-term consequences. Another alternative to achieve effective gene delivery is encapsulation or conjugating of genetic material, such as RNA, DNA, and siRNA, with nanoparticle NPs [13]. AD is one of the leading neurodegenerative diseases, with the most prominent form of dementia. The initial symptoms include deteriorating cognitive functions and impaired memory, eventually leading to motor system failure [14, 15]. Of the neurodegenerative disorders, PD is the most prevalent form. Selective cell death happens in the substantia nigra pars compacta dopaminergic neurons. That leads to the production of α-syncline in Lewy bodies [16]. Hereditary neurological disorders are Huntington's Disease (HD), characterized by chorea, a movement disorder, along with anxiety biopsies taken from. There have been some pieces of evidence of oxidative stress and mitochondrial defects in patients with neurodegenerative disorders such as Huntington's. Additionally, dysfunctional electron transport chains are present in the brains of individuals with HD [17, 18].

## CONCLUSION

Despite these challenges, ongoing research efforts are focused on addressing these issues and advancing CRISPR technology towards clinical applications for inherited neuropathies. With further refinement and validation, Therapies utilizing CRISPR have the potential to transform the management of these incapacitating conditions. CRISPR has significantly contributed to the elucidation of drug resistance pathways and metastasis. CRISPR-based screening also helps identify crucial carcinogens. A better understanding of the mechanism underlying it is needed to design targeted gene response treatments, as well as identify genes and therapeutic targets. In clinical research, loss-of-function screening can aid in treatment decisions and assess the efficacy of associated drugs. With accurate gene editing, the cost of production can be minimized, and off-target effects can be prevented. Important clinical trials are being conducted on lymphoma, myeloma, and leukemia. CAR T-cell therapy is another advancement in gene therapy research with tremendous potential for treating many diseases. CRISPR and CAR T-cell therapy complement each other to enhance the accuracy of gene editing and strengthen the immune system's defense against affected tissues. However, the full potential of this technology has yet to be realized and faces several challenges: immune checkpoint inhibition, off-target effects, and maintaining the survival of modified T cells. Additionally, iPSC-based disease models, combined with CRISPR/Cas9 technology, can be utilized to explore a range of genetic diseases. Genetic mutations can be corrected using targeted genome editing made possible by CRISPR/Cas technology. Cas9 has been applied to modify gene expression and for gene knockouts. The expansion of Cas13 applications against target RNA has increased its therapeutic use. Efficient strategies for distributing this technology ensure that it provides higher therapeutic benefits with safety measures.

## REFERENCES

[1] Gonçalves GAR, Paiva RMA. Gene therapy: advances, challenges and perspectives. Einstein (Sao Paulo) 2017; 15(3): 369-75.
[http://dx.doi.org/10.1590/s1679-45082017rb4024] [PMID: 29091160]

[2] Wu X, He X, Liu F, *et al.* Development and clinical translation of *ex vivo* gene therapy. Comput Struct Biotechnol J 2022; 20: 2986-3003.
[http://dx.doi.org/10.1016/j.csbj.2022.06.015] [PMID: 35782737]

[3] Kaur G, Arora J, Sodhi AS, Bhatia S, Batra N. Nanotechnology and CRISPR/Cas-Mediated Gene Therapy Strategies: Potential Role for Treating Genetic Disorders. Mol Biotechnol 2024; 1-23.
[http://dx.doi.org/10.1007/s12033-024-01301-8] [PMID: 39446301]

[4] Hosseinkhani H, Domb AJ, Sharifzadeh G, Nahum V. Gene therapy for regenerative medicine. Pharmaceutics 2023; 15(3): 856.
[http://dx.doi.org/10.3390/pharmaceutics15030856] [PMID: 36986717]

[5] Shah P, Magar ND, Barbadikar KM. Current technological interventions and applications of CRISPR/Cas for crop improvement. Mol Biol Rep 2022; 49(6): 5751-70.
[http://dx.doi.org/10.1007/s11033-021-06926-5] [PMID: 34807378]

[6] Kumar R, Kaur A, Pandey A, Mamrutha HM, Singh GP. CRISPR-based genome editing in wheat: a comprehensive review and future prospects. Mol Biol Rep 2019; 46(3): 3557-69.

[http://dx.doi.org/10.1007/s11033-019-04761-3] [PMID: 30941642]

[7] Balakrishnan B, Jayandharan G. Basic biology of adeno-associated virus (AAV) vectors used in gene therapy. Curr Gene Ther 2014; 14(2): 86-100. [http://dx.doi.org/10.2174/1566523214666140302193709] [PMID: 24588706]

[8] Goswami R, Subramanian G, Silayeva L, *et al.* Gene therapy leaves a vicious cycle. Front Oncol 2019; 9: 297. [http://dx.doi.org/10.3389/fonc.2019.00297] [PMID: 31069169]

[9] Vachey G, Déglon N. CRISPR/Cas9-mediated genome editing for Huntington's disease. Methods Mol Biol 2018; 1780: 463-81. [http://dx.doi.org/10.1007/978-1-4939-7825-0_21] [PMID: 29856031]

[10] Malankhanova TB, Malakhova AA, Medvedev SP, Zakian SM. Modern genome editing technologies in Huntington's disease research. J Huntingtons Dis 2017; 6(1): 19-31. [http://dx.doi.org/10.3233/JHD-160222] [PMID: 28128770]

[11] Naso MF, Tomkowicz B, Perry WL III, Strohl WR. Adeno-associated virus (AAV) as a vector for gene therapy. BioDrugs 2017; 31(4): 317-34. [http://dx.doi.org/10.1007/s40259-017-0234-5] [PMID: 28669112]

[12] Milone MC, O'Doherty U. Clinical use of lentiviral vectors. Leukemia 2018; 32(7): 1529-41. [http://dx.doi.org/10.1038/s41375-018-0106-0] [PMID: 29654266]

[13] Tan W, Wang K, He X, *et al.* Bionanotechnology based on silica nanoparticles. Med Res Rev 2004; 24(5): 621-38. [http://dx.doi.org/10.1002/med.20003] [PMID: 15224383]

[14] Sonawane SK, Ahmad A, Chinnathambi S. Protein- capped metal nanoparticles inhibit tau aggregation in Alzheimer's disease. ACS Omega 2019; 4(7): 12833-40. [http://dx.doi.org/10.1021/acsomega.9b01411] [PMID: 31460408]

[15] Sánchez-López E, Ettcheto M, Egea MA, *et al.* Memantine loaded PLGA PEGylated nanoparticles for Alzheimer's disease: *in vitro* and *in vivo* characterization. J Nanobiotechnology 2018; 16(1): 32. [http://dx.doi.org/10.1186/s12951-018-0356-z] [PMID: 29587747]

[16] Bekris LM, Mata IF, Zabetian CP. The genetics of Parkinson disease. J Geriatr Psychiatry Neurol 2010; 23(4): 228-42. [http://dx.doi.org/10.1177/0891988710383572] [PMID: 20938043]

[17] Montoya A, Price BH, Menear M, Lepage M. Brain imaging and cognitive dysfunctions in Huntington's disease. J Psychiatry Neurosci 2006; 31(1): 21-9. [PMID: 16496032]

[18] Lin MT, Beal MF. Mitochondrial dysfunction and oxidative stress in neurodegenerative diseases. Nature 2006; 443(7113): 787-95. [http://dx.doi.org/10.1038/nature05292] [PMID: 17051205]

## CHAPTER 22

# Small Molecule Therapies for CMT1A

**Abstract:** The treatment of Charcot-Marie-Tooth (CMT) disease with small molecules includes PXT3003 alongside ascorbic acid, curcumin, tirasemtiv, EGCG, and HDAC inhibitors, which target key disease-related pathways. The therapeutic drug PXT3003 targets CMT1A patients by enhancing myelination while decreasing the excessive expression of the PMP22 gene. The antioxidant properties of ascorbic acid contribute to collagen synthesis and protect nerve cells from damage. The antioxidant and anti-inflammatory properties of curcumin, tirasemtiv, and EGCG may have beneficial effects on nerve health in CMT patients. HDAC inhibitors show promise for enhancing nerve function and promoting myelination in preclinical and early clinical studies of CMT treatment; however, their safety and long-term effectiveness require further investigation. Since each patient responds differently to these treatments, customized therapeutic plans must be developed. The field of CMT research relies on ongoing clinical trials to thoroughly investigate the potential benefits of these therapeutic approaches. Medical treatment using small molecules has shown promise in improving outcomes for those suffering from CMT, especially those with CMT1A.

These therapies target specific disease pathways that help protect nerve cells by providing antioxidant protection and nourishing neural tissue. Additional research is needed to fully determine the clinical effectiveness and long-term outcomes of these therapies in CMT treatment, emphasizing the importance of continued exploration and individualized approaches in CMT research.

Type 1A Charcot-Marie-Tooth disease (CMT1A) is the most common form of CMT, accounting for nearly half of all cases. It is caused by a duplication of the peripheral myelin protein 22 (PMP22) gene. Overexpression of the PMP22 protein activates the unfolded protein response, which overwhelms Schwann cell protein folding systems. Neurological progression occurs as Schwann cell death leads to secondary axonal degeneration and dysmyelination and demyelination of peripheral nerves.

To treat CMT1A, several distinct gene therapies have been developed in recent decades. Most are still in the preclinical stage, using animal models that overexpress PMP22. By directly or indirectly suppressing gene expression, the CMT1A genetic pathway can be reversed, allowing myelination to be restored and preventing axonal loss.

The rapid emergence of potential therapies highlights the need for clinically useful and treatment-responsive biomarkers. These biomarkers, along with sensitive clinical evaluation tools, will aid in the development and successful completion of upcoming clinical trials for CMT1A.

**Sumaira Kanwal & Shazia Perveen**

**Keywords:** Ascorbic acid, Epigallocatechin gallate, HDAC inhibitors, Neuroprotective effects, PXT3003.

## INTRODUCTION

Small molecule therapies for Charcot-Marie-Tooth (CMT) disease, particularly CMT type 1A (CMT1A), aim to target specific cellular pathways involved in the disease's pathology. The estimated overall prevalence of hereditary neuropathies due to CMT is around 1 in 2,500 individuals. Clinical characteristics, inheritance patterns, causative genes, and various mutations within these genes all contribute to the heterogeneity of CMT. To date, over 100 distinct genes associated with CMT have been identified; these genes serve diverse functions, resulting in various CMT subtypes and disease processes. While no small-molecule therapy has yet been approved specifically for CMT, several potential candidates have been explored in preclinical and early clinical studies [1]. Here are some examples:

**PXT3003:** PXT3003 is a combination therapy consisting of three small molecules: baclofen, naltrexone, and sorbitol. Studies have shown that this combination of already approved and marketed drugs works synergistically to improve myelination and reduce PMP22 mRNA expression. Additionally, PXT3003 has been demonstrated to enhance the imbalanced downstream PI3K-AKT/MEK-ERK signaling pathways, which are involved in regulating Schwann cell development. In CMT1A rat models, brief treatment with PXT3003 during early development has led to long-term improvements in phenotypic manifestations. Consequently, treatment for CMT1A patients should ideally begin as early as possible to maximize its impact on disease progression. PXT3003 has shown promise in preclinical studies and early clinical trials, aiming to improve myelination and reduce overexpression of the PMP22 gene, which is duplicated in CMT1A [2].

**Ascorbic Acid (Vitamin C):** Ascorbic acid has been studied for its potential neuroprotective effects in CMT1A. Preclinical studies suggested that high doses of vitamin C might improve myelination and reduce oxidative stress in peripheral nerves, leading to efforts to explore its role in downregulating PMP22 gene expression. As one of the early treatments evaluated for CMT, ascorbic acid has shown promise in laboratory models. However, translation to human trials has been disappointing. Clinical studies in individuals with CMT1A have not demonstrated significant positive effects. These trials highlight the challenges of converting preclinical success into clinical efficacy [3]. Clinical trials have been conducted to evaluate the safety and efficacy of ascorbic acid in CMT1A patients. The process of phenotypic screening is shown in Fig. (**1**).

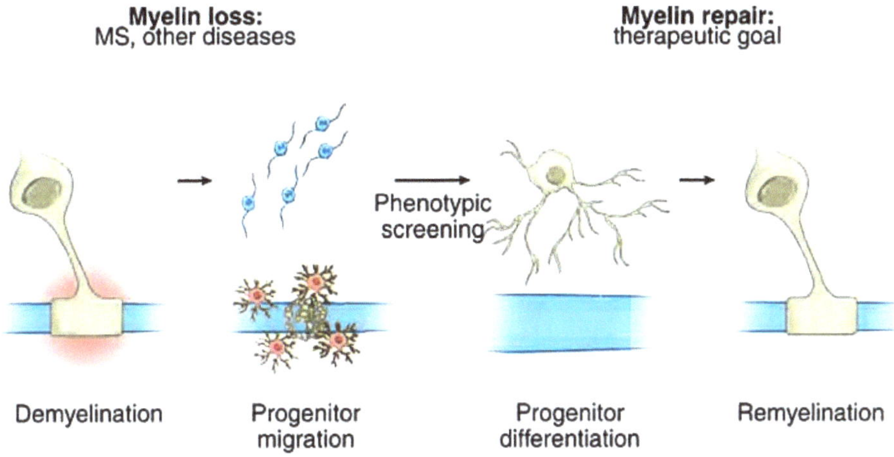


**Fig. (1).** Myelin loss and repair.

Ascorbic acid, commonly known as vitamin C, may play several potential roles in the treatment of peripheral neuropathy, including conditions like diabetic neuropathy and Charcot-Marie-Tooth disease (CMT). While its exact mechanisms are not yet fully understood, research suggests multiple ways in which ascorbic acid could benefit individuals with peripheral neuropathy:

## Antioxidant Activity

Ascorbic acid is a potent antioxidant that scavenges free radicals and reduces oxidative stress. Oxidative stress is implicated in the development and progression of peripheral neuropathy, particularly in conditions like diabetic neuropathy. The antioxidant transcription factor Nuclear factor (erythroid-derived 2)-like 2 (Nrf2) is often elevated in response to this antioxidant activity. Research shows that curcumin increases the production of antioxidant enzymes, including heme oxygenase 1 (HO-1) and detoxifying enzymes such as glutathione S-transferase P (GST-P) and NADPH quinone oxidoreductase-1 (NQO1) [4]. Through its ability to eliminate free radicals, ascorbic acid protects nerve cells and reduces the severity of neuropathic symptoms.

## Collagen Synthesis

The synthesis of collagen requires ascorbic acid, as it is essential for producing this structural protein found in connective tissues, including nerves. The integrity of nerve tissue depends on adequate collagen formation; therefore, individuals with hereditary neuropathies, such as Ehlers-Danlos syndrome or Marfan syndrome, may benefit from proper ascorbic acid levels to support nerve health.

### Neuroprotective Effects

Neuroprotective benefits of ascorbic acid treatment include support for nerve regeneration, improved myelination, and enhanced neuronal function. Animal studies have demonstrated that ascorbic acid enhances the production of Nerve Growth Factor (NGF), a crucial factor in nerve healing and tissue regeneration [5].

### Pain Management

Research findings suggest that taking ascorbic acid supplements may reduce neuropathic pain symptoms associated with peripheral neuropathy. The analgesic effects of ascorbic acid are believed to stem from its antioxidant and anti-inflammatory properties, although the exact mechanisms are not yet fully understood.

### Enhanced Nerve Conduction

Scientific research indicates that patients with peripheral neuropathy who take ascorbic acid supplements may experience improvements in nerve conduction velocity. By enhancing nerve signal transmission, ascorbic acid may help reduce the severity of symptoms such as numbness, tingling, and muscle weakness.

### Pathophysiology

Research indicates that improper Schwann cell differentiation contributes to the development of CMT1A disease symptoms. In one study, researchers used human induced pluripotent stem cells (hiPSCs) derived from two CMT1A patients to create an *in vitro* cell model. The duplication of the *PMP22* gene caused Schwann cells to deviate from their normal developmental path, from neural crest cells to endometrial fibroblast-like cells. This abnormal differentiation led to disrupted intracellular transport, altered lipid production and cholesterol metabolism, and negatively impacted both myelination and cell proliferation processes [6].

### Adjunct Therapy

Ascorbic acid should be considered an adjunct treatment alongside pain management medications, physical therapy, and lifestyle modifications for patients with peripheral neuropathy. Its antioxidant properties may complement other therapies in helping to manage neuropathic symptoms. However, further clinical trials are necessary to confirm its effectiveness and determine the optimal dosing regimen for various neuropathic conditions. Since individual responses to supplementation can vary, the decision to use ascorbic acid should be made in consultation with a healthcare provider.

## Curcumin

Curcumin, a compound found in turmeric, possesses well-documented antioxidant and anti-inflammatory properties. Early research suggests that curcumin-based therapies may offer neuroprotective benefits across a range of neuropathies. For example, localized application of a small amount of curcumin near a sciatic nerve injury accelerated functional recovery. In several models of demyelinating CMT neuropathies, curcumin was shown to improve pathogenic phenotypes. Its effects have also been studied in rats with diabetic peripheral neuropathy using both intraperitoneal injection and oral administration.

Curcumin is extracted from the rhizomes of *Curcuma longa* and belongs to the polyphenol class known as curcuminoids. Its pharmacological profile includes neuroprotective, anti-inflammatory, and antioxidant actions, which may reduce oxidative stress and inflammation in peripheral nerves, potentially offering therapeutic benefits in CMT.

However, curcumin has several limitations. It is poorly stable at neutral pH, has very low solubility in aqueous solutions (approximately 0.6 μg/mL), and breaks down rapidly. *In vitro* studies show that nearly 90% degrade within 30 minutes. These pharmacokinetic challenges necessitate the use of organic solvents or novel delivery systems for *in vivo* administration and may limit the therapeutic utility of the compound unless addressed.

## Tirasemtiv

Tirasemtiv is a small-molecule activator of the skeletal muscle troponin complex, which regulates muscle contraction. While initially developed for the treatment of Amyotrophic Lateral Sclerosis (ALS), tirasemtiv has also been investigated for its potential to improve muscle strength and function in CMT.

## Sensorimotor Disorder

Charcot-Marie-Tooth disease type 1A (CMT1A), a member of the sensorimotor disorder family known as CMT, is the most prevalent hereditary form of neuropathy. It is characterized by demyelination and axonal loss resulting from a duplication in the gene encoding Peripheral Myelin Protein 22 (PMP22). This genetic alteration leads to length-dependent degeneration of peripheral nerves, which manifests as reduced nerve conduction velocity and decreased compound muscle action potential.

The primary symptoms of CMT1A include atrophy of the lower limb muscles and foot deformities such as pes cavus, which often progress to the hands, leading to diminished tendon reflexes and distal sensory dysfunction. Although current treatment options for CMT1A are limited, most interventions aim to manage symptoms and improve quality of life [7].

### Epigallocatechin Gallate (EGCG)

EGCG is a polyphenol found in green tea with antioxidant and anti-inflammatory properties. Preclinical studies have suggested that EGCG may promote myelination and improve nerve function in CMT1A. Clinical trials have been conducted to assess the safety and efficacy of EGCG supplementation in individuals with CMT1A.

### Histone Deacetylase (HDAC) Inhibitors

HDAC inhibitors are a class of compounds that can modulate gene expression by altering chromatin structure. Research on preclinical levels suggests that some HDAC inhibitors show promise by enhancing nerve function and promoting myelination in CMT1A patients [8].

## CONCLUSION

These small-molecule treatments show promising therapeutic potential for Charcot-Marie-Tooth disease (CMT), but further research is needed to validate their safety, efficacy, and long-term effects in clinical practice. The wide variability in CMT manifestations among patients underscores the need for extensive clinical research and preclinical testing to determine how these therapies perform across different forms of CMT inheritance. The effectiveness of a specific treatment depends not only on genetic variations but also on individual biological factors and the severity of the disease. As a result, medical care for CMT must adopt a personalized approach, tailoring drug regimens to each patient's unique genetic and clinical profile.

The field of CMT research relies on personalized treatment strategies and ongoing clinical trials because patients show different responses to these therapies. Ongoing clinical studies, alongside research activities, will be necessary to develop these treatments so that they can safely enter standard medical practice. Through collaboration among patients, doctors, and researchers, better knowledge about these treatments can be gained to optimize their utility in CMT care.

## REFERENCES

[1] Stavrou M, Sargiannidou I, Georgiou E, Kagiava A, Kleopa KA. Emerging therapies for Charcot-Marie-Tooth inherited neuropathies. Int J Mol Sci 2021; 22(11): 6048. [http://dx.doi.org/10.3390/ijms22116048] [PMID: 34205075]

[2] Kimura Y, Schanberg LE, Tomlinson GA, *et al.* Optimizing the start time of biologics in polyarticular juvenile idiopathic arthritis: a comparative effectiveness study of Childhood Arthritis and Rheumatology Research Alliance consensus treatment plans. Arthritis Rheumatol 2021; 73(10): 1898-909.
[http://dx.doi.org/10.1002/art.41888] [PMID: 34105312]

[3] 3- Kato, T., Mizuno, T., Nakanishi, M., Lee, J. K., Yamada, S., Tsuboi, N., & Takahashi, K. (2023). Efficacy of ascorbic acid, thiamine, and hydrocortisone combination therapy: meta-analysis of randomized controlled trials. *in vivo, 37*(3), 1236-1245.

[4] García-Trejo SS, Gómez-Sierra T, Eugenio-Pérez D, Medina-Campos ON, Pedraza-Chaverri J. Protective effect of curcumin on D-galactose-induced senescence and oxidative stress in LLC-PK1 and HK-2 cells. Antioxidants 2024; 13(4): 415.
[http://dx.doi.org/10.3390/antiox13040415] [PMID: 38671863]

[5] Narra F, Piragine E, Benedetti G, *et al.* Impact of thermal processing on polyphenols, carotenoids, glucosinolates, and ascorbic acid in fruit and vegetables and their cardiovascular benefits. Compr Rev Food Sci Food Saf 2024; 23(6)e13426.
[http://dx.doi.org/10.1111/1541-4337.13426] [PMID: 39169551]

[6] Park S, Jung N, Myung S, *et al.* Differentiation of human tonsil-derived mesenchymal stem cells into schwann-like cells improves neuromuscular function in a mouse model of charcot-marie-tooth disease type 1A. Int J Mol Sci 2018; 19(8): 2393.
[http://dx.doi.org/10.3390/ijms19082393] [PMID: 30110925]

[7] Bondar A, Popa A, Papanas N, *et al.* Diabetic neuropathy: A narrative review of risk factors, classification, screening and current pathogenic treatment options (Review). Exp Ther Med 2021; 22(1): 690.
[http://dx.doi.org/10.3892/etm.2021.10122] [PMID: 33986855]

[8] Zaikos TD, Painter MM, Sebastian Kettinger NT, Terry VH, Collins KL. Class 1-selective histone deacetylase (HDAC) inhibitors enhance HIV latency reversal while preserving the activity of HDAC isoforms necessary for maximal HIV gene expression. J Virol 2018; 92(6)e02110-17.
[http://dx.doi.org/10.1128/JVI.02110-17] [PMID: 29298886]

# CHAPTER 23

# Latest Scientific Trends for Neuropathies

**Abstract:** There are various trends emerging in neuropathy as far as science is concerned. Precision or personalized medicine involves tailoring therapy to each person's unique DNA profile and disease characteristics, making it more specific. Treatment of inherited neurological disorders using gene therapy or gene editing to correct gene mutations or modify gene expression is now possible. This includes neurogenesis aimed at stimulating nerve regeneration, neurokinesis, and targeting molecular pathways involved in axial growth. Immunotherapy using immunomodulatory therapies is directed against immunotherapy-induced neurological disorders, such as Guillain-Barré Syndrome and CIDP. Early diagnosis and monitoring of disease progression require testing for biomarkers. Symptoms are monitored through digital health tools or wearable technology, and data is collected on neuropathic patients. Patient-centered care and quality of life initiatives aim to ameliorate the overall impact of neurological conditions on patients. The approach is multidisciplinary and relies on interdisciplinary collaboration in integrated neuropathy management. The ultimate goals of these trends are to improve prognosis and quality of life for individuals affected by these conditions.

**Keywords:** Biomarker discovery, Digital health, Gene therapy and editing, Guillain-barre syndrome, Multidisciplinary approaches.

## INTRODUCTION

### Precision Medicine

Increasingly, people are demanding treatment tailored to their individual genetic profile and disease characteristics. Doctors now have access to genomics and molecular diagnostics, which enable them to identify specific genetic mutations or biomarkers associated with different neuropathies, allowing for more targeted treatments. The way neuropathy is approached is evolving to account for an individual's genetics and physical characteristics, an approach known as personalized medicine. Recent research has identified several treatments capable of altering the course of disease by specifically targeting genetic changes, as seen in hereditary neuropathies such as Charcot-Marie-Tooth disease and hereditary amyloid neuropathy. Integrating genetic testing into routine healthcare practice will lead to more accurate diagnoses and more personalized treatment plans,

Sumaira Kanwal & Shazia Perveen

ultimately improving patient outcomes. Furthermore, new targeted therapies, including small molecules and RNA-based drugs, are showing promise in controlling diseases such as transthyretin hereditary amyloidosis [1].

## Gene Therapy and Editing

The use of gene therapy and gene editing technologies for treating inherited neuropathy by correcting gene mutations or regulating gene expression is becoming increasingly feasible. Gene-based interventions are currently being explored in clinical trials for conditions, such as Charcot-Marie-Tooth disease and hereditary neuropathy. Gene therapy is emerging as a pioneering approach to treat neuropathy, particularly when it results from genetic causes. The advent of gene editing technologies, such as CRISPR and RNA interference, has opened the door for addressing genetic problems at the molecular level [2]. Several studies have demonstrated the effectiveness of gene therapy in trials for conditions, such as peroneal muscular atrophy, resulting in significant improvements in neurological function and myelination. These treatments are currently under investigation in clinical trials to determine their safety and effectiveness for human use, with preliminary results showing promise for conditions, such as giant axonal neuropathy. Moreover, long-term observations in monotherapy suggest that gene therapy could be transformative in the treatment of neuropathy [3].

## Nerve Repair and Regeneration

Several strategies are being explored to promote nerve regeneration and neuropathy recovery, including stem cell therapy, neurotrophic factors, and small molecules that target pathways involved in axon growth and myelination. Due to new developments offering promising treatments, nerve regeneration and the repair of neurological injury and degenerative disease have become important topics. These strategies work by improving mitochondrial function, a key component for nerve regeneration and recovery. Mitochondrial dysfunction can impair the energy needed for the repair process [4]. Drugs aimed at promoting mitochondrial health are being explored to accelerate nerve regeneration. Furthermore, stem cell therapy is a promising strategy, as stem cells have been shown to differentiate into Schwann cells. These cells are especially valuable for demyelinating neuropathies because they are essential for myelination, the process of forming protective sheaths around nerves. Additionally, stem cells release neurotrophic substances that support neuronal survival.

At the same time, for the treatment of power loss, a new method for repairing nerves is emerging. To improve nerve regeneration and function, this therapy includes electrical stimulation. Reports from early studies suggest that electrotherapy can be used as an adjunct to non-surgical treatments, aiding in the acceleration of nerve fiber healing [5].

The synergy of (1) these strategies, drugs, stem cell therapy, and electrical interventions, and (2) their combined effects at the site of neuropathy has the potential to revolutionize neuropathy treatment into a personalized, multiphase therapy. However, the answers to these questions are still far from clear. Nerve damage is a complex condition, and these advances have yet to yield definitive clinical confirmation. Nevertheless, there is a strong possibility that these regenerative approaches will transform neuropathy treatment and markedly improve patient outcomes as we continue to expand knowledge and conduct clinical trials [6].

**Immune Modulation**

Immunotherapy has become a key focus in treating conditions, such as Guillain-Barré syndrome and Chronic Inflammatory Demyelinating Polyneuropathy (CIDP). The development of new therapies for these diseases is driven by a better understanding of the immune mechanisms behind them. Another promising approach for treating neuropathy involves managing the immune response through targeted stimulation [7]. Recently, immune signaling pathways involved in diseases, such as chronic demyelination and inflammatory neuropathies, have been extensively investigated. Currently, therapies aimed at modulating the immune response, such as monoclonal antibodies and cytokine inhibitors, are being studied to determine if they can mitigate symptoms or improve neural function. By blocking specific immune pathways, treatment outcomes may improve while minimizing side effects, making immune response management a growing area of neuropathy research [8].

**Biomarker Discovery**

Early diagnosis of neuropathy relies on the identification of reliable biomarkers. Biomarkers can be studied through various methods, including genetics, imaging, electrophysiology, and biochemistry. Detecting biomarkers is crucial for the rapid diagnosis of neuropathy. Several biomarkers of nerve pain and injury have been identified in recent studies, which can be used to tailor patient care through specific treatments. Identification of specific proteins in cerebrospinal fluid has been found to be closely associated with the nervous system. According to research, providing information on disease progression, therapeutic efficacy, and the standardization of these biomarkers will be essential for advancing the cure of neuropathy through precision medicine [9].

## Digital Health and Wearable Technologies

To monitor symptoms, track disease progression, and collect continuous data from individuals with neuropathy, wearable devices and digital health platforms are used. These technologies enable patients to remotely monitor their condition, personalize interventions, and facilitate large-scale data analysis.

Continuous health monitoring and real-time data collection offered by digital health technologies have the potential to transform how neuropathy is managed. For example, patients with diabetic neuropathy can monitor their health metrics using tools like smart insoles and Continuous Glucose Monitors (CGMs). It is important to integrate new devices with these tools to assist in tracking the progression of diabetes [10]. These devices help identify abnormal pressure points and elevated skin temperatures, which are early indicators of foot ulcer development and potential future ulcers. Furthermore, the incorporation of Health Event Analytics (HEA) into existing technologies can enhance predictive analytics and lead to personalized intervention systems that could be highly beneficial for patients.

New studies have shown that practical and accurate estimates of mobility and balance can be made in people with peripheral neuropathy, including those with Parkinson's disease, stroke, and amyotrophic lateral sclerosis, and that such tools can be further developed. The dynamics and objective stability measured by Gait Analysis Tools (GAT) complement traditional clinical assessments. Additionally, recent advances in sensor technology, such as photoplethysmography (PPG), provide valuable non-invasive monitoring techniques for patients with heart disease, particularly those with diabetic neuropathy. These tools enable consistent data collection across patients, which can inform clinical decisions while also empowering patients to take control of their health [11].

## Patient-Centered Care and Quality of Life

The focus is on enhancing patient-centered care and quality of life for individuals with neuropathy. Extensive research is being conducted to understand the global impact of neuropathic conditions on the physical, psychological, and social well-being of patients, as well as the role of integrative support care interventions.

The traumatic nature of neuropathy makes a patient-centered approach essential, tailored to meet the individual needs and preferences of each patient. This approach involves using patient feedback to foster shared decision-making and personalized care plans, which contribute to improved compliance and satisfaction. Given the many disorders that impair daily activities and emotional well-being, quality of life assessment has become an increasingly important component of neuropathy management.

In recent years, there has been growing interest in collaborative patient involvement in clinical practice to better address the specific challenges people with neuropathy face when seeking care [12].

Technology used in patient care can provide real-time feedback on health status as well as treatment success. For example, smart devices and health apps enable patients to track their symptoms and communicate efficiently with healthcare providers in a collaborative manner, supporting a patient-centered care approach. This combination of technology and patient engagement not only improves clinical outcomes but also enhances the overall quality of life for patients with neuropathic conditions [13].

### Multidisciplinary Approaches

Integrated management of neuropathy requires collaboration among multiple specialties, including neurology, genetics, rehabilitation, pain management, and psychiatry. To support integrated care and research efforts, multidisciplinary clinics and research alliances are being established. Neuropathy is a complex disease; therefore, a combined approach is essential. Effective management depends on teamwork among neurologists, physical therapists, occupational therapists, and other healthcare professionals. Together, this collaboration provides a comprehensive neuropathy care plan addressing physical, emotional, and social factors [14].

Recent literature emphasizes creating models that combine various treatment modalities, including medication, physiotherapy, and mental health support, as the most effective way to optimize patient care. Additionally, advances in digital health and wearable technology enhance coordination and communication among multidisciplinary team members. For example, patient data can be shared with the care team to prompt treatment adjustments and monitor progress. This teamwork not only improves the treatment pathway but also enhances patients' lifestyle and quality of life [15].

## CONCLUSION

Treatments for neuropathy are expected to benefit from new discoveries in precision medicine, gene therapy, and other emerging strategies. These advances enable us to study neuropathy more comprehensively and develop more effective ways to help patients lead healthier lives. Gene therapy offers novel approaches to treating genetic disorders, while precision medicine aims to provide individualized treatment for everyone. Key areas of focus include nerve regeneration and immune regulation, which involve repairing damaged nerves and controlling inflammation. Biomarkers enable us to expand diagnostic capabilities and develop personalized treatment plans based on specific patient information.

Moreover, digital health tools empower patients to become active participants in their own care, shifting the focus from providers to patients. To effectively address the challenges of neuropathy, these advances must be integrated into collaborative teamwork among care providers. A continuous flow of science-based, reliable information from researchers and healthcare professionals is essential for everyone involved, including patients. This collaborative approach ensures that all parties can effectively apply new strategies to better manage neuropathy and improve the lives of those affected.

## REFERENCES

[1] Saidia AR, Ruel J, Bahloul A, Chaix B, Venail F, Wang J. Current advances in gene therapies of genetic auditory neuropathy spectrum disorder. J Clin Med 2023; 12(3): 738. [http://dx.doi.org/10.3390/jcm12030738] [PMID: 36769387]

[2] Ozes B, Myers M, Moss K, *et al.* AAV1.NT-3 gene therapy for X-linked Charcot–Marie–Tooth neuropathy type 1. Gene Ther 2022; 29(3-4): 127-37. [http://dx.doi.org/10.1038/s41434-021-00231-3] [PMID: 33542455]

[3] Vignal-Clermont C, Girmens JF, Audo I, *et al.* Safety of intravitreal gene therapy for treatment of subjects with Leber hereditary optic neuropathy due to mutations in the mitochondrial ND4 gene: the REVEAL study. BioDrugs 2021; 35(2): 201-14. [http://dx.doi.org/10.1007/s40259-021-00468-9] [PMID: 33566264]

[4] Wang Y, Liu C, Ren Y, *et al.* Nanomaterial-based strategies for attenuating T-cell-mediated immunodepression in stroke patients: Advancing research perspectives. Int J Nanomedicine 2024; 19: 5793-812. [http://dx.doi.org/10.2147/IJN.S456632] [PMID: 38882535]

[5] Khatami M. Immune neuroplasticity (power within) is weakened by vaccines and drugs (power without): mitochondrial sink holes, genomic destabilization and immune disorders—hypothesis Clin Transl Med 2021; 11(1): e286.

[6] Smith EL, Mailankody S, Stachr M, *et al.* BCMA-targctcd CAR T-ccll thcrapy plus radiothcrapy for the treatment of refractory myeloma reveals potential synergy. Cancer Immunol Res 2019; 7(7): 1047-53. [http://dx.doi.org/10.1158/2326-6066.CIR-18-0551] [PMID: 31113804]

[7] Mastrangelo S, Rivetti S, Triarico S, *et al.* Mechanisms, characteristics, and treatment of neuropathic pain and peripheral neuropathy associated with dinutuximab in neuroblastoma patients. Int J Mol Sci 2021; 22(23): 12648. [http://dx.doi.org/10.3390/ijms222312648] [PMID: 34884452]

[8] Meade E, Garvey M. The role of neuro-immune interaction in chronic pain conditions; functional somatic syndrome, neurogenic inflammation, and peripheral neuropathy. Int J Mol Sci 2022; 23(15): 8574. [http://dx.doi.org/10.3390/ijms23158574] [PMID: 35955708]

[9] Murad AM, Majeed MJ, Al-Ameri RB, AL-Haidari AS. Serum myelin oligodendrocyte glycoprotein and myelin protein zero as diagnostic biomarkers in diabetic neuropathy. AL-Kindy College Medical Journal 2023; 19(1): 42-7.
[http://dx.doi.org/10.47723/kcmj.v19i1.859]

[10] Eleftheriadou A, Spallone V, Tahrani AA, Alam U. Cardiovascular autonomic neuropathy in diabetes: an update with a focus on management. Diabetologia 2024; 67(12): 2611-25.
[http://dx.doi.org/10.1007/s00125-024-06242-0] [PMID: 39120767]

[11] Sukur E, Akar A, Uyar AÇ, *et al.* Vacuum-assisted closure *versus* moist dressings in the treatment of diabetic wound ulcers after partial foot amputation: A retrospective analysis in 65 patients. J Orthop Surg (Hong Kong) 2018; 26(3): 2309499018799769.
[http://dx.doi.org/10.1177/2309499018799769] [PMID: 30235975]

[12] Ragab I, Wahman M, bu Aqoulah E, Alhalabi M, Jabir M, Atef A. Effect of implementing bundle of care on breast cancer patients paclitaxel induced peripheral neuropathy and quality of life. Tanta Scientific Nursing Journal 2024; 33(2): 287-309.
[http://dx.doi.org/10.21608/tsnj.2024.351232]

[13] Groenier M, Spijkerboer K, Venix L, *et al.* Evaluation of the impact of technical physicians on improving individual patient care with technology. BMC Med Educ 2023; 23(1): 181.
[http://dx.doi.org/10.1186/s12909-023-04137-z] [PMID: 36959581]

[14] Kulkarni A, Thool AR, Daigavane S, Aditi S. Understanding the clinical relationship between diabetic retinopathy, nephropathy, and neuropathy: a comprehensive review. Cureus 2024; 16(3): e56674.
[http://dx.doi.org/10.7759/cureus.56674] [PMID: 38646317]

[15] Wang C, Tachimori H, Yamaguchi H, Sekiguchi A, Li Y, Yamashita Y. A multimodal deep learning approach for the prediction of cognitive decline and its effectiveness in clinical trials for Alzheimer's disease. Transl Psychiatry 2024; 14(1): 105.
[http://dx.doi.org/10.1038/s41398-024-02819-w] [PMID: 38383536]

# CHAPTER 24

# Quality of Life with Neuropathy

**Abstract:** Neuropathy leads to symptoms including pain, insensibility, and reduced sensation, all of which influence an individual's quality of life. The extent of its impact depends on the severity, available treatments, and the level of social support. Neuropathy severely impacts the quality of life by weakening muscles, reducing coordination, diminishing sensory perception, and making everyday tasks challenging. Neuropathic pain, marked by sensations of burning, tingling, shooting, or stabbing, can deeply affect daily life by disrupting sleep patterns, cognitive function, and emotional well-being. Chronic pain and physical impairments caused by neuropathy can deeply affect emotional well-being. It may also disrupt social relationships, as limited mobility, persistent pain, and fatigue make it harder to engage with others, often contributing to isolation. Beyond these struggles, neuropathy can create occupational and financial consequences, making it difficult to maintain employment and manage medical expenses. Managing neuropathy can be challenging and substantially affects overall quality of life. Conditions, such as Hereditary Neuropathy with liability to Pressure Palsies (HNPP), can significantly affect a person's routine depending on severity, treatment success, and coping ability. Despite these challenges, an individual can achieve a meaningful life with proper support, effective coping techniques, and integrated healthcare. Effective management strategies, such as maintaining a balanced diet and exercise, contribute to an improved overall lifestyle. Furthermore, educating individuals about neuropathy and its symptoms can empower them to make informed decisions about their healthcare.

**Keywords:** Chronic pain, Coping mechanisms, Hereditary neuropathy with pressure, Neuropathy, Physical limitations.

## INTRODUCTION

Neuropathies can significantly impact the quality of life due to the diverse array of symptoms, including pain, numbness, weakness, and impaired sensation. The specific effects on quality of life vary depending on factors, such as the type and severity of the neuropathy, individual coping mechanisms, available support systems, and access to treatment. Here are some common ways in which neuropathies can affect quality of life:

**Physical Functioning:** People with neuropathy often struggle with physical functioning, mobility, and daily life activities. Peripheral neuropathy is associated

**Sumaira Kanwal & Shazia Perveen**

with slow walking speed and balance deficits, both of which are crucial for maintaining independence and overall quality of life. A study revealed that women with neuropathy walk at a slower pace (2.7 feet per second) compared to those without the condition (3.6 feet per second) [1]. These impairments not only impact daily life activities but also increase the risk of falls and subsequent injuries, further complicating their life. Neuropathy and physical ability are closely linked, as declining motor function can lead to a cycle of deterioration [2]. Evidence suggests that rehabilitation therapy and structured exercise programs can effectively enhance the chances of regaining movement and improve overall health outcomes of neuropathic patients. By focusing on physical therapy, healthcare professionals can help reduce mobility restrictions and enable patients to lead more active and fulfilling lives [3].

**Pain and Discomfort**: Neuropathic pain, characterized by burning, tingling, shooting, or stabbing sensations, can be chronic and debilitating. It can interfere with sleep, concentration, and overall well-being, affecting mood and emotional health [4].

**Emotional Well-being:** Living with chronic pain and physical limitations can take a toll on emotional health, leading to feelings of frustration, anxiety, depression, and social isolation. Coping with the uncertainty of the condition and its impact on daily life can also contribute to emotional distress.

**Social Relationships**: Neuropathies may affect social interactions and relationships with family, friends, and colleagues. Limited mobility, pain, and fatigue can make it challenging to participate in social activities, leading to feelings of isolation and loneliness.

**Occupational and Financial Impact**: Neuropathies, particularly Diabetic Peripheral Neuropathy (DPN), affect job performance and financial stability due to symptoms like severe pain, sensory impairments, and motor functioning, often causing missed workdays, which may lead to reduced workplace productivity. As a result, financial struggles arise, not only from lower income but also from the high cost of medical expenses, treatments, and mobility aids. Beyond these physical limitations, anxiety and depression further disrupt professional life, creating a cycle where reduced job performance leads to financial stress and impacts the overall well-being of neuropathic patients [5].

For individuals with neuropathy, employment barriers are significant, with research indicating that it is partly due to employer discrimination and lack of awareness about their condition. Many individuals require special equipment or workplace adjustments, which can be expensive. Furthermore, continuous medical treatments and rehabilitation services add to their financial burden, making life even more complex for them and their families [6].

**Self-esteem and Body Image**: Visible symptoms, such as muscle weakness, gait abnormalities, or the use of orthopedic devices, may impact self-esteem and body image. Individuals with neuropathies may experience feelings of self-consciousness or insecurity about their appearance and abilities [7].

**Treatment Burden**: Managing neuropathies often involves complex treatment regimens, including medications, physical therapy, and lifestyle modifications. Adhering to treatment plans and coping with side effects can be burdensome and may affect overall quality of life [8].

Despite these challenges, it is important to note that individuals with neuropathies can still lead fulfilling lives with appropriate support, coping strategies, and access to comprehensive care. Multidisciplinary approaches that address physical, emotional, and social aspects of well-being are essential for optimizing the quality of life in individuals living with neuropathies. Support from healthcare professionals, peer support groups, and family members can play an important role in helping persons manage to tackle associated issues with neuropathic conditions.

The quality of life for individuals with neuropathies, including conditions like Hereditary Neuropathy with Liability to Pressure Palsies (HNPP) and others, can differ considerably based on the severity of the neuropathy, the definite symptoms experienced, the effectiveness of treatment, and individual coping mechanisms [9]. Here are some factors that can influence the quality of life for people with neuropathies:

**Symptom Severity**: Neuropathies can range from mild to severe. Mild cases may cause occasional discomfort or tingling, while severe cases can lead to debilitating pain, muscle weakness, loss of sensation, and mobility issues.

**Pain Management**: Persistent pain is a frequent symptom of numerous neuropathies and can considerably affect the quality of life. Effective pain management strategies, including medications, physical therapy, nerve blocks, and alternative therapies, can help improve quality of life by reducing pain levels [10].

**Functional Limitations:** Neuropathies can affect mobility, coordination, and dexterity, making it challenging to perform daily activities, such as walking, standing, writing, or even holding objects. Assistive devices and adaptive strategies may be necessary to uphold liberty and improve quality of life.

**Emotional Well-being**: Living with a chronic condition like neuropathy can lead to emotional challenges, such as anxiety, depression, frustration, and social isolation. Support from family, friends, support groups, and mental health professionals can be invaluable in addressing these emotional aspects and improving overall well-being.

**Impact on Work and Social Life**: Neuropathies may affect an individual's ability to work, participate in social activities, and maintain relationships. Accommodations in the workplace, adjustments to social activities, and open communication with employers, colleagues, and friends can help mitigate these challenges and enhance the quality of life.

**Treatment Options:** Neuropathy appears as a complex challenge, as the majority of neuropathies remain incurable. Although individuals affected by neuropathy can take steps to improve their quality of life by changing their lifestyle, eating a balanced diet, exercising regularly, and using alternative therapies, a combination of these medical treatments plays a crucial role in alleviating discomfort, improving functional outcomes, and preventing further nerve damage. One of the most common ways to manage neuropathic symptoms is through medications. Doctors often prescribe anticonvulsants like anticonvulsants (*e.g.*, gabapentin or pregabalin), antidepressants (*e.g.*, amitriptyline and duloxetine), and topical agents, such as capsaicin cream or lidocaine patches, all of which have efficacy in reducing neuropathic pain [11].

Beyond medications, non-pharmacological approaches have proven to be effective in neuropathy care, such as lifestyle modification including a balanced or nutrient-rich diet (including vitamins B12, D, and E), regular exercise (yoga, swimming, or walking), and smoking cessation to support nerve health, prevent muscle weakness, and slow the process of disease progression. Physical therapy can enhance mobility and reduce the risk of falls associated with motor impairments [12].

In addition to pharmacological measures, non-pharmacological strategies, such as physiotherapy and cognitive behavioral therapy, have gained recognition for their significant contribution to the treatment of neuropathic symptoms. Silva's systematic review emphasizes the critical nature of rehabilitation interventions that focus on improving activity levels and promoting participation in daily life while emphasizing the need for a holistic approach to patient care. In addition, neuroscience education for pain has emerged as an important method of treating the biopsychosocial elements of chronic pain associated with neuropathy, which may facilitate better adherence to treatment and improve overall health outcomes [13].

**Education and Self-Management:** Education and self-care are essential components in improving the quality of life for people with neuropathy. Effective self-care strategies can help people take charge of their health and achieve better outcomes. According to research, educational therapies, such as Pain Neuroscience Education (PNE), can increase patients' understanding of their condition, increase self-efficacy, and reduce pain perception [14]. For example, a supportive educational intervention has been shown to dramatically improve self-care knowledge and skills in women with type 2 diabetes and diabetic peripheral neuropathy, thereby improving glucose control and overall health (2020).

Additionally, self-management education programs, including Diabetes Self-Management Education (DSME), have been shown to improve confidence, psychological well-being, and self-efficacy in older people with diabetes. To manage the chronic nature of neuropathy, these programs often incorporate elements that address coping mechanisms, pain management practices, and lifestyle changes. Incorporating educational tools into routine care can lead to upgraded health outcomes and improved patient understanding of the disease [15].

## CONCLUSION

Neuropathy has a profound impact on quality of life by affecting numerous dimensions of a person's well-being, including physical, emotional, cognitive, and social aspects. The manifestation of various symptoms, such as chronic pain, numbness, tingling sensations, muscle weakness, and poor coordination, can significantly hinder daily activities, reduce self-reliance, and contribute to psychological problems, such as anxiety, depression, and social isolation. As a result, these physical and mental health problems are often associated with low self-esteem, strained interpersonal relationships, and overall low satisfaction with life.

Effective treatment of neuropathy requires a multidisciplinary approach, which requires addressing both physical symptoms and psychological effects. Pharmacological interventions are used to control symptoms, including analgesics, anticonvulsants, and antidepressants; however, these treatments often produce only partial relief. Complementary therapies, such as physical rehabilitation, occupational therapy, Cognitive Behavioral Therapy (CBT), and mindfulness-based stress reduction, are used to reinforce coping strategies and improve functional abilities. Additionally, lifestyle changes, including regular physical activity, a balanced diet, proper foot care, and stress management techniques, have demonstrated positive effects on patient outcomes. The importance of early diagnosis is paramount. Timely intervention is essential to slow disease progression, prevent complications, and improve overall prognosis.

The best outcomes depend on personalized treatment plans tailored to the specific type of neuropathy and the unique needs of the patient. This approach not only addresses the physical manifestations of neuropathy but also integrates emotional support and social inclusion as important elements of comprehensive care. Future research should prioritize the exploration of novel modalities, such as regenerative medicine, gene therapy, and neuroprotective agents, aimed at addressing the underlying etiologies of neuropathy rather than its symptoms. Additionally, research is warranted to examine the effectiveness of a comprehensive care framework that integrates medical, psychological, and social support systems. A patient-centered approach to care, one that emphasizes participation in decision-making and self-care education, has the potential to improve the quality of life for people with neuropathy significantly.

In brief, neuropathy is a multifaceted disease that has a profound impact on a person's life. An integrated, patient-centered strategy that combines medical interventions with psychosocial support, lifestyle changes, and community resources provides the most effective means of improving quality of life. Promoting awareness, encouraging research initiatives, and promoting a comprehensive approach to care are essential for healthcare providers seeking to reduce the burden of neuropathy and improve the well-being of those affected.

## REFERENCES

[1] Ylitalo KR, Herman WH, Harlow SD. Performance-based physical functioning and peripheral neuropathy in a population-based cohort of women at midlife. Am J Epidemiol 2013; 177(8): 810-7. [http://dx.doi.org/10.1093/aje/kws327] [PMID: 23524038]

[2] Sugimoto K, Hoshino T, Tamura A, Yamazaki T, Suzuki S, Shimbo T. The relationship of one-leg standing time with peripheral nerve function and clinical neuropathy in patients with type 2 diabetes. Diabetol Int 2018; 9(4): 243-56. [http://dx.doi.org/10.1007/s13340-018-0354-2] [PMID: 30603374]

[3] Perrin BM, Southon J, McCaig J, Skinner I, Skinner TC, Kingsley MIC. The effect of structured exercise compared with education on neuropathic signs and symptoms in people at risk of neuropathic diabetic foot ulcers: a randomized clinical trial. Medicina (Kaunas) 2021; 58(1): 59. [http://dx.doi.org/10.3390/medicina58010059] [PMID: 35056367]

[4] Szewczyk A, Jamroz-Wiśniewska A, Haratym N, Rejdak K. Neuropathic pain and chronic pain as an underestimated interdisciplinary problem. Int J Occup Med Environ Health 2022; 35(3): 249-64. [http://dx.doi.org/10.13075/ijomeh.1896.01676] [PMID: 35040826]

[5] Selvarajah D, Kar D, Khunti K, *et al.* Diabetic peripheral neuropathy: advances in diagnosis and strategies for screening and early intervention. Lancet Diabetes Endocrinol 2019; 7(12): 938-48. [http://dx.doi.org/10.1016/S2213-8587(19)30081-6] [PMID: 31624024]

[6] Keesing S, Rosenwax L, McNamara B. The implications of women's activity limitations and role disruptions during breast cancer survivorship. Womens Health (Lond Engl) 2018; 14. [http://dx.doi.org/10.1177/1745505718756381] [PMID: 29409399]

[7] Flaubert JL, Spicer CM, Jette AM, Eds. The promise of assistive technology to enhance activity and work participation. 2017.

[8] National Academies of Sciences, Engineering, and MedicineMedications in single-dose vials:

implications of discarded drugs. 2021.

[9] Chrestian N. Hereditary neuropathy with liability to pressure palsies 2020.

[10] Bril V, Breiner A, Perkins BA, Zochodne D. Neuropathy. Can J Diabetes 2018; 42 (Suppl. 1): S217-21.
[http://dx.doi.org/10.1016/j.jcjd.2017.10.028] [PMID: 29650100]

[11] Feldman EL, Callaghan BC, Pop-Busui R, *et al.* Diabetic neuropathy. Nat Rev Dis Primers 2019; 5(1): 41.
[http://dx.doi.org/10.1038/s41572-019-0092-1] [PMID: 31197153]

[12] Silva, S. F., Magalhães, H. L. d., Deus, F. A. d., Andrade, K. K. S., Lima, V. P., & Gaiad, T. P. (2024). Rehabilitation interventions targeting the activity and participation of patient with neuromuscular diseases: what do we know? a systematic review. Arquivos De Neuro-Psiquiatria, 82(02), 001-012. [http://dx.doi.org/10.1055/s-0044-1779295]

[13] Nijs J, Wijma AJ, Willaert W, *et al.* Integrating motivational interviewing in pain neuroscience education for people with chronic pain: a practical guide for clinicians. Phys Ther 2020; 100(5): 846-59.
[http://dx.doi.org/10.1093/ptj/pzaa021] [PMID: 31995191]

[14] Wuri Kartika A, Widyatuti W, Rekawati E. The effectiveness of home-based nursing intervention in the elderly with recurrent diabetic foot ulcers: A case report. J Public Health Res 2021; 10(2).
[http://dx.doi.org/10.4081/jphr.2021.2162] [PMID: 33855395]

[15] Felix HC, Narcisse MR, Long CR, *et al.* The effect of family diabetes self-management education on self-care behaviors of marshallese adults with type 2 diabetes. Am J Health Behav 2019; 43(3): 490-7.
[http://dx.doi.org/10.5993/AJHB.43.3.4] [PMID: 31046880]

# CHAPTER 25

# Depression Among Neuropathy Patients

**Abstract:** Neuropathy patients often experience depression due to chronic pain, functional limitations, sleep disturbances, Impact on Work and Financial Concerns, Chronic Illness Burden, Biological factors, and social isolation. Chronic pain can lead to feelings of hopelessness, frustration, and sadness. For people with neuropathy, chronic pain has a significant impact on their ability to perform at work and their financial stability. Functional limitations can affect mobility and daily functioning, leading to a decline in independence and participation in activities. Sleep disturbances can exacerbate depression symptoms. Feelings of worthlessness and hopelessness brought on by losing one's job or being less productive might make depression worse. Neuropathy can impact work and financial stability, leading to feelings of worthlessness and depression. Stress, anxiety, and melancholy can result from the overwhelming weight of managing a chronic illness. Chronic illness management can be overwhelming, causing stress and anxiety. Pro-inflammatory cytokines, notably IL-6 and TNF-α, were significantly higher in neuropathy patients with concurrent depression than in those without depression. Biological factors like neurotransmitter imbalances can increase the risk of depression. Social isolation, resulting from pain and functional limitations, can contribute to feelings of isolation. Healthcare professionals should screen patients for depression and provide appropriate treatment, including psychotherapy, medication, lifestyle modifications, and support. Combining neuropathy treatment with depression can improve overall outcomes and quality of life.

**Keywords:** Chronic pain, Depression, Functional limitations, Neuropathy, Social isolation.

## INTRODUCTION

Recent studies have shown a strong comorbidity between neuropathy and depression, indicating a complex reciprocal link between the two disorders. Depression and neuropathic pain, which is defined by harm or malfunction of the somatosensory nerve system, commonly interact, resulting in a lower quality of life and a greater financial burden on healthcare [1]. Research shows that between 30 and 50 percent of neuropathy patients have clinically severe depression symptoms, with diabetic neuropathy patients experiencing higher rates [2]. Neurotransmitter dysregulation, altered neuronal plasticity, and common inflammatory pathways are the pathophysiological mechanisms that connect neuropathy with depression. Studies have revealed decreased neurotrophic factors

**Sumaira Kanwal & Shazia Perveen**

and increased pro-inflammatory cytokine levels in both disorders, pointing to a shared biological basis [3]. Furthermore, disturbed sleep patterns, social isolation, and functional impairment are all consequences of chronic neuropathic pain that can exacerbate and sustain depressive symptoms [4]. Early intervention that addresses both neuropathy and depression produces greater results than treating either ailment alone, according to recent clinical research. To manage this dual load, integrated treatment techniques that include psychological and pharmaceutical therapies have demonstrated encouraging outcomes [5]. Additionally, new research indicates that some antidepressants may be beneficial for both neuropathic pain and depression by affecting similar brain circuits. Depression among neuropathy patients is not uncommon and can significantly impact their overall well-being and quality of life. There are several reasons why neuropathy patients may experience depression [6].

**Chronic Pain:** Neuropathic pain can be persistent and debilitating, leading to feelings of hopelessness, frustration, and sadness. Dealing with constant pain can wear down a person's mental and emotional resilience, increasing the risk of depression. Chronic pain and neuropathic pain are interdisciplinary issues that lie at the intersection of economics, psychology, sociology, and medicine. The magnitude of this issue appears to be underestimated, but it is likely to expand as the population ages and the prevalence of lifestyle illnesses rises. Individuals working in a variety of occupational areas may also struggle with these illnesses, which have an impact on their productivity at work, mental health, and quality of life. According to research, musculoskeletal disorders are becoming more common in persons who are actively employed and can cause impairment or leave them unable to work. However, pain-related presenteeism and/or absenteeism not only result in financial hardships but also cause employee burnout, exhaustion, and depressive syndromes [7]. Major depressive disorder may be more common in chronic pain patients than in the general population; 36% of chronic pain patients are thought to have depressive symptoms [8].

**Functional Limitations:** Neuropathy can affect mobility, coordination, and daily functioning, making it challenging for individuals to perform tasks they once enjoyed. The decline in independence and limited capacity to participate in activities may lead to feelings of sadness and depression. The loss of muscle strength, power, and endurance caused by Peripheral Neuropathy (PN) causes neurogenic muscle atrophy, which can lead to falls, bone fractures, altered gait and impaired balance, recurrent infections, and amputations. According to a symptom questionnaire, a neurologic examination of the legs, and nerve conduction investigations, people with confirmed polyneuropathy were more likely to fall, sustain injuries, and become dependent on their instrumental and basic daily activities. With several symptoms originating from several organs, autonomic neuropathy frequently develops in tandem with sensory neuropathy [9]. Having trouble with basic tasks can make us feel worthless and helpless, especially if we are also depressed. These physical difficulties can also prevent us from participating in social activities, thereby exacerbating our emotional problems [10].

**Sleep Disturbances:** Neuropathic pain and other neuropathy symptoms, such as tingling or burning sensations, can disrupt sleep patterns, leading to insomnia or poor sleep quality. Sleep disturbances are strongly associated with depression and can exacerbate depressive symptoms. People with chronic illnesses, especially those with neuropathic pain, frequently have trouble sleeping [10]. Studies show that patients with chronic neuropathy frequently have severe sleep disturbances, which include increased sleep latency, increased wakefulness after sleep onset, and changes in sleep architecture. For example, a reduction in slow-wave sleep. In addition to being a result of pain, these disruptions intensify the pain itself, resulting in a vicious cycle whereby insufficient sleep causes increased sensitivity to pain [11].

**Social Isolation:** Another principal factor affecting people with chronic pain, especially neuropathic pain, is social isolation. Feelings of a lack of companionship and isolation are frequently caused by functional limitations brought on by chronic diseases that limit social connections and enterprise [12]. The biopsychosocial model of pain highlights the strong correlation between social participation and pain perception as well as psychological variables like anxiety and sadness [13]. Patients suffering from excruciating diabetic neuropathy, for example, report a reduced quality of life and focus attention on social isolation, which exacerbates their emotional distress and functional diminution. Neuropathy-related pain and limitations can lead to social withdrawal and isolation. Experiencing difficulty in participating in social activities or maintaining relationships may contribute to feelings of loneliness, which are vulnerabilities for depression [14].

**Impact on Work and Financial Concerns**: Neuropathy may influence an individual's capability to work, resulting in financial strain and uncertainty about the future. Loss of implementation or reduced productivity can lead to feelings of worthlessness and despair, contributing to depression. Chronic neuropathic pain patients occasionally struggle to keep a job because of their disease, which results in reduced productivity and higher medical expenses. Chronic pain has a remarkable impact on work and financial issues. These people's worry and anxiety are exacerbated by the substantial economic burden of managing chronic pain, which includes prescription drug prices and consultations. Due to cost concerns, patients may postpone or renounce critical treatments, which can result in a cycle of worsening health outcomes [15].

**Chronic Illness Burden:** Managing a chronic condition like neuropathy requires continuous medical appointments, treatments, and lifestyle adaptation. The burden of dealing with a chronic illness can be very profound. Feelings of stress, anxiety, and depression can lead to various emotional challenges.

Chronic pain related to functional impairments has a significant influence on day-to-day activities and overall quality of life. Normal workloads are frequently demanding for patients to complete, which can result in a deterioration in their physical condition and a greater reliance on others. Mobility problems and a reduced capacity for physical activity are among the functional impairments linked to chronic pain syndromes, especially neuropathic pain, which can exacerbate mental discomfort and social isolation. Depression-stricken neuropathy patients deal with a complex web of mental and physical challenges that substantially increase the challenges associated with chronic ailments. Compared to patients with neuropathy alone, patients with multiple disorders consumed healthcare at a rate that was 45% higher, resulting in higher medical costs and a lower quality of life [16].

**Biological Factors:** Biological factors may also be at play, such as neurotransmitter imbalances or changes in brain chemistry. That increases the risk of depression in patients with neuropathy. A complex interaction of biological, psychological, and social variables leads to chronic pain in neuropathy. A multidisciplinary strategy that takes into account the psychological and social elements of pain in addition to its physical manifestations is frequently obligatory for the management of neuropathic pain. Pain and sleep quality have been demonstrated to be improved by productive interventions like physical activity and cognitive-behavioral therapy, underscoring the importance of a comprehensive treatment approach. Patients with neuropathy who also feel pain from depression exhibit altered connectivity in the default mode network and decreased gray matter volume in the hippocampus and prefrontal cortex, putting forward structural brain abnormalities that may play a key role in both conditions.

## CONCLUSION

Medical professionals must evaluate patients with neuropathy for depression and provide suitable support and awareness. Persistent pain can diminish the emotional and mental resilience of a person, increasing the risk of depression. Chronic pain significantly affects a person's capacity to function at work and their financial security if they have neuropathy. Losing one's independence and ability to participate in activities can lead to feelings of dejection and misery. The burden of treating a chronic illness can be so inconvenient that it can lead to stress, anxiety, and regret. Neurotransmitters, inflammatory indicators, and pain circuits interact intricately with the molecular causes of depression in neuropathy patients. Reduced gray matter volume in the hippocampus and prefrontal cortex, as well as altered connections in the default mode network, are perceived in neuropathy patients who also have depression, indicating structural brain abnormalities that may contribute to both disorders. Treatment may include situation modifications, medication, psychotherapy, and encouragement from friends, family, and support groups. Treating depression concurrently with neuropathy can amplify overall results and the quality of life for patients. Medical assistance is required when an individual begins to express the symptoms of depression.

## REFERENCES

[1] Liu Q, Li R, Yang W, Cui R, Li B. Role of neuroglia in neuropathic pain and depression. Pharmacol Res 2021; 174: 105957.
[http://dx.doi.org/10.1016/j.phrs.2021.105957] [PMID: 34688904]

[2] Zhang X, Ma L, Mu S, Yin Y. The hidden burden—exploring depression risk in patients with diabetic nephropathy: A systematic review and meta-analysis. Diabetes Ther 2023; 14(9): 1481-502.
[http://dx.doi.org/10.1007/s13300-023-01436-y] [PMID: 37368150]

[3] M SL, O P. Inflammatory biomarkers as a part of diagnosis in diabetic peripheral neuropathy. J Diabetes Metab Disord 2021; 20(1): 869-82.
[http://dx.doi.org/10.1007/s40200-021-00734-1] [PMID: 34222094]

[4] Attal N, Bouhassira D. Advances in the treatment of neuropathic pain. Curr Opin Neurol 2021; 34(5): 631-7.
[http://dx.doi.org/10.1097/WCO.0000000000000980] [PMID: 34310363]

[5] Coelho DRA, Gersten M, Jimenez AS, Fregni F, Cassano P, Vieira WF. Treating neuropathic pain and comorbid affective disorders: Preclinical and clinical evidence. Pain Pract 2024; 24(7): 937-55.
[http://dx.doi.org/10.1111/papr.13370] [PMID: 38572653]

[6] Syed O, Jancic P, Knezevic NN. A review of recent pharmacological advances in the management of diabetes-associated peripheral neuropathy. Pharmaceuticals (Basel) 2023; 16(6): 801.
[http://dx.doi.org/10.3390/ph16060801] [PMID: 37375749]

[7] Szewczyk A, Jamroz-Wiśniewska A, Haratym N, Rejdak K. Neuropathic pain and chronic pain as an underestimated interdisciplinary problem. Int J Occup Med Environ Health 2022; 35(3): 249-64.
[http://dx.doi.org/10.13075/ijomeh.1896.01676] [PMID: 35040826]

[8] Meda RT, Nuguru SP, Rachakonda S, Sripathi S, Khan MI, Patel N. Chronic pain-induced depression: a review of prevalence and management. Cureus 2022; 14(8): e28416.
[http://dx.doi.org/10.7759/cureus.28416] [PMID: 36171845]

[9] Elafros MA, Andersen H, Bennett DL, *et al.* Towards prevention of diabetic peripheral neuropathy: clinical presentation, pathogenesis, and new treatments. Lancet Neurol 2022; 21(10): 922-36.
[http://dx.doi.org/10.1016/S1474-4422(22)00188-0] [PMID: 36115364]

[10] Giovannini S, Coraci D, Brau F, *et al.* Neuropathic pain in the elderly. Diagnostics (Basel) 2021; 11(4): 613.
[http://dx.doi.org/10.3390/diagnostics11040613] [PMID: 33808121]

[11] McParland AL, Bhatia A, Matelski J, *et al.* Evaluating the impact of cannabinoids on sleep health and pain in patients with chronic neuropathic pain: a systematic review and meta-analysis of randomized controlled trials. Reg Anesth Pain Med 2023; 48(4): 180-90.

[http://dx.doi.org/10.1136/rapm-2021-103431] [PMID: 36598058]

[12] Gierthmühlen J. What is associated with painful polyneuropathy? A cross-sectional analysis of symptoms and signs in patients with painful and painless polyneuropathy. 2022.

[13] Carreño-Hernández I, Cassol-Spanemberg J, de Rivera-Campillo E, Estrugo-Devesa A, López-López J. Is burning mouth syndrome a neuropathic pain disorder? A systematic review. J Oral Facial Pain Headache 2021; 35(3): 218-29.
[http://dx.doi.org/10.11607/ofph.2861] [PMID: 34609380]

[14] Pop-Busui R. Diagnosis and treatment of painful diabetic peripheral neuropathy 2022.
[http://dx.doi.org/10.2337/db2022-01]

[15] Røikjer J, Borbjerg MK, Andresen T, *et al.* Diabetic peripheral neuropathy: Emerging treatments of neuropathic pain and novel diagnostic methods. J Diabetes Sci Technol 2024; 19322968241279553.
[http://dx.doi.org/10.1177/19322968241279553] [PMID: 39282925]

[16] Kec D, Rajdova A, Raputova J, *et al.* Risk factors for depression and anxiety in painful and painless diabetic polyneuropathy: A multicentre observational cross-sectional study. Eur J Pain 2022; 26(2): 370-89.
[http://dx.doi.org/10.1002/ejp.1865] [PMID: 34592017]

# Glossary

**Action Potential**

An action potential is a rapid and transient change in the membrane potential of a neuron or muscle cell.

***Alzheimer's***

Alzheimer's disease is a progressive neurodegenerative disorder that affects the brain, leading to a decline in cognitive function, memory, and behavior. It is the most common cause of dementia, accounting for the majority of dementia cases in older adults.

**Amyotrophic Lateral Sclerosis (ALS)**

ALS is a fatal motor neuron disease. It is characterized by progressive degeneration of nerve cells in the spinal cord and brain. ALS affects voluntary control of arms and legs, and leads to trouble breathing.

**Anxiety**

Anxiety is a feeling of fear, dread, and uneasiness. It might cause you to sweat, feel restless and tense, and have a rapid heartbeat. It can be a normal reaction to stress. For example, you might feel anxious when faced with a difficult problem at work, before taking a test, or before making an important decision.

**Autoimmune Disorders**

Autoimmune disease happens when the body's natural defense system can't tell the difference between your own cells and foreign cells, causing the body to mistakenly attack normal cells. There are more than 80 types of autoimmune diseases that affect a wide range of body parts.

**Autonomic Dysfunction**

An autonomic dysfunction occurs when the autonomic nervous system, which controls functions responsible for well-being and maintaining balance, does not regulate properly.

**Autonomic Nervous System**

The autonomic nervous system is a component of the peripheral nervous system that regulates involuntary physiologic processes including heart rate, blood pressure, respiration, digestion, and sexual arousal.

**Blurred Vision**

A visual disturbance described as hazy or double vision, commonly occuring in neurological disorders-especially multiple scleriosis.

**Sumaira Kanwal & Shazia Perveen**

**Cognitive Changes**

Cognitive changes refer to alterations in mental processes such as thinking, memory, attention, reasoning, and perception. These changes can occur for various reasons, including normal aging, neurological conditions, psychiatric disorders, medication side effects, or other medical conditions.

**Cognitive Function**

Cognitive function is a broad term that refers to mental processes involved in the acquisition of knowledge, manipulation of information, and reasoning.

**CT**

A Computerized Tomography (CT) scan combines a series of X-ray images taken from different angles around your body and uses computer processing to create cross-sectional

images (slices) of the bones, blood vessels and soft tissues inside your body. CT scan images provide more-detailed information than plain X-rays do.

**CT Scan**

A computed tomography scan is a medical imaging technique used to obtain detailed internal images of the body. The personnel that perform CT scans are called radiographers or radiology technologists.

**Diabetic Neuropathy**

Diabetic neuropathy can affect nerves throughout the body, but it most commonly affects the peripheral nerves, which are the nerves that transmit information between the brain and spinal cord and the rest of the body.

**Dementia**

Dementia is a broad term that describes a group of symptoms characterized by a decline in cognitive function severe enough to interfere with daily activities and independent functioning.

**Depression**

Depressive disorder (also known as depression) is a common mental disorder. It involves a depressed mood or loss of pleasure or interest in activities for long periods of time. Depression is different from regular mood changes and feelings about everyday life.

**Disease**

A disease is a pathological condition that adversely affects the structure or function of an organism, resulting in specific symptoms or signs.

### Epilepsy

Epilepsy is a disorder of the brain characterized by repeated seizures.

### Foot Deformities

It is the structural abnormality of the foot that develop due to the neropathy-related muscle weakness and wasting. These deformities contribute to the foot problems, imbalance and increased risk of complications.

### Hyposmia

is a medical term used to describe a decreased or reduced sense of smell. It can occur as a temporary or chronic condition and may vary in severity from mild to severe.

### Idiopathic Neuropathy

Neuropathy is when nerve damage interferes with the functioning of the Peripheral Nervous System (PNS). When the cause can't be determined, it's called idiopathic neuropathy.

### Lewy Bodies

Lewy bodies are abnormal aggregates of protein that develop inside nerve cells in certain areas of the brain. They are primarily composed of a protein called alpha-synuclein, along with other proteins and cellular components. Lewy bodies are a characteristic feature of several neurodegenerative disorders, including Parkinson's Disease with Dementia (PDD), Dementia with Lewy Bodies (DLB), and Parkinson's Disease Dementia (PDD).

### Loss of Reflexes

Loss of reflexes refers to the absence or diminished response of certain reflexes in the body, which are typically automatic and involuntary responses to stimuli. Reflexes are controlled by the nervous system and can be indicative of various underlying conditions or injuries when they are diminished or absent.

### Metabolic Disorders

Metabolic disorders are inherited genetic conditions that result in problems with the body's metabolism. The condition leads to an enzyme deficiency because of a defective gene. There are more than six hundred genetic metabolic disorders, all having different symptoms.

### MRI

MRI is a type of diagnostic test that can create detailed images of nearly every structure and organ inside the body. MRI uses magnets and radio waves to produce images on a computer. MRI does not use ionizing radiation. Images produced by an MRI scan can show organs, bones, muscles and blood vessels.

**Motor Neuron**

Carry signals from the central nervous system to muscles or glands, controlling movement or glandular secretion.

**Muscle Rigidity**

Muscle rigidity is a symptom characterized by stiff, inflexible muscles that can hinder movement and cause discomfort. It's often associated with neurological conditions such as Parkinson's disease, where it's a prominent feature.

**Multiple Sclerosis**

Multiple Sclerosis (MS) is a condition that can affect the brain and spinal cord, causing a wide range of potential symptoms, including problems with vision, arm or leg movement, sensation or balance. It's a lifelong condition that can sometimes cause serious disability, although it can occasionally be mild.

**Neurology**

Neurology is the branch of medicine concerned with the study and treatment of disorders of the nervous system.

**Neurons**

Neurons, also known as nerve cells, are the fundamental building blocks of the nervous system.

**Neuropathy**

is a disease it occurs when nerve damage leads to pain, weakness, numbness or tingling in one or more parts of your body. The nerve damage may be because of disease, infection, injury, medicines, long-term alcohol abuse or another reason.

**Neurotransmitters**

A chemical substance used by the nerve cells to communicate with each other. Dopamine is one of the example of neurotransmitters, is involved in controlling movement and motor functions.

**Numbness**

Describes a loss of feeling in a part of the body. It also is often used to describe other changes in sensation, such as burning or a pins-and-needles feeling. Numbness can occur along a single nerve on one side of the body.

**Parkinson's Disease**

This is the most common cause of Parkinsonism. It is a progressive neurodegenerative disorder characterized by the loss of dopamine-producing neurons in the substantia nigra region of the brain. The exact cause of Parkinson's disease is not fully understood, but both genetic and environmental factors are thought to play a role.

**Parkinsonism**

Parkinsonism refers to a group of neurological disorders that share similar symptoms with Parkinson's disease but have different underlying causes. The primary characteristic of Parkinsonism is the presence of movement abnormalities, such as tremors, rigidity, bradykinesia (slowness of movement), and postural instability.

**Partial Seizure**

A partial seizure, also known as a focal seizure, is a type of seizure that originates in a specific area of the brain, rather than involving the entire brain at once. These seizures are caused by abnormal electrical activity in a localized part of the brain.

**Peripheral Nerves**

Peripheral nerves are the nerves that branch out from the brain and spinal cord to the rest of the body,

**Postural Instability**

Postural instability refers to difficulty maintaining an upright position and balance while standing or walking. It is often associated with neurological conditions, particularly Parkinson's disease, but can also occur due to other factors such as aging, musculoskeletal issues, or inner ear problems.

**Reduced Arm Swing**

Reduced arm swing refers to a decrease or absence of the natural swinging motion of the arms while walking. Typically, when a person walks, their arms swing rhythmically in opposition to their legs, aiding in balance and efficiency of movement. However, in some cases, such as certain neurological conditions or musculoskeletal issues, the arm swing may be reduced or absent.

**Seizure**

A seizure is a burst of uncontrolled electrical activity between brain cells (also called neurons or nerve cells) that causes temporary abnormalities in muscle tone or movements (stiffness, twitching or limpness), behaviors, sensations or states of awareness.

**Sensory Neuron**

Transmit sensory information from sensory receptors (*e.g.*, in the skin, eyes, ears) to the central nervous system.

### Shuffeling/Short Stepped Gait

A short-stepped gait, also known as shuffling gait, is a type of abnormal walking pattern characterized by taking small steps with minimal lifting of the feet. It is often associated with Parkinson's disease, a progressive neurological disorder that affects movement control. However, a short-stepped gait can also occur due to other neurological conditions, musculoskeletal issues, or as a result of aging.

### Spinal Cord

The spinal cord is a vital component of the Central Nervous System (CNS), extending from the base of the brain down through the vertebral column. It plays a crucial role in transmitting sensory information from the body to the brain and motor signals from the brain to the body.

### Stooped Posture

Stooped posture, also known as kyphosis or hunched back, refers to an abnormal forward curvature of the upper spine. This can result in a rounded or hunched appearance of the back, shoulders, and neck. Stooped posture can occur for various reasons.

### Syndrome

A syndrome refers to a collection of symptoms and signs that occur together and characterize a particular medical condition or disease.

### Tingling

It is a sign that a nerve is irritated and sending extra signals. Think of that pins and needles feeling as a traffic jam in your nervous system.

### *Toxins*

are substances created by plants and animals that are poisonous (toxic) to humans. Toxins may also include some medicines that are helpful in small doses, but poisonous in large amounts. Most toxins that cause problems in humans come from germs such as bacteria.

### Tremer

Tremors are involuntary, rhythmic muscle movements that typically involve shaking in one or more parts of the body. They can occur in various medical conditions, including neurological disorders, metabolic disorders, and certain medications' side effects.

### Ultrasound

Ultrasound refers to a medical imaging technique that uses high-frequency sound waves to create images of structures within the body. It is commonly used to visualize organs, tissues, and blood flow in real-time. During an ultrasound examination, a small handheld device called a transducer is placed against the skin, and a gel is applied to help transmit the sound waves.

## VNS Therapy

Vagus Nerve Stimulation therapy is a treatment for epilepsy that involves a stimulator (or 'pulse generator') which is connected, inside the body, to the left vagus nerve in the neck. The stimulator sends regular, mild electrical stimulations through this nerve to help calm down the irregular electrical brain activity that leads to seizures.

# SUBJECT INDEX

## A



## B



## C



## D

## M



## N



## O



## P



## Q



## R

www.ingramcontent.com/pod-product-compliance
Lightning Source LLC
LaVergne TN
LVHW070950210926
848482LV00002B/169

* 9 7 9 8 8 9 8 8 1 1 8 5 3 *